The Great Entrapment

The Great Entrapment

A BIBLICAL MODEL OF A WORKABLE CHURCH

in any Community of a Cross Cultural World.

Ralph Frederick Cater

Tanglewood Hill Press
P. O. Box 449
Dallas, OR 97338
Copyright 1998
by Ralph Frederick Cater

Published 1998

Printed in the United States of America

05 04 03 02 01 00 99 98 97 98
      5 4 3 2 1

Cater, Ralph Frederick
    The great entrapment : a Biblical model of a workable church in any community of a cross cultural world / by Ralph Frederick Cater.
    —1st ed.
    p. cm.
    Includes bibliographical references.
    Preassigned LCCN: 96-61988
    ISBN: 0-9654818-1-6

    1. Fundamentalist churches—Doctrines. 2. Dogma. 3. Church and the world. 4. Church renewal. I. Title.

    BT77.C38 1998   262.001'7
                               QB197-41171

Dedication

To any person who may patiently read this text along with a study of the Bible in order to gratify their burning desire to grow spiritually in the grace of the Lord Jesus Christ and to glorify Him in their daily life.

Foreword

Ralph Cater has produced an amazingly detailed study of Biblical doctrine and its daily application. His list of books he has studied in preparation for this work is impressive. The need for this book is plainly seen in the preaching of pastors throughout Christendom. Usually pastors utilize but a fraction of the doctrines listed in this work. To withstand the onslaught of the devil, the whole counsel of God is needed. It is included in this work. By knowledge of the basics of Christianity, Christians can stop the erosion of other believers into apostate groups, and turn the tide in the direction of true Christianity.

James B. Hoge, Ph.D.
Salem, Oregon

v

Acknowledgments

It is a pleasure to thank all those who helped me complete *The Great Entrapment.* A number of people, too numerous to mention, have encouraged and provided suggestions, typing, proofreading, and constructive criticism—notably the following: Dr. James Hoge, psychologist; Katie and Ron Imig of Child Evangelism Fellowship; Elsa Cater; Kay Dixon; Raechel and Robert Dow; John Engeln; Norman Fleck; Christina Frey; Carleen Olander; Lillie Flanders Overholt; Darrel Salisbury; Norvada Smedley; and others.

I am also indebted to Erma Armstrong who assisted in numerous revisions and provided the computer layout, design and editing.

Finally, I offer my salutation of thanks and patience to my wife, Pauline, who has been helpful in more ways than I can name.

- R. F. C.

Preface

This study is designed to make the believer and nonbeliever alike aware of conditions that prevail in the world that mankind is *not capable* of solving. The general plan is to study this nontechnical book along with any study Bible, since it will be far less comprehensible if the reader does not use the Bible. The text is only a primer to open up the real truth presented by the inspired Word of God—The Bible—which alone *is capable* of solving problems that exist in the world. By means of these Scriptural references, the reader can prepare for a thorough study of God's will in the Church Age.

There are many Bibles, books about the Bible, and various churches in the world; yet we live in a turmoil of confusion. Disagreement has been present for centuries. But there is a message to be read—God's message—which is there to be lived and understood.

In these last days, the standards, value judgments and attitudes of the world have infiltrated the Church to an alarming degree. Believers are alerted herein to ways to study and restudy their Bibles and to rethink their beliefs beyond church doctrine, denomination and indigenous misconceptions. There is much ignorance in regard to Bible doctrine. People don't know what they really believe. If people do not have a thorough knowledge of the Bible, how can they tell others about the Gospel of Christ?

Many people do not know the Gospel of Christ. It is the message that will make them free (John 8:32). It is a seed that must be sown, and the field is the world *(Matthew 13:38)*. Christians lack the confidence to witness to the world. We are all ministers and the life we live preaches to the world.

Therefore this book, in collaboration with a good study Bible, will aid the reader in mastering the rich content of God's Word for his personal spiritual growth and edification to glorify God.

Ralph Frederick Cater
1849 S. W. Boxwood Lane
Dallas, OR 97338-2396

Contents

CHAPTER ONE: Problems in the Church

Introduction

There are fundamental differences in the practices of various evangelical bodies of Christendom. Attempts to conform the practices of these various congregations reveal corresponding differences in their interpretations of Bible doctrine as well as a disregard for clear Bible doctrine.

In addition there is often indicated a fundamental misinterpretation of the Biblical word on the part of many church groups. Both the misinterpretations and the lack of basic regard for Bible doctrine are a cause for concern. Together the existence of these two kinds of institutions, fundamental and liberal, indicate the need for a return to responsible study and utilization of Biblical teaching which will reveal itself by conforming the practices of these various bodies of Christendom.

Background for the Study

Many ministers, Bible schools, and seminaries, though they may base their findings on the Bible, emphasize and believe that the key to their doctrine is found in their organi-

1

zational distinctives. Certain church groups, over the centuries, have come to believe that their doctrinal distinctives are superior to those of other persuasions. Many reverent, learned and spiritual men have developed their ideas, customs and traditions into an assembly. Their assembled traditions and doctrinal distinctives then may or may not be subject to worldly influences and to an erosion of the values and directives based on their original findings.

There are many reasons why the church has fallen away from the best of Biblical interpretations of the inspired Word of God. Men once were called by the Lord. Today men and groups desire recognition, money, affluence, entertainment, growth and popularity rather than to teach and obey the great principles of Old and New Covenant teachings.

New Bible versions and translations have not encouraged better study and teaching, but they have often resulted in confusion and a lack of serious study of God's Word. Therefore church members have often reverted to insipid, superficial and humanistic church activities.[1] Due to poor scholarship or the influence of other writings inside and outside an assembly, large segments of the church have been misled. Subtly the Devil and men with fleshly ambitions have had a destructive and critical effect on churches and their creation of doctrinal interpretative distinctives.

Where once the virtues of men were reinforced by kings and ministers, now the leaders of many nations are not great teachers—because they are not followers of the Word of God. In the nineteenth century we had leaders who lived godly lives under God's direction.[2]

Today we think more about improving our self esteem, personal worth and identity among men rather than the souls of men and the glory of God. For Christ laid down His life for the sins of every person, past, present, and future. Instead of focusing on these eternal things, we seek confidence through things of the flesh to enhance our conceit and self image. Our pride is puffed up. We have identified with the world's system.

> *III John 1:9 I wrote unto the church: but Diotrephes, who loveth to have the preeminence among them, receiveth us not.*

We are saying, in effect, nobody else is going to build me up, so I will accomplish personal worth by my own goodly achievements and activities. In the Bible, Diotrephes, the place hunter, nourished by self, did not walk in truth but desired self-exaltation and preeminence among Christians *(III John 1:9-11)*.

Our churches and their superficial leadership have allowed the world to contaminate many of the Evangelical Christian ministries. So many, like Diotrephes, have desired a self-centered identification and the admiration of others.

This study is confined to problems within evangelical fundamental Christendom, as it is conceived here in Protestant America. A consensus of problems was defined both before and during the research and investigation leading to the study. Here are some of the findings that were of concern to the researcher:

1. Dogmatic preaching and dynamic teaching are discouraged. The Word of God has gone by the wayside. This was noted as a lukewarm sign in the early Church of Laodicea. Its members were spiritually indifferent, poor, and blind, compromising the bland waters that came to the Metropolis. They had everything, except what God's love could offer, as the door had always been open *(Revelation 3:8)*.

2. Political and religious action contrive more and more to serve agendas and compromises of men rather than the Master Teacher and Savior.

3. Personality differences and conflict can often taint the

3

Revelation 3:8   I know thy works: behold, I have set before thee an open door, and no man can shut it; for thou hast a little strength, and hast kept my word, and hast not denied my name.

spiritual growth of persons desiring to grow in a Biblical ministry *(Galatians 5:17-18)*.

4. There is a prevalence of amplified instrumental music with lyrics that fail to offer an in-depth message to the unbeliever and believer. The carnality of the world has contaminated the music of some churches.5. Witnessing for Jesus, as He commanded of us, is not being done with vigor and dedication. Cults do a superior job of witnessing for their world organizations.

Significance of the Study

This study was conceived while ministering in numerous churches in the United States over the years. Gradually an understanding of spiritual and authentic church conditions was developed, as they existed then and as they exist yet today.

Galatians 5:17-18   For the flesh lusteth against the Spirit, and the Spirit against the flesh: and these are contrary the one to the other: so that ye cannot do the things that ye would. But if ye be led of the Spirit, ye are not under the law .

Because of the great diversity of church distinctives and interpretations among evangelical fundamental Christians (non-legalistic bodies), there is difficulty in forming a consensus. There are, indeed, few central bodies that collect and disseminate official information among believers about Bible doctrines.[3] [4] Today our faith is being challenged on every side, and many are compromising the truth.

There is a great need for

churches to stand squarely for the truth and to preach and teach the whole counsel of God. Men's personalities and backgrounds must not block the ministry of Jesus Christ. By God's grace, the church must be raised up by the brethren to take a position that will provide fellowship free from entangling alliances. The Savior Jesus Christ

> *I John 3:17 But whoso hath this world's good, and seeth his brother have need, and shutteth up his bowels of compassion from him, how dwelleth the love of God in him?*

loves man. If a man loves Jesus Christ, surely he should love all brethren alike and the unbeliever, also, in deed and truth *(I John 3:15-18)*

God is offering us a free gift. Take time to study the Bible legacies. We need them to survive. As Christians, we are in a spiritual battle every day. The events of history, yesterday and today, support this fact.

The church (believers) can play a significant role in times of war and in our temporary peace. People are coming to Christ in God's timetable and must move ahead until He comes again.

In this writing, and in the study upon which it is based, a model was developed that can be used by any church, without labeling it, in order to establish a church climate for influencing spiritual growth. People want to identify with a group. Some groups do a reasonably good job of teaching the Word of God by using the Bible along with their organizational format. However, people need to identify with the teaching of the Bible *alone* and place their total allegiance in Christ—through prayer and a study of the total Word of God, the Bible.

God's Word is rooted in faithfulness *(Isaiah 55:11; I Kings 8:56-61)*. Such allegiance has been found in isolated groups throughout our nation's history.

An example of such faithfulness is found in Old Salem,

North Carolina, on a local historical plaque which reads:
The Moravians broke from established forms of religion to find a simple heart felt faith. They regarded the return to Scriptures as the only source for fulfillment and meaning. Their liturgies stressed a personal religious experience and an inner joy. Such faith assured them that life could be more humane, more relevant to their needs.—Signed by Nickolas Lewis 1722.

In the same location John Amos Comenius (1592-1670), a Moravian theologian and a pioneer of modern pedagogy, in 1633 said:
The first care ought to be the soul, which is the principal part of a man. The next care is for the body that it may be a habitation fit and worthy of an immortal soul.

The above models serve as a basis for our discussion. What better way to combat false teaching, lukewarmness and indifference? We must join in keeping God's Word as the standard for living. There is a need for us to pray and study God's Word zealously in the church, in the workplace and in our home Bible study groups.

Here are some examples of what can and will happen if the current movement continues away from Bible teaching and Biblical living. We might say that now we are on a humanistic collision course gaining momentum.

First, the New Age Movement exemplifies pantheistic thinking[5]— the concept that all is God and God is all. Many hold to this belief. This philosophy continues to infiltrate the minds of Christians. Why? Because they do not study the total Word of God—the Bible *(II Timothy 1:13; II Peter 1:20,21; 2:1-3:9; Galatians1:6-12; II Corinthians. 11:4)*. Without God's standard and wisdom, they don't recognize false teaching.

A second area of deep concern is the charismatic controversy, which has prepared us for acceptance of an irrational illusion. While focusing on personality one is blind to ultimate truths. Satan lures one into that realm and to all kinds of societal problems that creep into the church unaware. The standard of the Canon is then missing, *in absentia*.

> *I Timothy 6:10 For the love of money is the root of all evil: which while some coveted after, they have erred from the faith, and pierced themselves through with many sorrows..*

We are thus bypassing the Bible in favor of our wants, desires, and professed needs *(I Timothy. 6:9-10)*.

We have seen how catastrophic this can be by observing what has happened to some media ministries in the last couple of decades.

These ministries are validated by people who stand up and give glowing testimonies of what God has done for them. Testimonies of experiences rather than a careful perusal of God's Word have masked the teachings of Jesus Christ. Acknowledging that changed lives provide a confirmation that God's power and grace are available in our day, we should not be trapped into accepting sensational testimonies as the final authority of what is truth, rather than God's truth and wisdom. The gospel is the power of God unto salvation (Romans 1:16-20).

A third concern is the new paganism or what is known as religious pluralism. People accept, lackadaisically, all the religions of the day. The writer has observed that churches have many who offer convincing arguments that one religion is as good as another and that one is entitled to his own opinion;.

What does this engender? It undermines the Bible as the bedrock of our values so that our present morals are determined by man's reasoning rather than by God's wisdom and revelation. The fact that family values are challenged on every side, yet defined in many differing ways, is an example.

A general definition of a Biblical Christian may be given as a grace believer who is redeemed through faith by the shed blood of a resurrected Christ, who has been brought out of spiritual darkness and given a divine nature, and who has been brought into the glorious liberty and will of God to serve and glorify Christ in the Spirit.

Christians need to be cognizant of the relentless pressures of the world cunningly controlled by the Prince of the power of the air. The Devil continues to contaminate the church. Therefore, we must be aware that God's love and freedom from bondage can be demonstrated in the lives of all those who follow and live for

> *Galatians 5:1 Stand fast therefore in the liberty wherewith Christ hath made us free, and be not entangled again with the yoke of bondage.*

Christ *(Galatians 5:1)*. He gave us the Comforter—The Holy Spirit—so that we can be spirit-controlled in our daily living.

When church bodies are overly preoccupied by the church remaking itself—through reimaging, building programs, faith pledges, credit-card syndromes, amplified music and yarns to entertain itching ears—then few lessons from scripture are taught.

This is called: The Great Entrapment. The Scriptures are inspired by God and written by many people under divine direction. Can anyone stop God? No! Who is the only supplier of Eternal Life? God!

Believers who use the Bible for daily living know that the omnipresent God places a high priority upon the legacy of the soul. Who is best qualified to be the largest supplier of life applications to feed man's soul, spirit, and body? Some people might think the answer would be a developer of good works or a philosopher to devise a cross-cultural society, or they would lean on their own understanding. These sources would appear very impressive to the world where sin, superficial education, and technology are competitors and distractors. Those entrapments are present.

> *John 10:9 I am the door: by me if any man enter in, he shall be saved, and shall go in and out, and find pasture.*

There are many religions that reach back prior to Christ's first coming to the earth that vie for the believer's attention. They represent an expansion of religious pluralism. Even with the advent of Christ there can be no guarantee that a religion that purports to call itself "Christian" will change the heart of man.

That is why God has never made the Gospel change for anyone. God loves all people and wants us to believe and come to repentance and forgiveness through His Son Jesus Christ. There is no other name given to man whereby we must be saved and gain eternal life *(Acts 4:12; 15:11; Ephesians 1:19-23; Philippians 2:9-12; Colossians 3:17; Revelation 2:17).* By faith each person must believe Christ died for the sins of the world *(John 14:6; 10:9; 8:32),* and specifically, He died for your sins and mine.

> *Acts 4:12 Neither is there salvation in any other: for there is none other name under heaven given among men, whereby we must be saved.*

Luke also supports this concept in *Acts 4:12.* God has said that Christ is the only way to save each living soul. Therefore no man will come to God but by Jesus Christ.

Christ is the way, truth, and the life. *(John 14:6; Acts 4:12; Romans 5:1-2; 6:14,18,22; Ephesians 1:20-23; Philippians 2:9-11; Colossians 3:17.)* He was the sinless Holy One who came to give His life as a ransom for the

> *II Timothy 3:16 But shun profance and vain babblings: for they will increase unto more ungodliness.*

> *Jeremiah 2:7 And I brought you into a plentiful country, to eat the fruit thereof and the goodness thereof; but when ye entered, ye defiled my land, and made mine heritage an abomination.*

sins of every human being.

The Bible doctrine found in II Timothy 3:14-17 and Jude 1:4 is a rich weave and texture of numerous threads of God's wisdom and instruction:

Jeremiah, like many others, was chosen by God, as one to whom all must give account. Jeremiah's lengthy ministry of warning revealed to Israel its hypocrisy and disobedience *(Jeremiah, Chapters 2, 3, 5, 7, 8, 28, 29)*. These chapters furnish prime examples of the lax oversight of the religious leaders and the exposure of rebellious peoples who violated God's plan for their lives. Their attitude was, as in the current vernacular, "Just do it!" No need for excuses or to ask questions about it. Disobey God and be in style. It is the fad. How could man think to prevail when he dared war against God? Jeremiah warned of the many entrapments

> *Genesis 12:1-2 Now the Lord had said unto Abram, Get thee out of thy country, and from thy kindred, and from thy father's house, unto a land that I will shew thee: And I will make of thee a great nation, and I will bless thee, and make thy name great; and thou shalt be a blessing*

Consider again the return of the Jews to Israel, as in Biblical times (Genesis *12:1-5*). They would become the caretakers of the land. But their preoccupation was to be free of the tyranny of other nations, not to glorify God. They would seek political and economic acclaim and live by tradition and ritual, but not in obedience to God according to the Scripture.

As the world observes and applauds the athletes of the Olympic Games, it witnesses awesome physical feats of humanity. Their rewards, however, are temporal. In contrast, God's church pursues a crown of life for eternity. Our spiritual life was meant to mesh with our earthly life.

> *I Thessalonians 4:13 But I would not have you to be ignorant, brethren, concerning them which are asleep, that ye sorrow not, even as others which have no hope.*

Children of God know the truth only from the Word of God and prayer. God's love moves through them to reach out to other Christians and the unsaved. Children of God should pray and encourage others by invitation to enter into God's dedicated service. No pressures, judgmental or legal demands should ever be placed on the will of a person. The Holy Spirit does the convincing and the saving. We can only witness for the Lord and live a godly life before the world. Real believers, called "the church," will receive their legacy someday. They will be caught up to be with Christ *(I Thessalonians. 4:13, 5:11)*.

People may abound in good but futile intentions. Here is a simple illustration: It is taken to be a personal achievement psychologically for anyone to climb Mt. McKinley, a 20,320 foot summit. About 1,000 people endeavor to climb the summit each season; half succeed. That our endeavors should not be futile we should ask ourselves, "Are my priorities for **self**?" Do we want to be able to say, **"I** did this; **I** am recognized?" Do we boast inwardly? A spiritual encounter with God far exceeds any psychological experience on land, water or air. God wants us to climb mountains through numerous obstacles and circumstances daily.

God wants us to grasp these lessons as major preparatory steps for eternal life with Him. When we stop studying scriptures for answers to our daily problems, we forsake our God-given spiritual resources. We open the door to options discovered outside the scriptures. We are trading temporal

11

human wisdom and achievement for eternal life.

Another brief illustration of futile endeavor is in the teachings of certain *oneness* groups. A growing movement of anti-trinitarianism is clouding men's minds. They mistakenly pursue a three-step teaching toward Salvation, saying that:

1) Baptism is necessary for salvation (unscriptural).

2) Baptism is administered in Jesus' name only (unscriptural).

3) Baptism of the Holy Spirit requires speaking in tongues for salvation (unscriptural).

In the above teaching, however, Faith, Trinity and the Blood of Christ are completely divorced from the Canon of Scripture.[6][7] Presently, there are about five million members in this apostatized entrapment.

We must continue to ask ourselves, are our Biblical priorities and spiritual values God-centered? Are we constantly yielding in our walk with Christ to glorify Him. We are a priesthood of grace believers.

> *I Corinthians 15:58*
> *Therefore, my beloved brethren, be ye stedfast, unmoveable, always abounding in the work of the Lord, forasmuch as ye know that your labour is not in vain in the Lord.*

The pursuits of religion, righteous works and performance will never yield an understanding of the divine plan of Jesus Christ *(I Corinthians 2:10-16)*. We should always give ourselves fully to the work of the Lord, because we must know our deeds in the Lord are not wasted *(I Corinthians. 15:58)*. We must pray for greater love and unity among all members of the Body of Christ.

The growth of Mideast and Far Eastern religions and cults are increasing in the United States at an alarming rate.

A few of the reasons are:

1. Many people have migrated from other nations.

2. Missionaries from other nations have introduced their religion to the United States, taking advantage that this country believes in religious freedom.

3. Christianity in the United States has become more liberal in its teaching and has extended its influence to other countries.

4. However, Biblical fundamental Christianity has taken a conservative view of all issues by remaining separated from the world. They, too, are supportive of their own missions in this country and in other nations.

True Biblical fundamental Christianity ought to take neither a liberal or conservative position outside of religion. It is unfortunate that evangelical fundamental Christians refer to themselves as conservatives. This position can be refuted if we ask ourselves these questions:

a - Is it conservative to share Christ without an argument?

b - Is it conservative to ask a person where he will spend eternity?

c - Is it conservative to ask a homosexual to turn his life around?
d - Is it conservative to talk to an AIDS victim about his soul?

Jesus would have shared the gospel with anyone under any circumstances. Why not you? All of the questions above are radical. The Christians in the early church were radical because they were moved out of their smug complacency by God's Holy Spirit. They were revolutionary! Christ was not conservative. He came with a sword to do the will of the sovereign God that sent Him to save sinners!

13

ENDNOTES

[1]. Stam, Cornelius R. *The Berean Searchlight.* Chicago, Ill: The Berean Bible Society, Vol. 51, No. 11, Feb., 1991, p. 330.

[2]. *Ibid.*, pp. 328-331.

[3]. Mead, Frank S.; Revised by Samuel S. Hill, *Handbook of Denominations in the United States; 9th ed.*, Nashville, TN: Abingdon Press, 1990, all.

[4]. Reid, Daniel G., Consulting Editors and Others. *Dictionary of Christianity in America*; Downers Grove, IL: Inter-Varsity Press, 1990.

[5]. *Ibid*, pp. 809-810.

[6]. Tucker, Bruce; "Are Oneness Groups Cultic?" *The Standard: The Newsmagazine of the Baptist General Conference*, Vol. 82, No. 3, April, 1992; pp. 18-19.

[7]. Boyd, Gregory A. *Oneness of Pentecostals And The Trinity.* Grand Rapids, MI: Baker Book House; 1992.

CHAPTER TWO: The Church in Question

A Review of Related Literature

From His unadulterated Word, God teaches, clearly and without apology, that Christ and His Church would be built upon a Rock, which is Christ, the Chief Cornerstone. The Church then signifies particular persons, who are faithful believers (Matthew 16:18); and Hades, death, the grave, and destruction shall not overcome them.

> *Matthew 16:18 And I say also unto thee, that thou art Peter, and upon this rock I will build my church, and the gates of hell shall not prevail against it.*

The chosen text is in the future tense: "I *will* build my church." This doctrine of ecclesiology is the Biblical position of the Church, for grace believers, throughout the Church Age. Pentecost is the birthday of the spiritual social institution called the Church (*I Corinthians 12:12-18; Acts 4:11-12; I Corinthians 3:10-23; Matthew 21:42-45*). Therefore, Christ's command needs to be of first concern to Christians as a continuation of Abraham's

15

faith and works, that men would believe God's promises *(Genesis 22:15-18; Galatians 3:8,18)*.

Herein the born-again grace believers, from Pentecost to the rapture, discover the Body of Christ as a living organism[1] *(I Thessalonians. 5:1-12)*. This "dispensation of grace" is the Church Age. It is a mystery that had not been revealed in the Old Testament. It is an arm of the Church that has been stated as "advancing the Kingdom," "bringing in the Kingdom," and, "establishing the Kingdom."

The Church is not a political institution. Men lose sight of the primary nature of the Church as a "called out" body of people "for His name," a heavenly people, one body separate from all other men of the world, with a superior covenant, as a one-of-a-kind heavenly bride of Christ. We must always see the distinctive nature of the Church both in its grace dispensation and in its membership, containing only the born-again. The Church is an earthly organization but also a heavenly organism *(Hebrews 8:1-13; 9:24-28)*. It is a new covenant, and it could not be enforced until the death of a testator *(Hebrews 9:14-18)* and the fulfillment of the Old Covenant.

Paul informs us that the Saints are not under law but under grace, espoused to Christ *(Romans 7:1-6)*. Paul contrasts our position now to that under the Law *(Galatians 4:4-7)*. He is a minister to the circumcision, for the truth of God confirms the promises made unto the fathers *(Romans 15:8,9)*.

Christ never established the Church while upon the earth. His utterance was, "I will build my church." *(Matthew 16:18-19)*. Our Sovereign God sent His Son to head the Church, *(I Corinthians 11:3; Ephesians 1:22, 5:23-24)* as the crucified, risen Lord; resurrected and ascended to the Father and glorified.

God sent the great Administrator of the Church, the Holy Spirit. In *Acts I*, the disciples were still waiting in expectation of the Holy Spirit. Immediately after Pentecost, the

Church as a corporate body was recognized *(Acts 2:47)*. There are many ecclesiological erroneous conceptions of the Church.[2] The Scriptures, however, interpret the difference between the visible and the invisible Church.

> *Acts 2:47... Praising God, and having favour with all the people. And the Lord added to the church daily such as should be saved.*

The Magnitude of the Church

What is the Church? It is God's house, assembly, or congregation. The Church is a called-out assembly, a gathering *(ekklesia, Hebrews 2:12)*.[3] The outward visible organization is not to be considered the true church of Christ. It may be far from it; it may be a synagogue *(sunagoge)* of Satan *(Acts 13:43-45; Revelation 2:9, 3:9)*.[4]

Yet the Church may have few who are hundred percent born-again believers, true members of Christ's body. Further, it is not the members that comprise a church for His name; but rather they establish a bride for His Son *(Acts 15:14)*. Moffat, a missionary for forty years without a convert, alone constituted the Church of Christ in Africa. The visible Church, though imperfect, may or may not be united, in local settings, by organizational features. The organized visible Church is restricted to living persons in a given time and place.

Fausset[5] and Best[6] interpret the visible Church in that which belongs to the invisible, in spite of Christ's warning in the "parable of the tares and wheat" *(Matthew 13:24-30, 36-50; I Corinthians 15:42, 53,58; Acts 28:23-31)*. To separate out the tares from the wheat prematurely has led to numerous divisions, and has created hard feelings among the brethren *(Romans 8:13; Colossians 3:2-10)*. By faith, believers are working patiently for Almighty God to resurrect His children. What you can see is the local, real and visible Church. This Church is holy, set apart by the Lord Jesus Christ

17

(Galatians 1:4; Ephesians 5:26-27). Our Lord gives unity and reality during any period of time in the dispensation of grace believers.

Evans[7] expresses the issue in this manner: "The visible Church is composed of Church members that are actually imperfect saints on the earth drawing after perfection" *(Galatians 1:1-6; Philippians1:1; Colossians 1:2)*.

Strong[8, 9] views the Church of believers in whom Christ lives, to whom and through whom He reveals God *(Ephesians 1:22-23)*. Certainly the visible Church would be all the members of all the churches made up of believers and unbelievers (sheep and goats). The New Testament refers to the Church in this way. It reaches out to Jew and Gentile with the same Gospel *(Acts 11:19-30; 13:1-3)* and calls those who profess Christ "Christians."

> *II Timothy 2:19*
> *Nevertheless the foundation of God standeth sure, having this seal, The Lord knoweth them that are his. And, Let every one that nameth the name of Christ depart from iniquity.*

In contrast,[10, 11, 12] the invisible Church is universal and ideal. The supreme goal of the invisible Church relates to the eternal purposes of God. It has specific and special value to our Lord Jesus Christ *(Ephesians 5:25-27; II Timothy 2:19)*. The invisible Church is all of the believers in the church that glorify God (both now alive and those with Christ). It is an ideal which possesses supreme perfection or completion *(Colossians 1:15-27; Hebrews 12:22-24; Romans 1:19-20; Ephesians 5:23-30,32; Revelation 2:28-29; 3:6; 21:27; 22:16-18)*. Other passages that refer to that ideal in this way are *Matthew 7:15-27; 13:47-50; and 25:1-46*.

Therefore, the righteous or ideal invisible Church will reign with Christ, and with His Saints as written in the Book of Life of the Holy Lamb. God definitely assigns precious promises to the Church: promises of election, predestination, adoption, spiritual priesthood, the direction of the Holy Spirit to all truth, and the sealing of the believer's salvation. Old Testament Saints by faith are mentioned for God has taken care of them.

> *Ephesians 1:22-23*
> *And hath put all things under his feet, and gave him to be the head over all things to the church, Which is his body, the fulness of him that filleth all in all*

Finally, we can say that the ideal church may be anointed *(Romans 12:1-2)* by the regeneration of the Holy Spirit *(Ephesians 1:22-23)*. The beauty and likeness of Christ is seen in the convert who glorifies God *(Matthew 5:14-16)*. Grace believers possess an edification complex which is the deep-felt power of the Holy Spirit to express Christ in their lives and known to others.

"Out of the fullness of the heart the mouth speaks.

"They are invisible insofar that it is God alone who can infallibly see who among professors are animated by a living, loving faith, and who are not."[13]

Each characteristic interpretation of Scripture among Biblical expositors reflects the members' values, attitudes, and beliefs, which thus become part of their formation. What is the larger contributing factor? It is the anointing of the Holy Spirit which brings the praying, comforting, leading, teaching, directing and convicting to the believer's daily fellowship with the Lord Jesus Christ in *(I John 2:20-21)*.

Reference to the Church *(Ecclesia)* —the called out ones *(Matthew 16:18-20; 18:15-20; I Thessalonians. 1:1)*—is found 102 times in the Book of Acts and in the epistles. The New Testament Church does not allude at all to a building, meeting house, denomination or organization. The church concept is also expressed in the New Testament as the *(Galatians 2:6-10)* fellowship *(koinonia)*[14] among converted believers directed by the Holy Spirit (*Acts 2:1-4, 32-44; Philippians 3:6-14*).

With this fellowship of sufferings, the Church continued steadfastly in the apostles' doctrine and fellowship. Note the commonality between fellow, fellow-servant (Colossians 1:7), fellow-worker (Romans 16:21), fellow-citizens (Ephesians 2:19), fellow-soldiers (Philippians 2:25), etc. Christians were sincerely loving and bonding to each other, and sharing material and spiritual possessions (Acts 2:44-47). "So the body of Christ is the Church of believing human beings in both *"ecclesia"* and *"koinonia."*[15] This fellowship is with one another and with the Lord Jesus Christ as the common denominator. The stabilizing power of the Holy Spirit indwells each believer whom God loves, chastens, and raises up for His glory alone. This visible local fellowship is not perfect, however, with its mixed company of spiritual and carnal believers and the unsaved. See *Matthew 18:15-17; Romans 14:1-5, 10, 13, 15; 15:1; 16:17-18, I Corinthians 3:1-4; 4:18-19; 11:18-19; II Corinthians 12:19-21; Galatians 2:11-14, 3:1, 4:9-18, 5:15, 6:1; I. Thessalonians. 3:8-11; II Thessalonians. 3:6, 14, 15; and II Timothy 4:3-4, 10.*

The Philadelphia Confession of Faith[16] ascertains that the "...purest churches under heaven are subject to mixture and error (*I Corinthians 5; Revelation 2 & 3*), and some have so degenerated as to become no Churches of Christ, but synagogues of Satan (*Revelations 18:2; II Thessalonians. 11:11,12*). Nevertheless Christ always hath, and ever shall have (*Matthew 16:18; Psalm 72:17; Psalm 102:28; Revelation 12:17*) a kingdom in the world to the end thereof, of such as believe in him, and make profession of his name."

The confession further interprets the Universal Church as being internally operated by the Holy Spirit and God's unmerited favor for the elect gathered into a whole with Christ as King, Lord, Priest, and Savior. The Church is the bride of Christ.[17] Study *Hebrews 12:23; Colossians 1:18, 24;*

Ephesians 1:10, 22-23; 5: 23, 27, 32.; I Peter 3:4.

Enns[18] epitomizes this age old distinctive taught by Augustine, Calvin and Luther, that the invisible Universal Church membership is not known, though the members are visible. A sovereign God does know this reality, and He will separate the sheep from the goats *(II Timothy 2:19; John 10:14, 27).*

> *Colossians 1:18 And he is the head of the body, the church: who is the beginning, the firstborn from the dead; that in all things he might have the preeminence.*

The Visible and Invisible Church

There are six different sets of words in contrast to one another:

Imperfect Church	True Church
1) Visible Church	1) Invisible Church
2) Local Earthly Church	2) Universal Heavenly Church
3) Real or earthly Church	3) Ideal Spiritual Church
4) Psychological Church	4) Spirit Directed Church
5) Lip Service	5) Life Service
6) Organization	6) Organism

The passages that refer to the Church in this way are *Acts 11:19-24; 13:4-12.* The invisible Church is all of the believers in all ages, including the present saints. God knows the ideal invisible Church, and the passages that refer to it in this way are *Colossians 1:21-27; Hebrews 12:22-24; I Corinthians 1:2-3; 12:12-31; I Peter 2:1-10.*

Although some deny that the Scriptures make such a distinction, claiming that every time the Church is studied in the New Testament the reference is to the local church, there is a practical, common sense distinction behind the dichotomy. Passages that support this kind of interpretation of a mixed church would include those such as *I John 2:4-29, and Acts 28:23-31* where the Bible refers to people leaving the Church because they were never really part of the Church. This clearly refers to a case where nonbelievers were a part of the local church in some significant way *(Matthew 7: 13-14; Luke 13: 23-27).*

> *Matthew 7:14 Because strait is the gate, and narrow is the way, which leadeth unto life, and few there be that find it.*

The parable concerning the tares and the wheat is another example of the mixed multitude *(Matthew 13:24-30, 36-43).* Jesus Himself indicated that false Christians will be hidden within the organized Church.[19] In addition, when the apostles told new converts how they could be saved, they never made involvement with the Church a condition. Some typical passages are *Acts 3:12-26* and *Acts 16*,[20] declaring the Gospel which extends our thoughts far beyond Paul's defense before King Agrippa.

Two facts become apparent in the foregoing analysis: that 1) some within the organized church are not true believers and, 2) some are true believers who may not yet be affiliated with the institutional Church. It seems clear, therefore, that it is possible to be part of the mystical body of Christ even if one is not part of the organized, earthly church. Likewise, it seems apparent that a person can be part of the organized, earthly church and still not be a part of Christ's true Church.

Some groups, such as the Quakers and the Plymouth

Brethren, point to the corruption within the institutional church, and belittle the importance of the institutional Church. They stress the relationship of the individual to God through Christ, and avoid the establishment of membership rolls and formal patterns of leadership and traditional organization.

Others, for example the Roman Catholic Church, trace their beginning to the establishment of the Church by Christ, and claim that they have inherited from the apostles the authority to forgive sins and convey the saving grace of Christ *(Matthew 16:18)*. They believe that the personal spirituality of the ministering authorities

> *Matthew 16:18 And I say also unto thee, That thou art Peter, and upon this rock I will build my church, and the gates of hell shall not prevail against it.*

is irrelevant, as long as they are the duly appointed representatives of the church. As a consequence, all manner of sin and abuse of authority has been tolerated. According to Catholic doctrine, confession of a specific sin must be heard by a priest to grant forgiveness. *This* is not Bible doctrine.

A middle position is best, which identifies from the Scriptures the need for local church autonomies, as a source of teaching applied Biblical doctrine as the authority for discipline, and the church as a place of service, prayer, and fellowship. The fact that hypocrisy exists within an institutional church does not justify a blanket condemnation of the church and its work. The earliest believers saw a need for united prayer, study and fellowship *(Acts 2:41-47)*. There is strength in true doctrinal unity that provides an impact on the world for Christ *(II Timothy 2:15; 3:16, 17)*.

But listen to Paul as he ad-

> *II Timothy 3:16 All scripture is given by inspiration of God, and is profitable for doctrine, for reproof, for correction, for instruction in righteousness...*

dresses the Church of Corinth. He speaks out in regard to the strife and division he sees among the brethren. Compare I *Corinthians, chapters one and two*, with similar problems in churches today.

The members argue over petty issues. They deny that a simple gospel is needed, not the wisdom of their words. Preach Christ to these brethren, proclaiming the Cross to all those that perish in their foolishness. They can be saved from their depravity only by the God-given grace of the precious blood of Christ.

Under Christ's call and instruction Paul admonishes us that we study the Scriptures, for the Spirit searches out and knows all things needful for us to learn. When we receive God's Spirit, we understand everything that God has given us *(I Corinthians 2:10-16)*. The Bible is inerrant in its content; it is immutable in its requirements. In addition, the Word of God or Bible is irreversible in its plan and is irrevocable in its judgments. There is no appeal to any source outside the Bible for divine judgments *(Psalm 119:160)*.

As described in *I Corinthians 11:18-24,* it is necessary for each of us to examine ourselves, repent of our sins, and to forgive and restore others who have wronged us. Then, we partake of the Lord's Supper, eat the bread and drink the cup, informing others about the Lord's death until He comes again. God issues a warning to the persons who take the emblems and are not worthy of them. They are guilty of sinning against the body and blood of the Lord Jesus Christ. Therefore, judge yourself carefully, for the Lord chastens and judges us so that we will not be destroyed with the world *(Proverbs 19:18; Hebrews 12:6-8)*.

> *Proverbs 19:18*
> *Chasten thy son while there is hope, and let not thy soul spare for his crying.*

The churches of today are having other contentions. Their

members may be worthy, but negligent. One problem begets another. We have the Bible in numerous, easy-to-read versions and excellent translations. The Church must not permit the world to contaminate it. Ministers and Bible teachers need to feed their flock with plenty of Scripture that is coherent and can be applied to daily living. Many Christians are feeding on mere skim milk of the Word. They are being fed scraps rather than a solid diet of Scripture which will make them mature, fruitful Christians.

They need solid food in order to ward off the devil. God sifts us for His service. The Spirit does this so we can glorify the Father, serve His plan on the earth.

Other problems are manifest. Secondly, the writer of Hebrews admonishes people not to neglect the assembling of themselves together (*Hebrews 10:25*). Thirdly, Paul stresses that each believer has at least one spiritual gift that is useful in the building up of other saints in the faith *(Romans 12:1-8; I Corinthians 12:12-27; Ephesians 4:11-16; I Peter 4:7-11)*. Gathered together, His servants can restore and sustain one another.

The invisible church, or true believers, follow Christ by the grace of the baptism of the Holy Spirit. This group of regenerated believers span history and geography *(I Peter 2:5; Hebrews 11:40; Ephesians 1:22-23)*. This is why R. B. Kuiper[21] refers to the visible church as a caricature of the invisible. The image of the invisible Church is glorious; the image of the visible church is sterile and has often brought dishonor to Christ and the name Christian *(John 10:14-18)*. Christian organizations and church groups and, in fact, persons not in a specific group, are all vessels which may contain the invisible Church of Jesus Christ. Only the content matters to God, since He alone has the all-knowing capacity to determine the invisible Church to be raptured someday.

In the verb *ekkaleo, ek* means "out" and *kaleo* "to call out" *(Ephesians 2:19-20)*. The Church *(II Tim 3:15)*, therefore, is composed of the true born-again children of God, called for God's purposes and sanctified from the world by a sovereign God to be used solely for His own plan and reasons.[22] *I Corinthians 12:13* and *Colossians 1:18,19,24* make it clear that all those who know Christ have been placed into His body, which is the true Church. It is important for each of us to be sure of our standing before God. The true or invisible Church refers to all regenerated persons from Pentecost to the second coming of Christ. This comprises all saved people everywhere who are baptized by the Holy Spirit—not water baptism alone—into one body called the Church with Jesus as the head or chief cornerstone *(Colossians 1:18-20; Ephesians 1:22-23, 4:15-16)*.

The Church may or may not be a denomination which meets in a building *(I Peter 2:3-10)*. It is comprised of those who truly in their hearts call Jesus Lord and Savior and serve Him *(Galatians 2:20-21)*—Him alone. Yet only God can faultlessly determine who belongs to the true church and who does not *(II Timothy 2:19-21; I Corinthians 3:11-17)*.

In the final analysis, the Good News reaches the human race all over the world. Believers have a personal relationship in Christ, not religion. Therefore, we pray for greater love and unity among the members of the Body of Christ. By their doctrine you can know them; by their fruits you can know them *(Proverbs 11:30; Colossians 1:10-12; Romans 7:4-5; John 15:7-10)*. The Church will serve the needy, the depraved, and its brethren and will administer the function of witnessing—in season and out of season—in a social and spiritual manner which glorifies and gives God the total preeminence. The gates of Hades shall not prevail against her *(Matthew 16:18-19)*. God is in control and Jesus is the rock.

ENDNOTES

[1]. Lockyer, Herbert. *All The Doctrines of The Bible.* Grand Rapids, MI: Lamplighter Books, Zondervan Publishing House, 1964, pp. 234-240.

[2] Walvoord, John F.. "Prophesy And The Seventies;" in *Where Is The Modern Church Going?* C. L. Feinberg, Ed. Chicago, IL: Moody Press, 1971, pp. 111-123.

[3] Vine, W. E. *An Expository Dictionary of Biblical Words*; New York: Thomas Nelson Publishers, 1985, pp. 122 & 42.

[4] Vine. *op. cit.* p. 100.

[5] Fausset, A. R. *Bible Encyclopedia And Dictionary.* Grand Rapids, MI: Zondervan Publishing House, 1902, p. 130.

[6] Best, W. E. *The Church - Her Authority And Mission*; Houston TX: Best Book Missionary Trust, pp. 17-23, 75.

[7] Evans, William. *The Great Doctrines of The Bible.* Chicago, IL: Moody Press, 1912, p. 183.

[8] Strong, Augustus Hopkins. *Systematic Theology: A Compendium Commonplace - A Book Designed For The Use of Theological Students - A Doctrine of Salvation.* Philadelphia, PA: Judson Press, 1909, pp. 888-889.

[9] Lockyer, Herbert. *op. cit.,* pp. 229-267.

[10] Fausset. *op. cit.,* p. 130.

[11] Tenny; Merrill C. *Pictorial Bible Dictionary* Grand Rapids, MI: Zondervan Publishing House, 1964, p. 171.

[12] Enns, Paul. *The Moody Book of Theology. Chicago*, IL: Moody Press, 1989, p. 348.

[13] Fausset. *op. cit.*

[14] Vine. *op. cit.,* pp. 42 , 233.

[15] *Ibid.*, pp. 42, 233.

[16] *The Philadelphia Confession of Faith with Catechism.* Grand Rapids, Michigan: Associated Publishers and Authors, Inc., 1869, pp. 52-53.

[17] *Ibid.*, pp. 47-48.

[18] Enns. *op. cit.*, p. 348.

[19] Fausset. *op. cit.*, p. 130.

[20] Hammond, T. C. *In Understanding, Be Men.* DownersGrove, IL: IFCA Press, 1978, pp. 154-155.

[21].Kuiper, Rienk Bouke. *The Glorious Body of Christ.* Grand Rapids, MI: Wm. Errdmans Publishing Company, 1958, pp. 29-30.

[22].Saucy, Robert L. *The Church in God's Program.* Chicago,Il: Moody Press, 1972, pp. 11-19.

CHAPTER THREE: The Bible, God's Standard

An attempt is made here to interpret a standard or model closer to God's Word and will, as a preventive measure to ward off apostasy in the visible church. That standard is, in fact, the Bible, and the interpretations do not diverge from that model.

It should be noted herein that when the Holy Scriptures are inset and in italics, they are based upon the King James version of the Bible. In this doctrinal treatise in defense of Scripture, however, other versions of the Bible are used occasionally, in which case those cited are in direct quotes within the text. These carry the punctuation, capitalization, and wording of those more modern sources.

In addition, it should be stated that certain positions in regard to those Scriptures are taken from those of the Independent Fundamental Churches of America (IFCA),[1, 2], from the writer's biblical interpretations, and from other relevant sources.

Faith in the Holy Scriptures

The Holy Bible, as originally written, was the verbally-inspired product of Spirit-controlled men and, therefore, has all truth without any admixture of error in its matter. The Bible is, therefore, meant to be the true center of all Christian union and the supreme standard by which all human conduct, creeds, and positions, shall be tested and judged *(Matthew 5:17-19; II Timothy 3:16-17; II Peter 1:19-21; Job 32:8; I Corinthians 2:9-14; Psalm 119:97-160).*

There is one, and only one, living and true God. There is but one infinite intelligent Spirit, the Maker and Supreme Ruler of Heaven and Earth, inexpressively glorious in holiness and worthy of all possible honor, confidence, and love. Yet in the Godhead there are three persons: the Father, the Son, and the Holy Spirit, equal in every divine perfection and executing distinct but harmonious offices in the glorious work of redemption *(Exodus 20:2-3; I Corinthians 8:6, Revelation 4:11; I John 5:7; Matthew 28:19; John 15:24; 14:11, 16, 17, 26).*

The immutable, incarnated Christ is the Word, who was with God, and was God *(John 1:1)* and became man *(John 1:14).* Jesus Christ is the Second Person of the Triune Godhead, who was born and lived a sinless life in a real human body on earth and died a vicarious death to provide salvation for depraved men. Therefore, every human being who trusts Christ by faith is guaranteed a sinless, deathless, glorified body, like Christ's present glorified body *(Matthew 27:52; John 5:21-28).*

Legacy of the Scriptures

All false religions are based on human teachings. Human teachings are totally inadequate for arriving at oneness with the Triune Godhead. All belief must be based on the inerrant, infallible Word of God, which is the Holy Bible.

It is therefore stated herein that the Holy Scriptures of the Old and New Testaments are the verbally-inspired Word of God, the final authority for faith and life, inerrant in the original writings, infallible, and God-breathed *(II Timothy 3:16, 17; II Peter 1:20,21; Matthew 5:18; John 16:12,13)*.

God's Own Word

This is stated, not as the word of men, but as it is in truth the Word of God, which works effectually, also, in the believer *(I Thessalonians. 2:13)*. When we read the Bible, we should realize that we are receiving God's own message. We must appreciate the Bible, not only as fine literature, but as the very Word of God *(Colossians 3:10-17)*.

> *I Thessalonians 2:13*
> *For this cause also thank we God without ceasing, because when ye heard of us, ye received it not as the word of men, but as it is in truth, the word of God, which effectually worketh also in you that believe.*

Holy Spirit Inspired

Holy men of God spoke as they were moved by the Holy Ghost *(II Peter 1:21)*. The writers of the books of the Bible knew just what to write, because the Holy Spirit put the message into their minds. The whole Bible extends equally and fully into all its writings as they appeared in their original manuscripts. This does not take away the personalities of the writers. Each writer has his own individual style.

The original Hebrew, Aramaic, and Greek writings were without mistakes, because every word was verbally inspired by the Holy Spirit *(Mark 13:11; I Corinthians 2:13; Matthew 10:19)*.

Some present-day translations are without error in setting forth the original message as the Spirit gave it to the men

31

who wrote the books. Recent findings in archaeology prove the accuracy of most of our present translations. But some modern translations should be carefully scrutinized as to their interpretation of the deity of Christ.[3]

All Scripture was given by the inspiration of God, and it is profitable for the teaching of doctrine, for reproof, for correction, and for instruction in righteousness: that the man of God may be perfect and thoroughly furnished unto all good works *(II Timothy 3:16,17)*.

Proofs of the Scriptures

1. Every prophecy concerning things which would happen up to the present has been literally fulfilled. For example, Jerusalem has been returned to Israel in the twentieth century. Some prophecies are about things still in the future, but they will also be fulfilled in God's own time and according to His plan.

2. The miraculous unity, and agreement, in the Bible exceeds that of any other book. It was written by approximately forty different writers, who lived in different locations during a period of 1600 years; yet unity is in every book. The real author of all of them was God, the Holy Spirit.

3. The miraculous results of the Scriptures, also, show that it is trustworthy. The Scriptures say, "Ye must be born again," and every person who has come to Christ in faith has experienced the miracle of a new birth and a changed life.[4]

4. The Scriptures will never be destroyed. Infidels, and scoffers have never succeeded in destroying God's Word, and they never will. Jesus said, "Heaven and earth shall pass away, but my words shall not pass away *(Matthew 24:35; Jude 18)*."

Attributes of the Godhead

There is one triune God, eternally existing in three persons: Father, Son, and Holy Spirit. These are co-eternal in being, co-identical in nature, co-equal in power and glory, and they have the same attributes and perfections. "Hear, O Israel: the Lord our God is one Lord *(Deuteronomy 6:4)*." "The grace of the Lord Jesus Christ, and the love of God, and the communion of the Holy Ghost be with you all *(II Corinthians 13:14)*." That Word is revealed also in *Matthew 28:18-19; Mark 12:29; John 1:14; Acts 5:3-4; Hebrews 1:1-3; Revelation 1:4-6.*

> *Mark 12:29 And Jesus answered him, The first of all the commandments is, Hear, O Israel; The Lord our God is one Lord...*

The Trinity reveals and expresses one God in three eternal distinct entities; who are equal persons in that Trinity, or Godhead. The equal persons are Father, Son and Holy Spirit. Note that each is distinct from the other, yet the three are united as one God. Triunity may best be expressed by Jesus Christ in *Matthew 28:18-20.* Jesus elaborates on the great commission. He tells His Church to go forth and preach: teach everywhere in the name of God, Jesus Christ and the Holy Spirit *(John 14:11, 16, 17, 26; II Corinthians 13:14; I Peter 1:2)*. The three persons in the Godhead (triune God) are one God in substance, equal in power, and glory. Search the Judeo-Christian sources of *Deuteronomy 6:4,5; Isaiah 43:10-11; Isaiah 44:6-8, 45:21-23; I Corinthians 8:5-6* and *Acts 17:29*; search even His eternal power and Godhead, so that men are without excuse. For the Godhead is not like man's devices and entrapments *(Romans 1:20)*.

> *Acts 17:29 Foreasmuch then as we are the offspring of God, we ought not to think that the Godhead is like unto gold, or silver, or stone, graven by art and man's device.*

In Christ dwells all the fullness of the Godhead *(Colossians 2:8-10)*. Yet the word Trinity is not found in Scripture. The doctrine of the Trinity is interpreted from Scripture, however, in order to comprehend the three united persons or relational modes without separate existence which form one true God. We are to understand that the holy divine nature subsists in three distinctions: the Father, Son, and Holy Spirit, but that God is undivided.[5]

Note the unity within three persons expressed in *Isaiah 48:16*: "Come close to me. Listen to this: from the beginning, I have not spoken in secret. Now, the Lord Jehovah and His Spirit has sent Me." We must then ask: "Sent who?" It is the Christ who is in unity with Jehovah God and His Spirit.[6] Therefore, three persons have a unique, distinct relationship, and are equal in authority, and function. Therefore, God is Father; God is Son; God is Spirit.[7] The Father is not begotten, nor does He proceed from any person; the Son is eternally begotten from the Father (*John 1:18, 3:16, 18; I John 4:9*).

The term *generation* suggests the Trinitarian relationship in the Son, who is eternally begotten of the Father. The Holy Spirit eternally proceeds from the Father, and the Son (*John 14:26, 16:7; I Thessalonians 1:2-5*). The word *proceeds* suggests the Trinitarian relationship of the Father and the Son sending the Spirit. These terms denote a *relationship* within the Trinity, and do not suggest inferiority in any way.[8] "Although terms like *generation* and *procession* may be used in referring to the functioning within the Trinity, it is important to realize that the three persons are equal in authority. The Father is recognized as authoritative, and supreme (*I Corinthians 8:6*); the Son is also recognized as equal to the Father in every respect (*John 5:21-23*); and the Spirit is likewise recognized as equal to

> *I Corinthians 8:6 But to us there is but one God, the Father, of whom are all things, and we in him; and one Lord Jesus Christ, by whom are all things, and we by him.*

the Father and Son *(Matthew 12:31-32)*."[9] Things equal to the same thing are equal to each other.

The qualities and characteristics of the nature of God are known as His attributes. Some of these are:

A. God is eternal.

"Before the mountains were created, or you have formed the earth and the world, even from everlasting to everlasting, thou art God *(Psalm 90:2)*." God never had a beginning and never will have an end. This also means that God has always had life in Himself, apart from any other being.

B. God is incomprehensible.

"O, the depths of the riches, both of the wisdom, and knowledge of God! How unsearchable are his judgments, and his ways past finding out *(Romans 11:33)*." God is beyond the grasp of human understanding. A God whom we could fully comprehend is beyond our imagination *(Matthew 11:27)*.

C. God is invisible

"No man has seen God at any time; the only born Son, who is in the bosom of the Father, He has declared Him *(John 1:18; 5:37)*." No one has ever seen God, because God is Spirit, and, therefore, cannot be seen with human eyes *(I Timothy 1:17; Colossians 1:15; Hebrews 11:27; John 4:24)*.

> *John 4:24   God is a Spirit; and they that worship him must worship him in spirit and in truth.*

D. God is immutable.

"I am the Lord, I change not *(Malachi 3:6)*." "Every good gift, and every perfect gift is from above, and comes down from the Father of lights, with whom is no variableness, neither shadow of turning *(James 1:17)."* God's immutability means that God never changes. As He was from eternity, so He is today and in the future[10] *(Hebrews 1:10-12; 13:8).*

E. God is omnipotent.

"I know that you can do everything *(Job 42:2)."* "Behold, I am the Lord, the God of all flesh; is there anything too hard for me *(Jeremiah. 32:27)*?" There is nothing impossible with God. "Jesus saw them, and said unto them, 'With men, this is impossible; but with God all things are possible' *(Matthew 19:26)."* Omnipotent means all powerful. There is nothing that God cannot do. God allows Satan and sin to reign for His sovereign reasons, which are often incompressible to us and for which He does not owe us an explanation *(Mark 1:27; John 5:19-21; I Peter 3:21-22).* Satan's doom is sure in God's own time.

F. God is omniscient.

"God is greater than our heart, and knows all things *(I John 3:20)."* "Great is our Lord, and of great power: His understanding is infinite *(Psalm 147:5)."* There is nothing that God does not know. He is omniscient *(Matthew 9:4; 12:25; Luke 6:8; 9:47; 11:17; Colossians 2:23).*

G. God is omnipresent.

"Where shall I go from Your Spirit? Where shall I flee from Your presence? If I ascend up into Heaven, You are there; and, if I make my bed in hell (Sheol, the place of departed spirits) behold, You are there. If I take the wings of the morning, and dwell in the uttermost parts of the sea; even there you shall lead me, and Your right hand shall hold me *(Psalm 139:7-10)."* Omnipresent means present everywhere. There is no place where we can hide from God's presence *(Matthew 28:26; John 1:48; 3:13).*

H. God is sovereign.

"For of Him, and through Him, and to him, are all things: To Him be the glory forever (Romans 11:36)." See also *Genesis 24:3; Exodus 15:18; 18:11; Psalm 113:4; John 19:11*; and *Act 17:24-26.*

God's divine plan of all things, including our salvation, was determined by Him, without consultation with any other being. God knew the end of all things, and all His creatures from the beginning; thus He ordained all things according to His own divine will and plan *(Colossians 1:12-18).* The sovereignty of God means that God has supreme power and is unlimited in all that He performs, and that He does not need to give an account of His doings to anyone *(I Samuel 2:6-10; I Chronicles. 29:11,12).* God's sovereignty is supreme and all-powerful, all-knowing, and present everywhere. Satan has not this capacity, or ability, and will be totally destroyed by God's sovereignty in the future. Study *Ephesians 1:11.*

God marks out, elects,[11] and selects those of His choosing—which will be teachers or evangelists, and which will be pastors—while others who hear the Good News will go their own way in this world. They are Gospel-hardened, or impermeable to His call *(Romans 9:15-19; Ephesians 1:5, 11; Romans 8:29; Acts 4:28; I Corinthians 2:7).*[12]

A good, moral, well-meaning person may still be depraved or sin-corrupted by God's standard of perfection. Mankind can do nothing for his own salvation. God has offered the gift of eter-

> *Ephesians 1:11 In whom also we have obtained an inheritance, being predestinated according to the purpose of him who worketh all things after the counsel of his own will...*

nal life to man, but a man must accept the gift of salvation only though faith in Jesus Christ.

God is sovereign. He does nothing contrary to His own nature and administers everything according to His divine plan. He chooses in love whom He wants *(Ephesians 1:3-14)*, but allows limited free will to those who respond and obey Him. Will the lost ever respond to His plan of salvation? Note that Saul, Cain, Pilate, Alexander, Demetrius, and Diotrephes are some examples of those who rejected God's way. Their sinful condition was not transformed into the new birth.

To this present day *(Romans 9:14-24)*, the above premises apply. God has mercy on whom He will, and whom He will He hardens. This is termed God's free will of purpose *(Romans 10:9-18)*. The Word is near you, in your mouth and heart *(Deuteronomy 30:11-14)*. All you do is confess your sins and believe sincerely in your heart. God in turn offers you His grace (unmerited favor) and His free gift of everlasting life *(Ephesians 2:8-9)*. Again the choices belong to you unless the Sovereign God distinctly chooses you for His purposes.

A few examples taken from Scripture, of those especially selected by God, are: David chosen of God *(Psalm 78:70)*; the conversion of Saul of Tarsus on the road to Damascus *(Acts 1:1-9)*; Peter chosen by Jesus to build His Church *(Matthew 16:17-19)*; Jeremiah the prophet is called out *(Jeremiah 1:4-19)*, and many others. Only God can change the sinful condition through the power of the Holy Spirit. You are tranformed as a new creature in Christ. Neither will human reasoning, eclectic philosphy, religiosity, nor high morals ever give you a transformed life in Christ to enter the Kingdom of God.

God has elected, chosen, selected, who He will. It is by God's eternal decree. Study *Romans 8:29* and *Ephesians 1:4, 5, 11* once again in this context.

The Person and Work of Christ

The following doctrinal statements are made to summarize the source, the origin, the nature and the destiny of our Lord, Jesus Christ:

1. The Lord Jesus Christ, the eternal Son of God, became man, without ceasing to be God, having been conceived by the Holy Spirit, and born of the Virgin Mary, in order that He might reveal God, and redeem sinful men *(John 1:1,2,14; Luke 1:35)*.

2. The Lord Jesus Christ accomplished our redemption through His death on the cross as an advocate, vicarious, substitutionary sacrifice; and our justification is made sure by His literal, physical resurrection from the dead *(Romans 3:24, 25; I Peter 2:24; Ephesians 1:7; I Peter 1:3-5; John 21:24, 25)*.

3. The Lord Jesus Christ ascended to Heaven, and is now exalted at the right hand of God. He is our High Priest. He fulfills the ministry of Intercessor, and Advocate *(Acts 1:9, 10; Hebrews 7:25, 9:24; Romans 8:34; I John 2:1, 2)*.

The Person of Christ

1. Christ is God

"In the beginning was the Word , and the Word was with God, and Word was God *(John 1:1)*."

"But, unto the Son, He (God, the Father) saith, Thy throne, O God, is forever and ever… *(Hebrews 1:8)*." From these passages and others *(Psalm 2:6-12)* we know that Christ is defined as God.

2. Christ became man

Christ, the son of God, became the Son of Man at His birth, and throughout His earthly life, was always both God, and man. "And the angel answered and said unto Mary, The

Holy Ghost shall come upon you, and the power of the Highest shall overshadow you; therefore, also that Holy child who shall be born of you shall be called the Son of God *(Luke 1:35).*"

"And the Word (Christ) was made flesh (man), and dwelt among us, (and we beheld his glory, the glory as of the only Begotten of the Father), full of grace and truth *(John 1:14)."*

Many today (Jehovah's Witnesses, Orthodox Jews, some liberals, and cults) deny that Christ was the Son of God. They do not believe that the Deity became a human and dwelt in the world.

"Hereby know you the Spirit of God: Every spirit that confesses that Jesus Christ is come in the flesh is of God and every spirit that confesses not that Jesus Christ is come in the flesh is not of God: and that spirit of Antichrist, whereof you have heard that it should come; and even now already is in the world *(I John 4:2, 3)."*

The only person who could redeem us from sin was God Himself, who became man for us *(Psalm 49:7,15).* As the sinless son of God, Christ could be a perfect sacrifice for our sins and satisfy the Justice of a Holy God.

Having made peace through His atoning death, He could become our great high priest before God *(Isaiah. 53).* Through the atonement of our sins by the son's death on the cross, God maintained His holiness while extending His mercy to a world of sinners, "that he might be just, and the justifier of him which believeth in Jesus *(Romans 3:26)."*

The Work of Christ[13]

1. Past—Christ became our Savior.

The purpose of Christ's coming into the world was the salvation of sinners, and this purpose was accomplished by His death as our substitute *(Romans 5:6-9; II Corinthians*

5:21).

"And she shall bring forth a Son, and you shall call His Name Jesus: for He shall save His people from their sins *(Matthew 1:21)*."

"Neither is there salvation in any other: for there is no other name (the name of Jesus, verse 10) under Heaven, given among men, whereby we must be saved *(Acts 4:12)*."

To be our Savior, it was necessary in God's plan for Him to die, to be buried, and to rise again.

"For I delivered unto you, first of all, that which I also received, how that Christ died for our sins according to the Scriptures; and that He was buried, and that He rose the third day, according to the Scriptures *(I Corinthians 15:3, 4)*."

2. The Triumph of the Resurrection

The uniqueness and glory of Christ's resurrected life is not acknowledged outside Christianity. Jesus Christ, the Son of God, provides the surety that the believer will also be resurrected to everlasting life. The gospels teach the physical resurrection of Christ by credible witnesses and examples *(Luke 24:1-48)*. Some infallible proofs of Christ's resurrection are the forerunner of ours. Marvel not at this, because an hour is coming when all believers who are in their graves shall hear His voice and shall come forth; and those alive in Christ will be resurrected. It is not too late for the living to believe that God's grace bestows eternal life and for them to be included in one of the many stages of the first resurrection *(I Thessalonians 4:13-18; Revelation 11:12; 20:4b, 12-13).*

Those who practice evil will be ushered into the resurrection of condemnation. We would not have you be ignorant like other men who have no hope. But if we really believe that Jesus died for our sins and has risen from death to life, ascending to heaven to reign as our Lord and Savior, our hope and faith in the Lord Jesus Christ is good not only for the present life but for eternity. Therefore stand firm and immovable in your faith, resist the devil and his advocates, and always abound in the productive work of the Lord *(I Corinthians 15:1-58)*.

The Doctrine of the Holy Spirit

The Holy Spirit is a divine person, is coequal with the Father and the Son, and is eternal and of the same essence, majesty and glory with the Father and the Son. Therefore, the Holy Spirit is truly God. *(I John 5:6-8; Romans 8:9-16; Matthew 28:19; John 16:7-16; Acts 5:3-4)*.

The Holy Spirit is the person who convicts the world of sin, of righteousness, and of judgement; and He is the supernatural agent in regeneration, baptizing all believers into the body (Church) of Christ, indwelling in them, and sealing them unto the day of redemption *(John 16:8-11; II Corinthians 3:6; 12:12-14; Romans 8:9; Ephesians 1:13-14)*.

He is the divine teacher who guides believers into all truth; and the saved are indwelled with His Holy Spirit *(John 16:13; I John 2:20, 27; Ephesians 5:18)*.

The Holy Spirit is a Person

"But when the Comforter comes, whom I will send unto you from the Father, the Spirit of Truth, who goes out from the Father, He will testify about me *(John 15:26)*."

Notice that the Holy Spirit is referred to by Christ as "He", using the masculine pronoun, even though the word *spirit* is neuter. This shows that it is always correct to refer to the Holy Spirit as "He" or "Him", but not as "It." Christ said, "He (the Holy Spirit) will speak of Me."

Work of the Holy Spirit in the World

And when He (the Holy Spirit) comes, in righteousness

and in judgment, He will rebuke the world for its sin. The work of the Holy Spirit is to convict the sinner of his sin. This is an important truth. Unless a sinner is convicted of sin, he will never turn to the Savior for salvation *(John 16:7-15).*

Work of the Holy Spirit in the Believer

1. Regeneration:

"Not by works of righteousness which we have done, but according to His mercy. He saved us, by the washing of regeneration, and renewing of the Holy Spirit *(Titus 3:5, 6). See also John 1:13; Ephesians 2:1, 5)."*

The Holy Spirit brings about a renewing, that is, a new life, as Jesus mentioned to Nicodemus: "Except a man be born of water, and of the Spirit, he cannot enter into the Kingdom of God *(John 3:1-18; 14:17)."* Christ told the woman at the well that whoever drinks of the living water that I give shall never thirst into everlasting life *(John 4:1-15).*

"For as many as are led by the Spirit of God, they are the sons of God *(Romans 8:9-14)."*

The Holy Spirit leads us into a Christian life if we yield ourselves wholly to Him *(Ezekiel. 36:27; Acts 16:10).*

"The Spirit, Himself bears, witness with our spirit that we are the children of God *(Romans 8:16)."* See also *Romans 5:6-9; II Samuel 3:2; Isaiah 59:21.*

The Holy Spirit gives us this assurance of our salvation through the evidence of our new life as it harmonizes with the Word of God *(I Corinthians 2:10).* See also *Romans 8:2-4.*

"Praying always with all prayer and supplication in the Spirit, and watching thereunto with all perseverance and suppli-

> *I Corinthians 6:19*
> *What? Know ye not that your body is the temple of the Holy Ghost which is in you which ye have of God, and ye are not your own?*

cation for all saints *(Ephesians 6:18)."*

The Holy Spirit helps, guides, and gives power to the believer when he prays *(Jude 20)*.

"But you are not in the flesh, but in the Spirit, if so be that the Spirit of God dwells in you. Now, if any man have not the Spirit of Christ, he is not of His *(Romans 8:9)."*

Every truly born-again Christian is indwelt by the Holy Spirit *(Matthew 3-11)*.

"For by one Spirit are we all baptized into one body *(I Corinthians 12:13)."*

2. Our relationship is with the Holy Spirit[14]

"Know you not that you are the temple of God, and that the Spirit of God dwells in you *(I Corinthians 3:16; 6:19)?"*

What an honor it is to have the Holy Spirit use our bodies as His temple, but what a serious thought that He is always present, wherever we go!

3. Indwelling Spirit

You are now not in the flesh, but in the Spirit, for the Spirit of God lives in you. Remember, any man who does not have the Spirit of Christ, is not born again (Romans 8:9). Your body then, is the temple of the Holy Spirit. You are not your own, but God's disciple or ambassador to do His will *(I Corinthians 6:19). It is the highest honor bestowed upon mankind when the Holy Spirit uses our bodies as His temple.* No man, religion, or even philosophy has the capacity to turn a child of wrath into a child of God. God is always present, wherever we go.

We pray for help to glorify God in our bodies. We pray thus: Not that I am sufficient to attain in myself any reasonable conclusion by my own righteousness and wisdom, but my sufficiency is from God *(II Corinthians 2:14-17; 3:5)*.

4. Spirit and Water Baptism

With one Holy Spirit, we are all spiritually baptized into one body, His Church *(I Corinthians 12:13)*. We are now members of the body of Jesus Christ, His invisible Church. Water baptism, whatever mode is used, identifies the believer with other members of the church. The water baptism is a symbol of spiritual baptism. Jesus Christ commanded the new Christian to be baptized, for this is a sign of the Christian's fellowship with Him in His death *(Romans 6:3-5; Colossians 2:12; Galatians 3:27)*.

Baptism is also a sign of His resurrection *(Mark 1:4; Acts 26:16)* and of His giving himself up to God, through our Lord Jesus Christ, to live and walk in the newness of life *(Romans 6:2,4)*. The condition is that those persons must profess Christ *(Mark 16:16; Acts 8:36, 37)*. True repentance is a change in mind and a change of will toward God, through total faith and obedience to Jesus Christ. Water is used, and the convert is baptized in the name of the Father, the Son, and the Holy Spirit.[15]

Remember, the teaching of a particular baptism was especially distasteful to many, for just as Jewish believers taught by the Old Testament found it hard to give up physical circumcision, so the church, today, has stubbornly clung to its water baptism, which is merely symbolic of Holy Spirit baptism *(Matthew 3:5, 6, 11; Acts 2:38; 8:14-17; 10:44-48; 19:2-5)*. Indeed, water baptism is the circumcision of Christendom. It is actually the Holy Spirit who circumcises the deceitful heart of man. It is the Trinity who cleans up a person and gives him a new nature. The old nature becomes submissive to the new nature as the Holy Spirit directs, teaches, and comforts that person in all his inadequacies *(John 14:26; Galatians 3:13; 6:15)*.

So we must remember, it is the riches of God's grace alone *(Ephesians 1:7; Philippians 3:4-9)*, and not religion, which places the believer in "one body" and "one baptism" in Christ, and its heavenly position and blessings are innumerable. How can Bible preaching and teaching in our present day continue to be largely humanistic, superficial, and insipid?[16] God forbid!

God gave us His precious promise that His Word will not return void *(Isaiah 55:11)*. The decision is ours, and it can be a living decision for Christ—and immortality—or a deadly decision of eternal torment with Satan and his demons. This is a stark reality.

5. Sealing

We were sealed by that Holy Spirit of promise *(Revelation 7:3)*. The Spirit is the unconditional guarantee of our inheritance, when the soul, spirit, and glorified body will again be united in Christ to the praises of His glory *(Ephesians 1:13; 4:30; John 3:33; 6:27)*. We have a common inheritance, a complete redemption of His purchased property. We were bought with a price; but our assurance is sound, because God always keeps His Word. If we go back on our faith in Jesus Christ as Lord and Savior, have we really experienced a true conversion? This is not an emotional experience alone, but a spiritual truth in a persons's life.

6. Filling

"Be filled with the Spirit *(Ephesians 5:18; I John 5:6-9)*." This is a time when we are threading our way through a very complicated process, We are subduing our old nature while our new nature is being nurtured and comforted by the Holy Spirit in progressive sanctification. Sanctification is a condition after the rebirth, of being set apart from worldly and sinful acts, unto a holy purpose. We surrender our lives to Him in complete yieldedness. We give Him the full right-of-way. We must yield to Him daily as the Spirit prays, teaches, and comforts the believer *(Genesis 6:3; Isaiah 11:2; Matthew 10:12, 24, 40-42; John 14:16-17, 26)*. "Repent, and be baptized." You will receive the gift of the Holy Spirit *(Acts 2:38, 39)*.

We grieve Him when we wilfully sin, when we harbor sinful thoughts, when we yield to temptations, when we lose our tempers, when we neglect our spiritual responsibilities, and when we wilfully resist Him *(Ephesians 4:30)*.

"Quench not the Spirit *(I Thessalonians. 5:19)*." We are sanctified by God the Father, God the Son, and God the Holy Spirit *(I Thessalonians 5:23; Ephesians 5:26; Romans 15:16)*.

Just as fire is put out with water, so the fire of the Holy Spirit in our lives can be quenched by worldliness, lack of prayer and testimony, and other sins (such as pride, jealousy, falsehood, deceitfulness, backbiting, etc.).

Peter said, "Ananias, why has Satan filled your heart to lie to the Holy Spirit, and to keep back part of the price of the land *(Acts 5:3)*?" Ananias told a half-truth, and Peter called this "lying to the Holy Spirit."

"All manner of sin, and blasphemy shall be forgiven unto men; but the blasphemy against the Holy Spirit shall not be forgiven unto men *(Matthew 12:31)*."

This dreadful sin was committed by the Pharisees when they attributed to Satan the work of the Holy Spirit, in the ministry of Jesus when He cast out a demon.

Blasphemy against the Holy Spirit cannot be committed by a truly born-again Christian. "He is able to keep that confidence which I have committed to Him ..." my soul which is "kept by the power of God unto salvation *(Philippians 1:6)*."

ENDNOTES

[1]. *This We Believe*. Westchester, IL: Independent Fundamental Churches of America, Vol. 1, 1970.

2. *This We Believe*. Grandville, MI: Independent Fundamental Churches of America, Vol. ll, 1980.

3. Torrey, R. A. *What The Bible Teaches*. Fleming H Revell Co., 1898-1933, pp. 245-268.

4. Zuck, Roy B. *Basic Bible Interpretation* . Wheaton, IL: Victor Books, Division of Scripture Press Pub., Inc., 1991, pp. 70-75.

5. Enns, Paul. *The Moody Handbook of Theology*; Chicago, IL: Moody Press, 1989, pp. 199-200.

6. Green, Jay P., Sr. *The Interlinear Hebrew-Aramaic Old Testament*. Peabody, MA: Hendricksen Publishing, 1985, p. 1702.

7. Enns. *op. cit.*, pp. 198-203.

8. *Ibid.*, p. 200.

9. *Ibid.*, p. 200.

10. Torrey, R. A. *op. cit.*, pp. 21, 23, 30-33; 70-74.

11. Worrell, A. S. *The New Testament Revised and Translated*. Philadelphia, PA: American Baptist Publication Society, 1904, Appendix D, p. 12.

12. Enns, Paul. *op. cit.*, pp. 340-341, & 480-482.

13. Bancroft, Emery H. *Elemental Theology, Doctrinal and Conservative*. Grand Rapids, MI: Zondervan Publications, 1970, pp. 311-312.

14. Scofield, C. I. *The New Life In Jesus Christ*. Chicago, IL: The Bible Institute of the Colportage Association, 1915, pp. 67-74.

15. *The Philadelphia Confession of Faith With Catechism*. Grand Rapids, MI: Associated Publishers and Authors, Inc., 1869, pp. 52-53.

16. Stam, Cornelius R. *The Berean Searchlight*. Chicago, IL: 1991, p. 330.

CHAPTER FOUR: The Promise of Salvation

The Depravity of Man

Doctrinal Statement

Man was created in the image and likeness of God, but in Adam's sin the whole human race fell, inherited a sinful nature, and became alienated from God. Man is totally depraved. He is unable to remedy his lost condition *(Genesis 21:26, 17; Romans 3:22, 23; 5:12; Ephesians 2:1-3, 12)*. In this section Bible Doctrine will be reviewed which describes the total depravity of man, his fall from grace, and the salvation God has offered. Yet man was created in the image of God.

Man was created in the image of God

In the Scriptures we read: "And God said, Let us make man in our own image, after our own likeness... So God created man in his own image, in the image of God created He him, male and female created He them *(Genesis 1:26, 27)*."

49

> *Colossians 3:10 And have put on the new man, which is renewed in knowledge after the image of Him that created him...*

This does not mean that man was created in the likeness of God bodily, because God has no body. He is a Spirit. It means, however, that man was created in the image, or likeness of God's righteousness and holiness.

We are told: "And be renewed in spirit of your mind, and that you put on the new man, which, after God, is created in righteousness and true holiness *(Ephesians 4:23, 24).*'

The image of God in which man was first created was lost by man through sin, but God sent His Son to pay the price for our sins, and offer us the gift of eternal life, by faith in Jesus Christ *(Colossians 3:10).*

Man was made the head of creation

After mankind was created in the image of God, "God blessed them, and said unto them, Be fruitful and multiply, and replenish the earth, and subdue it, and have dominion over the fish of the sea, and over the fowl of the air, and over every living thing that moves upon the earth *(Genesis 1:28).*" Man, however, disobeyed God.

Man disobeyed God and thus fell in sin

Why? We are perplexed that God allowed man to fall from perfection. Only God knows all the reasons. We can only come to understand that man in God's image could not be required. God allowed that man be given a choice. Given that choice, however, man fell from grace.

"When the woman saw that the tree was good for food, and that it was pleasant to the eyes, and a tree to be desired to make one wise, she took of the fruit thereof, and did eat, and gave also unto her husband with her; and he did eat *(Genesis*

3:6)."

Adam was the head of the human race; therefore, in him the whole human race fell in sin *(Romans 5:12)*. So death passed upon all men, for that all have sinned.

By one man's disobedience, all were made sinners *(Romans 5:19)*.

> *Romans 5:19 For as by one man's disobedience many were made sinners, so by the obedience of one shall many be made righteous.*

After Adam sinned, every man in the world has been born in sin, having a sinful nature *Psalm 58:3).* ;The sole exception was Jesus Christ, who was not conceived by an earthly father, but by the Holy Spirit (

This is the true picture of every person who was ever born or ever will be born. Man is totally depraved and capable of any sin. Man can do nothing to save himself or help himself out of his sinful condition. It is only by the grace of God that this fallen image can be changed. "For all have sinned, and come short of the glory of God *(Romans 3:23)."*

"As it is written, there is none righteous, no not one *(Romans 3:10)."* Read also *Romans 3:11-18*. This is the true picture of an unregenerate person. "For there is not a just man upon the earth that does good, and sins not *(Ecclesiastes. 7:20)."*

Man needs a Savior

It becomes evident that man is in need of a Savior. "For as in Adam all die, even so, in Christ shall all be made alive *(I Corinthians 15:22)."* One must understand, however, that this is an etermal promise for believers only.

All who will come to Christ, believing and accepting Him as Savior, will be saved. Through the obedience of one (Christ), many will be made righteous *(Romans 5:19)*. Christ as the son of God taught us: "Verily, verily, I say unto you, unless a man be born again, he cannot see the kingdom of God *(John 3:3)*."

Man's destiny is overwhelming[1]

The grace that God manifests toward those who believe in Him seems at times overwhelming. Indeed, His promise is: "For God so loved the world, that He gave His only begotten Son, that whosoever believes in Him should not perish, but have everlasting life *(John 3:16, 36)*."

"It is appointed unto men once to die, but after this, the judgement *(Hebrews 9:27)*." We are promised a place of no night, where we need neither candle nor light of the sun *(Revelation 21:4-8)* where we will abide in His eternal grace *(Revelation 22:21)*.

Man has one of two choices, heaven or hell. We can gain heaven only by faith in the Lord Jesus Christ. Hell is the destiny of all those who reject Christ as their Lord and Savior. If you are indifferent about salvation, what will happen to your soul (Ezekiel 18:4, 20; Mark 8:36-37)?

Salvation-Regeneration-Sanctification

Salvation is the gift of God brought to man by grace and received by personal faith in the Lord Jesus Christ, whose precious blood was shed on Calvary *(Luke 23:33-43)* for the forgiveness of our sins *(John 1:12; Ephesians 1:7-10; I Peter 1:18)*. One of the greatest God-given gifts we have is the power to respond. God then effects changes in the direction of our lives. Christ came to offer regeneration and forgiveness to the ungodly, who were not saved. Study

> *John 1:12 But as many as received him, to them gave he power to become the sons of God, even to them that believe on his name...*

and analyze *I Timothy 1:15; Luke 19:10; II Corinthians 5:21; Hebrews 2:14-15* for further understanding.

Regeneration, or new birth,[2] is defined as impartation of new, righteous, Christ-like spirit by the Holy Spirit of God*(Matthew 19:28; Titus 3:5-8)*. Regeneration can never be repeated. It is to be forever with God. It is Christ within us; the Spirit produces a new birth *(John 3:3-10)*. One must meet God face to face to give an account of himself *(Romans 14:12; Hebrews 9:27-28)*. Every person must see conversion as a turning to God. Therefore, regeneration or rebirth *(John 3:3-7)* is brought about by the Holy Spirit indwelling in the believer.

Therefore, salvation is confession, repentance of sin, and conversion through faith, believing in Christ. Then God forgives us of our sins immediately. The Holy Spirit comes into the soul and spirit of the believer and changes that person, making him a new creature in Christ. It is not the result of human effort, but it is an act of God which imparts a divine new nature *(II Peter 1:4)* and a new self *(Ephesians 4:24)*.

> *II Peter 1:4 Whereby are given unto us exceeding great and precious promises: that by these ye might be partakers of the divine nature, having escaped the corruption that is in the world through lust.*

The believer now has the capacity for righteous living because he is a new creature in Christ. He has been given a divine nature and a new heart *(Romans 5:5)* to love God (*I John 4:9*), and a new will *(Romans 6:13)* so that the believer's soul has the capacity to obey God. The believer is set apart or sanctified before God, and he grows more spiritual and able to serve and glorify the Savior in a Christlike manner.

In the plan of salvation there is a sequential order to the elements which constitute it. First, faith and repentance must precede justification; second, justification must precede sanctification; and, third, sanctification must precede glorification. There is an irreversibility to the plan of salvation for the saved. To reverse the order is heresy.

By grace you are saved

"For by grace are you saved through faith; and that not of yourselves, it is the gift of God; not of works, lest any man should boast *(Ephesians 2: 8-9)*."

These verses summarize God's way of salvation. A person will vacillate because of his conscious strong will, sinful nature and spiritual blindness *(Romans 9:18; 11:7; 14:23; I Corinthians 2:14-15 contrast)*, "being justified freely by His grace through the redemption that is in Christ Jesus *(Romans 3:24)*."

However, "where sin abounded, grace did much more abound; that as sin has reigned unto death, even so, might grace reign through righteousness unto eternal life by Jesus Christ, our Lord *(Romans 5:20,21)*."

Furthermore, God's grace brings salvation to all men, schooling us to renounce evil*(Titus 2:11-12)*.

Salvation through faith

"Now faith is the substance (confident assurance) of things hoped for, the evidence (conviction of their reality) of things not seen *(Hebrews 11:1)*." We can now have confident assurance that God's grace is a reality *(Galatians 5:6; I Corinthians 2:5; II Corinthians 4:16)*. We can know the power of God as faith works through love.

If we believe, if we have faith in the Lord Jesus Christ, we shall be saved *(Acts 16:31; Acts 17:11-12; John 4:41-42; Mark 9:23)*.

Faith is the manner in which the person has personal confidence in God *(James 2:17)*. Unger[3] analyzes the expression of faith in several ways:

1. A saving faith is induced by the Spirit, causing a person to trust Christ as his sin-bearer *(Hebrews 9:28).*

2. A serving faith prompts the child of God, with the help of the Holy Spirit, to bend his redeemed life to God's will, rather than his own will *(Romans 12:1-5; Corinthians 1:18-25).*

3. A sanctifying faith demonstrates that the believer has grace, and a divine power from Christ *(Romans 6:11).*

4. A responsive faith is a growing likeness to Christ which bears the fruit of the Holy Spirit *(Galatians 5:22,23).*

5. A doctrinal faith is a loving, living trust in the body of Biblical truth *(I Corinthians 16:13; Colossians 1:23; 2:7; Jude 1:3).*

Faith satisfies, pleases and honors the triune God. The believer comes to God and has faith that God is the rewarder of all that diligently seek Him *(Hebrews 11:6; Matthew 6:33).* We must remember that this is through Christ's atoning death on the cross *(Romans 5:13-21).* Because of the trespass of one man, Adam, many die, but much more did the grace of God and the free gift of one man, Christ, bring salvation to all men.

Grace is unmerited favor bestowed on us by God, but it must be received through faith. Grace is the reservoir of God's abundant supply of salvation; Faith is but the heart's trustful, sincere sure response to the precious promise of God *(Hebrews 11:1-3).*

We have many Scriptural assurances of that promise:

"But to him that works not, but believes on Him that justifies the ungodly, his faith is counted for righteousness *(Romans 4:5)."*

"But as many as receive Him (through faith), to them gave He power to become the sons of God, even to them that believe on His name *(John 1:12)."*

"He that believes on the Son has everlasting life *(John 3:36)."*

"For God so loved the world that He gave His only begotten Son, that whosoever believes in Him should not perish, but have everlasting life *(John 3:16)*." The Lord... is not willing that any should perish, but that all should come to repentance *(II Peter 3:9)*.

"Therefore, being justified by faith, we have peace with God through our Lord Jesus Christ *(Romans 5:1)*." "Believe on the Lord Jesus Christ, and you will be saved *(Acts 16:31)*."

How simple God made the way of salvation—simply believe! But, to believe is a heart transaction, and not a mere head transaction. Many people believe in Jesus Christ through their intellect, but they never come to Him by faith, trusting in Him alone, through no merit of their own *(Romans 10: 9, 10)*. God determined in eternities past whatever was necessary to accomplish His purposes, through Christ, our Saviour *(Ephesians 1:5,11)*. God is all-knowing, and he allows those with a believing heart and mind to be saved by the Holy Spirit. So why trouble God with your unbelief?

Salvation is the gift of God

Remember Christ's parables: "Jesus answered and said unto her, if you knew the gift of God, and who it is that said to you, give me to drink; you would have asked of Him, and he would have given you living water *(John 4:10)*." He would have given you, as it were, everlasting life!

These words were spoken symbolically of salvation—a universal call. The redemption of the soul is above any price or value a man could pay or assess. God himself paid the price in the atoning death of His Son.

"For the wages of sin is death; but the gift of God is eternal life through Jesus Christ our Lord *(Romans 6:23)*."

And we say, "Thanks be to God for His unspeakable gift *(II Corinthians 9:15)*."

A gift is not a gift if we pay the smallest price for it or

work the least for it. A gift is free, and must be received. It will not be forced upon us *(Ephesians 4:7-8)*. Are we ready to accept this gift? Read on.

Salvation is not of works

God tests salvation by good works *(James 2:14-26)*.
"Not by works of righteousness which we have done, but according to His mercy He saved us... (Titus 3:5)." See also *Romans 4:5*.

No one will ever obtain salvation and go to heaven by just doing the best he can. Christ paid it all through His shed blood on the cross of Calvary. He arose, and was resurrected to be at one with the triune God. Salvation is a gift from God (I Corinthians 3:9-15).

> *Romans 4:5   But to him that worketh not, but believeth on him that justifieth the ungodly, his faith is counted for righteousness.*

Today, receive forgiveness of your sins, past, present and future and the gift of eternal life as a child of God. God will rejoice as you come to share His peace—the peace of God which passes all understanding *(II Peter l:3-10; Phillippians 4:7)*. In peace, you are saved from your sins.

Eternal Security and Assurance

All who are saved are kept by God's power and are thus secure in Christ forever. This is the final perseverance *(Isaiah 45:17; John 3:15, 16; 6:37-40; 10:27-29; 17:11-12; Romans 8:1, 29-39; Hebrews 5:9; 9:12, 24; I John 5:12-13; Jude 1)*.

It is the privilege of believers to rejoice in the assurance of their salvation through the testimony of God's Word; which, clearly forbids the use of Christian liberty as an occasion to the flesh, to fulfill the lusts thereof *(Romans 13:13, 14;*

Galatians 5:13; Titus 2:11-15).

"Eternal Security" is the belief that one has received life eternal, a gift that cannot be taken away. The believer's eternal state is already and permanently secured *(Galatians 4:5-9; Ephesians 1:11-18; II Corinthians 1:21-22).* His faith is sealed until the day of redemption by God *(Ecclesiastes 3:14).*

> *Galatians 4:5-6   To redeem them that were under the law, that we might receive the adoption of sons. And because ye are sons, God hath sent forth the Spirit of his son into your hearts crying, Abba, Father.*

The assurance of the believer is the confidence that he has in God, that he is presently and eternally saved from all his sin. This assurance is instilled by the Word of God and confirmed in the heart by the Holy Spirit.

There are Christians who do not believe this glorious truth. They contend that a person can be saved one day, and lost the next. It is important to know what God has said about eternal salvation *(Philippians 1:6; I John 5:12; Romans 8:1:29-39; John 5:12-13).*

Those of the Arminian[4, 5] persuasion are convinced that man cannot be assured of God's grace. Their church assemblies have debated the security of believers for centuries. Our survey shows that 80 percent of their members are unsure of their own salvation.

Enns[6] describes the doctrines of Jacobus Arminius (1560-1609), which are quite different from those founded on Calvinism. His followers affirm a five-point postulation, which differs from John Calvin's position on man's assurance of salvation. According to the analysis of Enns, the Arminians believe in:

1) conditional election based on God's foreknowledge;

2) unlimited atonement;

3) the premise that although man has a free will, he cannot save himself;

4) grace, operating on one's will before one turns to God, enables man to cooperate with God in salvation; and

5) a conditional perseverance—that the believer can be lost.[7]

The belief here is that "....no one is condemned eternally because of original sin. Man is condemned because of his own sins." This is quite at variance with *Romans 5:12-21*.[8] Man is not subject to a sudden loss of salvation *(Hebrews 6:4-6; I Peter 1:10-25; II Timothy 2:5-26)*. There is assurance in these Scriptures.

> *Romans 5:18*
> *Therefore as by the offence of one judgment came upon all men to condemnation; even so by the righteousness of one the free gift came upon all men unto justification of life.*

Eternal security must be interpreted on Biblical truth, not on emotions, church doctrines based on men's traditions, private theological views, or scholarly arguments.

Eternal security is the unlimited guarantee by a sovereign God. This gift of salvation delivers us from eternal death and torment *(Revelation 20:11-15; 21:8; 22:15-19)*. Man must understand that without salvation he is separated from God, and not really saved *(John 3:16-18; Matthew 25:46)*.

Jesus taught this loud and clear by presenting two different paths for man, cited in Scripture. A paramount problem in man's life is his separation from God, and the lack of recognition that he is sinful. He needs to believe and accept God's free gift from Jesus

> *Matthew 25:46 And these shall go away into everlasting punishment: but the righteous into life eternal.*

Christ. It certainly can not be purchased any other way (Psalms 49:7-9, 15; I Peter 1:18-19).

Secondly, the old nature problem is man's strong will

and rebellion against God. This world and the devil have many distractions which sidetrack man's understanding and distort his thinking and belief. The sinful nature of mankind blinds him from truth *(I Corinthians 2:12-16; Hebrews 5:14; Romans 5:6)*.

Can we change our condition? According to *Romans 5:12-21*, repentance, faith, and belief take place in the mind, heart and behavior. The Holy Spirit really changes our condition and attitude. Our condition must be changed by Jesus Christ, who died on the cross, arose and was resurrected to God the Father.

Christ is the complete and final blood sacrifice which atones for everyone's sin in this strife-ridden world. Without the shedding of His blood, there is no remission, or forgiveness of sin *(Hebrews 9:22; Matthew 26:28)*. Christ died for our sins, a gift that was paid in full for our sinful depravity.

> *Matthew 26:28 For this is my blood of the new testament, which is shed for many for the remission of sins.*

Only the risen Christ can save us from our sinful condition. Only Christ can preserve us through His Spirit residing in us, and sealing us, and adopting us as children of God, so that we are no longer children of wrath *(Revelation 7:1-10)*. God gives the certainty of divine approval to all believers. Christ has delivered us from eternal death to eternal life by His once for all time sacrifice of Himself.

The Synod of Dort (1619) supported Frenchman John Calvin's "tulip doctrine" in five points:

(1 total depravity of man
(2 unconditional election
(3 limited atonement
(4 irresistible grace
(5 perseverance of the believers

Churches not wanting to lose control of their members

or fearful of letting others see them weak, have engaged in private, verbally-heated, and but sometimes threatening dialogue about doctrine.[9] God, however, would want us to be secure in the knowledge of divine approval.

In Psalm 16, David expresses his own experience through the leading of the Holy Spirit. He remarks in the Psalms that the Lord is his refuge. The Lord takes care of each of us daily. Security and trust in Him offer stability in our faith. Our present and future are secure forever. We must confess our sins daily, with genuine repentance before God, and yield to Christ all known and unknown sins. He will forgive us immediately.

What if sins prevail over you, and your sins are repeated *(James 4:13-17)*? We need to be careful how we interpret Scripture. There is nothing more injurious to the soul than failing God. Regardless of the sin, Jesus Christ, the son of God, who knew no sin, put himself in the place of all sinners by paying the complete price for the forgiveness of sins, in His death by the shedding of His blood on the cross. Christ gave us this magnificent gift so we could have eternal life, by simply, humbly, believing in Him for life beyond this earthly life.

Every person needs to consider carefully, however, the sins of omission, which the conscience does not readily protest against as it does against the sins of commission *(John 13:2-21; Luke 12:47-48; Numbers 15:29-30)*.

Why must we not leave God out of our plans *(II Peter 2:21; I Peter 2:21-25)*? Even though we suffer and experience trials, our Sovereign God wants us to be humble and dependent upon Him in our Christian walk. It is absurd

> *II Peter 2:21 For it had been better for them not to have known the way of righteousness, than, after they have known it, to turn from the holy commandment delivered unto them.*

to will against God and ourselves by committing sins, deliberately, when we know what is right.

Again, we can repent, have faith, and believe in Christ. Or, we can persist in our sins and expire someday, finding the real truth too late. Now is the day of salvation, not after we are dead. The unsaved will receive everlasting life also, but in torment and suffering. We need not fear other men, but we must make the decision today to accept a loving God and His Son, as Lord and Savior forever. Why should we be tormented, leaning on our own reasoning and self-justification?

You, as a person, cannot improve your soul with money, appearance, reputation, or achievement. Each of us has to accept the free gift that has already been paid in full. Boastfully comparing yourself with your neighbor and excusing yourself to others will do you no good when you stand before God to be judged. Recognize your condition. You are a sinner—a condemned criminal in the sight of God. But God can change that condition for you.

The promise in the Scriptures is: "I give unto them eternal life; and they shall never perish. Neither shall any man pluck them out of my hand. My Father, which gave them me, is greater than all; and no man is able to pluck them out of my Father's hand *(John 10:28-30)*." This message is confirmed also in *John 6:37; Ephesians 2:8-9; I John 5:1-13; Romans 18:35-39; Philippians 1:6; II Thessalonians. 3:3; II Timothy 1:12; 4:18; Jude 24* and *Hebrews 13:8*

Those who do not believe in the eternal security of the believer say, "Yes, no man can pluck them out, but Satan can," or "I can fall out of His hand." Is Satan stronger than God? Are you stronger than God? The answer is no! God is faithful in His promises and will keep us permanently *(Hebrews 10:23; Genesis 21:22)*. Our final perseverance is retained by the measure of our faith *(Romans 12:1-3; 2:7; Hebrews 3:14, Ecclesiastes 3:14)*.

True regeneration is a divine act of the Holy Spirit and

cannot be repeated. Our union with the Godhead is never cut off. It is only man that twists God's doctrines with his limited human reasoning, but His children will not perish. Christ has mastered death and the grave. Thus, the sinner is pardoned from his sins permanently *(Ephesians 1:7; Colossians 1:14; Psalm 103:12; Isaiah 38:17; Hebrews 10:17; Isaiah 44:22).*

Christ has finished the work by returning to be with the Father, and He reigns eternally. Christ is the High Priest, our advocate defense attorney, who pleads our case, for the remission of our sins, before the Father *(I John 2:1).*

This does not mean that Christians never sin. Each believer is a new creation, a new creature, and he continues to struggle against the flesh, which continues to rebel against the Spirit. This causes a life in conflict, a life imperfect in most circumstantial performances in comparison to his new character. No doubt all Christians commit fleshly, or carnal acts. Sinful behavior finds its source in the flesh *(I Corinthians 3:3-11; I Peter 2:11; II Peter 2:18; Galatians 5:17-26)* and sinful persons are guilty of acting according to the flesh.

All true believers, by virtue of their relationship with the Savior, walk obediently, but not perfectly, as disciples of Christ. In spite of their transgressions, their earnest, instant confession of sin is covered by the blood of Christ *(Mark 14:24; Luke 22:20; John 6:53-59).* Spiritual man has a fellowship with Christ, whose divine nature will be communicated to the believer by the working of the Holy Spirit.

This is a sanctified concept, progressive in the convert, and held as a result of the sovereignty of the Godhead. The Holy Spirit leads, blesses, comforts, and counsels the believer, from within, by not permitting sin to control his mind, soul and life *(Ephesians 1:13-14; 4:30; I Corinthians 3:17; II Corinthians 9:8).*

Lastly, Christ returns for His very own. Our Savior will present His true believers—the invisible Church—as faultless before God *(Jude 24-25; I Corinthians 1:7; Ephesians*

5:7; I Pet 1:13). All will be a finished work, as Christ prays for us and asks that we remain ever with Him *(John 17:24; I Thessalonians 4:17; John 14:3).* Thus, the Lord Jesus Christ is the believer's security throughout eternity.

"All that the Father gives Me shall come to Me; and him that comes to Me, I will by no means cast out *(John 6:37)."* This is a thrilling and precious promise *(II Timothy 1:12).*

We will abide in His presence forever! No one else can cast us out, and God will not. This promise makes us eternally secure and gives rest to our soul *(Colossians 2:2).*

"And this is the Father's will, which hath sent me, that of all which He hath given me, I should lose nothing, but should raise them up again at the last day *(John 6:39-40)."* This message is contained likewise in *Colossians 3:2-4* and *John 5:24.*

"I know that, whatsoever God does, it shall be forever *(Ecclesiastes. 3:14)."* "The counsel of the Lord standeth for ever, the thoughts of His heart to all generations *(Psalm 33:11)."* God would not be omnipotent if He were unable to keep His own eternally secure.

Satan and the flesh offer eternal damnation. God says of those He has chosen: "And I gave unto them eternal life *(John 10:28)."* God loves His children. It would not be eternal life if it could be lost at any time. Eternal life continues forever. God loves man. Can man really fathom this?

"He that hears my word, and believes on Him that sent me, has already received everlasting life, and shall not come into condemnation, but is passed from death unto life *(John 5:24)."*

"There is therefore now no condemnation to them which are in Christ Jesus *(Romans 8:1)."* God repeats this promise in *John 3:16-20,* and we are urged to examine ourselves *(II Corinthians 13:5)* and be baptized *(I John 3:21-22).*

All this is true, because Jesus bore condemnation on the cross for our sins, for all who would receive Him as their personal Savior. The Bible makes it clear that God "hath made him (Christ) to be sin for us, who knew no sin; that we might be made the righteousness of God in him *(II Corinthians 5:21)*."

The final blood sacrifice of death on the cross was made by Christ Himself, for the remission of our sins. "Wherefore, he is able also to save them to the uttermost that come unto God by him, seeing he ever lives to make intercession for them *(Hebrews 7:25)*." Christ will intercede for us, completely and forever.

Christ is now at the right hand of God as our intercessory high priest. Whenever we sin and repent, He pleads our case and reminds the Father that He died for us. To Peter, Jesus said, "Behold, Satan has desired to have you, that he may sift you as wheat, but I have prayed for you, that your faith fail not *(Luke 22:31-32)*."

Should God Forget

Should God forget to send the rain,
And let the sparrow fall;
Nor send His blessed sunlight
To shine upon us all;
Should moon and stars cease to appear
Because of His neglect;
And darkness fall upon the earth
And bring a retrospect—
Then, we'll remember.

Should God forget to comfort give
When sorrows o'er us fall;
Should the lilies be forgotten
By the maker of us all;
Should God forget the seed we sow
In fields where once it grew,
And water fail the hydrant
Where once we freely drew—
Then, we'll remember.

Should God forget to stay the hand
When anger flashes thru;
Should that sweet peace He doth provide
Pass out from me and you;
Should He withhold the faith we know
In superhuman power

To keep, sustain, uphold and guide
Thru every trying hour—
Then, we'll remember.

Should God forget His promise
Ne'er again to flood the earth;
Should He forget to keep His word
About a "second birth";
Should He forget to ope' the gate,
And not be at the door
To welcome us when we arrive
Upon the other shore—
THEN, WE'LL REMEMBER!

by Lillie Flanders Overholt

ENDNOTES

[1]. Bancroft, Emery H. *Elemental Theology - Doctrinal and Conservative* Grand Rapids, MI: Zondervan Publishers, 1970, pp. 311-312.

[2]. Enns, Paul. *The Moody Handbook of Theology*. Chicago, IL: Moody Press, p. 340.

[3]. Unger, Merrill F. *Unger's Guide to the Bible*. Wheaton, IL: Tyndale House Publishers, Inc., 1974, p. 490.

[4] *This We Believe*. Westchester, Ill.: Independent Fundamental Churches of America 1970 Vol. 1 and 1980 Vol 11.

[5]. Thiessen, Henry Clarence. *Introductory Lectures in Systematic Theology*. Grand Rapids, MI: Eerdmans Publishing Co., 1949, pp. 261-262.

[6]. Enns, Paul. *op. cit.*, pp. 628, 499.

[7]. *Ibid.*, p. 628.

[8]. *Ibid.*, p. 499.

[9]. *Ibid.*, pp. 479-480.

CHAPTER FIVE: The Established Church

The Believer's Two Natures

Doctrinal Statement

Every saved person possesses two natures, with provision made for victory of the new nature over the old nature through the power of the indwelling Holy Spirit *(I John 5:1-5; I Corinthians 15:50-58; Colossians 3:8-14; Ephesians 4:22-32; Romans 7:14-25; I Peter 2:11-12)* Claims of the eradication of the old nature in this life are unscriptural.

Is the true believer aware of the two natures struggling within himself? The Scriptures are very clear about this, and mankind cannot rid himself of the old nature with any rationalization.

Paul, Peter, and assuredly all of the apostles had this struggle within. Sinfulness is in the flesh, not in the divine new nature which

I Peter 2:11   Dearly beloved, I beseech you as strangers and pilgrims, abstain from fleshly lusts, which war against the soul...

has been regenerated by the Holy Spirit. Study prayerfully the following passages relating to the two natures. You will discover you are not alone in your dilemma: *Romans 7:14-25; 8:1-39; I Corinthians 6:19; Galatians 5:1-26; Colossians 3:1-11; Ephesians 4:22-24; I Peter 2:11-12; I John 1:5-10.* "For sin shall not have dominion over you: for ye are not under the law, but under grace *(Romans 6:14);*" does this mean we are now free from sin? You need to be cautious how you interpret the Scriptures.

The heretic or fractious Christian has the stubborn mind-set that the true believer does not have two natures. Perhaps that person is inserting his own understandings rather than searching the Scriptures thoroughly. A person may misinterpret that the Christian does not possess the sinfulness of the flesh *(Ephesians 4: 17-22).* Even though the phrase *human* or *old nature* does not appear in Scriptures, it still exists. The Lord cautions those directed by the Spirit, however, not to allow their hearts to become hardened from truth and thought. The old man or old nature does prevail.

If not so, why then does a person still quench or grieve the Spirit after his conversion? Why does a person confess his sins before partaking of the Lord's Supper? In our personal prayers and in the apostle's prayer Christ gave us, why then do we ask for forgiveness of sins?

Therefore, let not your heart become hardened. Unless you can judge your own need for forgiveness, God will certainly harden your heart. He will offer you mercy and grace no longer *(Hebrew 3:7-19).*

The apostle Paul was left boasting, in his feeble infirmities and sinfulness, wholly dependent on the mercy and grace of God amidst all his honorable distinctions. His extraordinary and multiple revelations were therefore soon followed by humiliating affliction *(II Corinthians ll:1-33;12:1-7).* God would not allow Paul the incentives he wanted to obtain spiritual pride. The visions he saw in a third heaven suggest that, in his own nature, he felt a need for pride. What he received was a humbling, that the power of the Lord might rest upon him.

Yet Paul endured in spite of his own inadequacies through Christ's love and strength as recorded in the epistles*(II Corinthians 2:14-17; 3:5)*. God's mercy and grace was sufficient for Paul, with a thorn in his life, to serve in his physical and spiritual condition unequivocally to glorify God. Another highly revered example is in the tribulations of Job. He learned valuable lessons in acknowledging his inadequacies and finding his sufficiency in God. God is pitiful and merciful. You too can trust Him patiently in all your adversities *(Job 42:1-16; James 5:11)*.

When we abide in the light of Christ, the Spirit has the ability to control our old nature. With that indwelling power in our hearts we can put off sinfulness. We are reconciled in Christ instantly. We are told to love one another *(I Peter 1:22-25)* though the struggle of the sinful flesh within us is ever present *(I Peter 2:11-12)*. We are justified by faith in God.

When love is absent, the Holy Spirit is quenched among the brethren. There is no reconciliation. A story illustrates this tendency among us. In 1961, the late Dr. M. R. DeHaan, founder of Radio Bible Class, was scheduled to teach at Estes Park, Colorado. A Christian organization, representing four states, gave little publicity to the Bible conference and selfishly did not want outsiders to attend the meetings. The rejection of one family's attendance was evident. Dr. DeHaan observed the hardened hearts of conference leaders who had no desire to share the event with others. He then bluntly remarked that unless the family was admitted to the conference, he would not speak.

Although the speaker was able to change their decision without prayer, one can see how some Christians, who may represent the visible Church, are alienated in a variety of entrapments and identifiable activities with the world. A Holy

Spirit reconciliation is absent.

There are certain sects, known as "holiness" groups, who believe in a second act of God's grace after they are saved, which they call "being sanctified" or "the baptism of the Holy Spirit." They believe that when this is experienced, a person does not sin anymore. This is unscriptural and in error. Sinless perfection will not be attained until we reach the glories of Heaven. Only then will our glorified bodies be like our Savior's, when sin will reign no more *(Romans 8:16-18,30; Philippians 3:20-21)*.

"Walk in the Spirit, and you shall not fulfill the lusts of the flesh. For the flesh lusts against the Spirit, and the Spirit against the flesh; and these are contrary, the one to the other, so that you cannot do the things that you would. But if you are led by the Spirit, you are not under the law" *(Galatians 5:16-18)*.

When a person is saved, his old nature remains just as vicious as ever. But he is given a new nature by the Holy Spirit, which resides in him. The indwelling Holy Spirit gives us victory over our old nature, or flesh, and Satan still tries to influence us. The flesh remains with us until physical death. How important it is to yield ourselves daily to the Holy Spirit, so that He may continually fill us and enable us to live victorious Christian lives.

"Let not sin, therefore, reign in your mortal body, that you should obey it in the lusts thereof. Neither yield your members as instruments of unrighteousness to sin; but yield yourselves unto God, as those that are alive from the dead, and your members as instruments of righteousness to God... Know you not, that to whom you yield yourselves servants to obey, his servants you are to whom you obey; whether of sin unto death, or of obedience unto righteousness *(Romans 6:12,13,16)*?" If we should yield any part of our bodies—our ears, hands, mind, tongue, or any other part—to unrighteousness, we are subject to a spiritual death.

God does not force us to do His will. He loves us and has given us a new nature to obey Him, but we can fail and disobey God if we allow the old nature, or the *old man* to corrupt us *(Ephesians 4:22; Colossians 3:9)*. How important it is to yield our will to God's will, and thus have victory over sin and evil! Again, the Holy Spirit prays, comforts, and directs our lives away from the manifestations of sin *(I Corinthians 2:10-16)*. "Submit yourselves, therefore to God. Resist the devil, and he will flee from you. Draw close to God (in prayer), and he will draw close to you *(James 4:7-8)*." "Take heart, I have overcome the world *(John 16:33)*."

> *Colossians 3:9 Lie not one to another, seeing that ye have put off the old man with his deeds.*

A child of God is overcoming the world; and our faith is the victory that has upset the world *(I John 5:4)*. When we resist the devil and draw near to God, in constant fellowship and prayer, we live in victory over our old nature *(Ephesians 6:10-18)*. We will have taken a stand against evil. We will have run from temptation.

> *I Corinthians 2:10 But God hath revealed them unto us by his Spirit: for the Spirit searcheth all things, yea, the deep things of God.*

"For they that are after the flesh do mind the things of the flesh; but they that are after the Spirit the things of the Spirit. For to be carnally minded is death; but, to be spiritually minded, is life and peace... For as many as are led by the Spirit of God, they are the sons of God *(Romans 8:5, 6, 14)*." If we mind only the things of the flesh, we will merit a spiritual death.

We must seek daily the leading of the Holy Spirit. "You put on the Lord Jesus Christ and make not provision for the flesh, to fulfill the lusts thereof *(Romans 13:14)*." See also

Galatians 5:16. In the original language of the New Testament, "to put on a person" meant to imitate a person and become like him. Apply this to Christ; we are the free servants of Christ. We are not to feed the lusts of our flesh to satisfy our own desires. Obeying God's commands—*to put on Christ*—denying self, gives us spiritual victory.

Separation

How do we maintain a separation between the plan of God and the stratagems of the world? Before we look at apostasy around us, let us look into our own hearts!

Therefore, meditate on God's knowledge and wisdom and dare to be different. Those that love God still work under the adversities the believer must endure. He is called by God to serve Him and is sanctified to become more like Christ according to His purpose. For God knew infallibly those believers he would predestine, foreordain, justify and glorify, those saints whom he had chosen but allowed others a limited free will to carry out His divine plan. Further, He allowed the Holy Spirit to prayerfully intercede on behalf of our weaknesses.

Why then is it that the good that I personally intend to do I do not, but the evil which I do not intend, I am practicing? I do the very thing I do not intend to do, and it extends beyond hypocrisy and those observable world views. Yes, it is the sin that constantly appears and resides in me.One example is stubbornness and unyielding of soul which is seen as a barrier to the will and obedience of God. Such stubborness in any saint can condemn the soul. When a person refuses to recognize and relate to it, stubbornness may preclude change in a sanctified life *(Galatians 5:16-26; Mark 2:18-22). Study the charts on pages 94-95.*

Another condition that may wear upon the believer can be the consequence of hardened doubts. Though intending to do the will of God, this burden is a barrier to submission. We are His! We live a separated, sanctified life in Christ, through adversity and in prosperity, until Christ calls us to our heavenly home with a glorified body to serve the living Messiah forever. Jesus the Christ is constantly washing us of our sins. We confess, and the Living High Priest forgives our iniquities immediately. Careful study of the first eight chapters of Romans will reveal that we can be joyful in our hearts with Him into eternity.

Biblical Christians defend their faith—not their egos, projects, strategies, and programs. To do otherwise would violate the eternal plan of God. Maintaining a separation between the plan of God and the stratagems of the world is our most difficult task.

All converted people should live in such a manner as not to bring reproach upon their Lord and Savior, separate from all religious apostasy, worldly strife and sinful pleasures, practices, and associations—as commanded by God *(II Timothy 3:1-5; Romans 12:1,2; 14,13; I John 2:15-17; II John 9-11; II Corinthians 6:14-7:1).*

The Christian and the World

The Christian has been saved from God's everlasting condemnation; therefore, we should live apart from the world's contamination. God has washed us from our sin, and now He teaches us to live apart from the things that will defile us. Separation is God's way of keeping His children clean, so that He can bless them and use them for His glory.

The scope and sequence of believing in Christ immediately leads to sanctification *(II Thessalonians 2:13-17).* The act of sanctification means to be set apart by the strength of the Spirit for God's purpose. The Spirit strengthens the disciple's new dependance upon God. The immortal soul and spirit have been set free from sin, but the mortal body is corrupt and incapable and will consistently fail, due to sin, until we receive a glorified body after physical death *(Romans, chapters 6-8)*.

Separated from Apostate Groups

An apostate is "one who deserts professed principles of faith." Professed principles of faith are those vital truths of the Word of God, especially the deity of Christ, His miracles, and the inspiration of the Scriptures. Apostate groups have departed from those Bible *truths* and professed principles of faith and are specifically denying those truths and not separating themselves from the things of the world.

Legalism, sensationalism, private interpretations, and even other gospels are the specific features of the apostates. Social issues such as population control, altering the economic system to erase poverty, politics, and fighting for social justice, which are worthy issues in other settings—have displaced the true gospel and doctrine in many churches. This constitutes apostasy.

Distinctives of Apostate Teaching:

1) Secret words, and gestures required to reach God

2) Sinless perfection

3). Hidden mysteries of other religions

4). Spiritual encounters with the dead

5). Oaths of allegiance to church authorities and specific organizations

6). Defining God as an exalted man

7). Exalting men to become as gods

8). Unbelief in the Godhead and resurrection of Christ

Certain organizations, with specific distinctives, will inform and assure people that they are the only true church. Beware of these man-made or demonically-inspired religions. The exalted logic and claims to wisdom of those whom Satan has deceived can lure others into the same entrapment, satisfying the pride of man. Apostate teachings, cults, and the occult are subtle, perverted forms of evil.

Many groups design themselves to deceive, and they practice mind-abuse of their members with prescribed life styles, such as Satanic rituals and exorcisms or secret ceremonies, with a *modus vivendi* that masks their emotional and financial exploitation. Such apostate influences manipulate minds with a high degree of success.

There are even those who profit in illegal activities such as drug trafficking; prostitution, and pornography by attracting strong peer groups at vulnerable points in young lives. In such abominable activities, the old nature makes a concerted effort to please the flesh to the final degree. Young fledglings are subjected to demonic activities of the mind and body to an unthinkable degree. Study *I Timothy 6:9; Thessalonians. 3:5.*

We need not be fearful of Satan and his demonic influence when our faith remains strong (*Ephesians* 6:11-18). God, the Holy Spirit carefully instructs us to flee from Satan. We are to be anxious for nothing as we pray. The Holy Spirit as a person prays with us. God will supply our needs, and we will thank God and accept His answers *(Philippians 4:6-19).*

It is the object of this section of the chapter to make people aware of organizations or individuals which are taking root in their lives. The power of evil is part of the nature of man. There are those who have a demonic dominance over others to blind them to the truth of God. They are capable of taking control of the mind of the ignorant, causing them to taking control of the mind of the ignorant, causing them to depend solely on distorted alliances and activities that are contrary to the will of God *(II Timothy 3:10-17; 4:1-22)*. We must be ever mindful of these dangers.

"Know this, that in the last days perilous times shall come. For men shall be lovers of their own selves... lovers of pleasure more than lovers of God; having a form of godliness, but rejecting the power thereof... *(II Timothy 3 and 4)*." And we are instructed to have nothing to do with distorted alliances.

We are now living in some of the last days which Paul prophesied. It is well for us to take a firm stand and study God's Word, so that we can contend for the truth, and the faith which was once delivered to the saints *(Jude 3)*. We should be so well-informed by the teachings of the Word of God that we can readily detect every false doctrine and teacher, and the subtle perversions of liberal, distorted teachings and writings. Study *I Corinthians 1:10* and *Romans 16:17-20.*

God pleads, "If any man teach otherwise, and consent not to wholesome words, even the words of our Lord Jesus Christ, and to the doctrine which is according to godliness... from such withdraw yourself *(I Timothy 6:3, 5)*." Bible doctrine is essential in the church age of grace for some will depart from the faith. We have witnessed a denunciation of specific doctrines such as the seriousness of marriage, divorce, and the sacredness and sanctity of life, etc.

"Have no fellowship with the unfruitful works of darkness, but, rather reprove them *(Ephesians 5:11)*." Witness to them, as the Lord Jesus Christ taught us to do *(Jeremiah. 42:5; John 4:21-24; John 6: 53-54; Matthew 5:20)*. We are admonished to reprove them, which means that we expose them. This can only be done when we gain a thorough understanding of the Word of God *(II Timothy 3:16-17; 2:15-16)*.

"Be you not unequally yoked together with unbelievers... but come out from among them, and be you separate, says the Lord, and touch not any unclean thing; and I will receive you *(II Corinthians 6:14-7:1)*.

Apostates are unbelievers with a belief system and behavior contrary to Christ's teachings. Therefore, we should not be yoked to them. An "unequal yoke" borrows its meaning from the yoke used with animals in ancient times. Two different kinds of animals were not to be yoked together in work, but mules with mules, oxen with oxen, and horses with horses. Christians ought to be yoked with Christians in their church relationships, marriage relationships, and often in their business partnerships and social fellowships. God never blesses an unequal relationship (*Ezekiel* 18:25-27, 29; *II Corinthians* 6:14).

"If there come any unto you, and bring not this doctrine, receive him not into your house, neither bid him Godspeed , for he that wishes him Godspeed is partaker of his evil deeds *(II John 10:11)*." See also *Titus 3:9*. It is possible, however, in today's world, that we encounter many every day of our lives, who are evil, to whom we may say, "God bless you."

How dangerous it is to fellowship with those who deny the true teachings of God's Word *(I Timothy 1:19; 4:1; II. Timothy 4:4-10; Hebrews 3:12; 6:6; II Peter 3:17; I John 2:19)*.! We may, of course, be very selective about whom we associate with.

Separation from the World

"Be not conformed to this world *(do not imitate its ways and practices)*, but be changed by the renewing of your mind, that you may prove what is that good, and acceptable, and perfect, will of God *(Romans 12:1-18)*." Strong, indeed, is the Christian who resists a contact that would influence him away from the true teachings of Christ.

What influence Christians would have in the world if they gave attention to this command! The world does not conform to our way and practices—why should we to theirs? The Spirit-controlled Christian will not conform to this world, but he will bear witness to Jesus' message. Christians can speak out to assist those who must break free from bondage. Prayer and the Holy Spirit can free someone who is under a spell, when he is willfully blind to the truth, even when an erroneous mindset and demonic workings are in control.

Pray and study the Word. The Holy Spirit comforts, teaches, and provides escape from demonic mind-sets and temptations. We need to look inside ourselves and discover what is missing. We are drifting radically away from the citadel of free speech when we do not involve ourselves in witnessing for that which is God's truth and will. "The Spirit himself beareth witness with our spirit, that we are the children of God *(Romans 8:16)*. Where persecution is becoming severe and discriminatory in the world *(Romans 8:14-25 9:17-18; 11:7; 14:23; Matthew 28:18-20)*, may we set an example of love and acceptance, influencing any we may encounter along the way.

"Love not the world, neither the things that are in the world. If any man love the world, the love of the Father is not in him. *(That is a serious indictment.)* For all that is in the world, the lust of the flesh *(things that our carnal nature craves)*, and the lust of the eyes *(things we allow our eyes to look at with a covetous longing)*, and the pride of life *(things we pride ourselves on as our accomplishments or possessions)* is not of the Father, but is of the world. And the world passes away, and the lust thereof, but he that does the will of God abides forever *(I John 2:15-17)*." This is indeed a beautiful Scripture.

We are chosen out of this World[1]

"I have chosen you out of this world, therefore the world hates you *(John 15:19)*." Even persons with a limited free will will be persecuted *(Proverbs. 16:4; Romans 8:26-33; 9:11; Ephesians 1:4; 3:10-11; I Peter 1:18-21).*

We should not be alarmed when we take our stand against the world, and ungodly men hate us. Jesus said: "Blessed are you, when men shall hate you, and when they shall separate you from their company, and shall reproach you, and cast out your name as evil, for the Son of Man's sake. Rejoice you in that day, and leap for joy! for, behold, your reward is great in Heaven *(Luke 6:22,23)*."

Separation from Evil

"Let every one that names the name of Christ *(as his Savior)* depart from iniquity *(II Timothy 2:19)*."

"I pray not that you should take them out of the world, but that you should keep them from the evil *(John 17:15)*."

Separation unto God

"And you shall be holy unto Me; for I, the Lord, am holy, and have severed *(separated)* you from other people, that you should be mine *(Leviticus 20:26)*." See also *Numbers 11:18; 23:9;* and *Romans 1.*

> *II Timothy 2:19*
> *Nevertheless the foundation of God standeth sure, having this seal, The Lord knoweth them that are his. And Let every one that nameth the name of Christ depart from iniquity.*

This was said to Israel of old, but it is just as applicable to us today. God is jealous of His honor. He wants all that we are for Himself. He has a right to us, for He purchased us with the precious blood of His own dear Son.

Separation from the world, the flesh, and the devil is important; but leaving these must also imply the soul is going to do the things the Spirit tells us to. We say, "No" to sin, but also say, "Yes" to God. By God's grace, we do good things

Separation from sins without a dedication to God is Pharisaism, but dedication to God with separation from sins, is righteous, holy and joyful.

> *Ezekiel 18:4 Behold, all souls are mine; as the soul of the father, so also the soul of the son is mine: the soul that sinneth, it shall die.*

Great Commission of Souls

"Thus it is written, and thus it behooved Christ to suffer, and to rise from the dead the third day, that repentance and remission of sins should be preached in his name among all nations, beginning at Jerusalem... And it came to pass, while he blessed them, he was parted from them, and carried up into heaven *(Luke 24:46-51)*."

It is accountable of the saved to witness by word, deed, love and truth as the Scripture instructs, and to seek to proclaim the gospel to all mankind. *(Mark 16:15; II Corinthians 5:10; Matthew 28:18-20; Proverbs 11:30; I John 3:18; Daniel 12:2-3; Revelation 14:6-7).*

You are my Witnesses

> *Mark 16:15 And he said unto them, Go ye into all the world, and preach the gospel to every creature.*

"You shall be witnesses to Me, both in Jerusalem *(home community)*, and in all Judea *(our state)*, and in Samaria *(the adjoining country)*, and to the uttermost part of the earth *(foreign countries) (Acts 1:8)*." See also *Ephesians 1:13; Romans 8:1, 2, 16.*

A witness is a person who is called upon to testify concerning what he personally knows. Every true Christian should be willing, glad, and able to tell what he knows concerning his Savior. Peter said: "Be ready, always, to give an answer to every man that asks you a reason of the hope that is in you, with meekness and fear *(I Peter 3:15)*." The Psalmist said, "Let the redeemed of the Lord say so, whom He has redeemed from the hand of the enemy *(Psalm 107:2)*." See also *I John 5:6-9; John 15:27; Acts 5:20-21; 22:14-15; Titus 2:15.*

If we know we have been redeemed (brought out of Satan's domain), we should say so as often as we have opportunity. God honors a faithful witness. We can witness by word of mouth, by handing out the printed Word (portions of Scripture, tracts, and so forth), and by our personal Christian life, and deeds. Remember, our responsibility is to witness.

Convicting of sin, and convincing of the truth are the work of the Holy Spirit. The Church body is afraid to witness verbally to the unsaved. Why? Some are not really saved, or fearful of witnessing, or afraid of what others may think. With some the love of Jesus Christ has grown cold. Others are unwilling to endure persecution and embarrassment. The Apostle Paul was willing to suffer pain and hardship, and was glad and willing to be thought a fool for Christ sake.

Some must go to Foreign Missions

"And He said to them, 'You go into all the world, and preach the gospel to every creature *(Mark 16:15)*.'" See also *John 21:18, 24, 25; Matthew 28:16-20.*

"How beautiful are the feet of them that preach the gospel of peace, and bring glad tidings of good things *(Romans 10:15)*." In the sight of God, the feet of missionaries are beautiful. We are ambassadors or representatives of Christ.

"Now we are ambassadors for Christ, as though God did beseech you by us; we pray in Christ's stead, that you be reconciled to God *(II Corinthians 5:20)*." See also *Ephesians 6:18-20.*

An ambassador is a person who lives in another country as a representative of the land in which he has his citizenship.

Our spiritual citizenship is in Heaven *(Philippians 3:13-21)*. This world should be to us a foreign land, in which we represent Heaven. Let us be true representatives and witness daily as the Spirit directs and comforts.

Our Mission Perspective

In chapter one of Colossians, Paul's message is, I am now rejoicing in my sufferings on your behalf at Colosse; and I am filling up in my own body what is yet lacking of the sufferings of Christ in behalf of the Church. Our present-day perspective for Christian witness focuses on the "10/40 window" that extends from West Africa across Asia, between ten degrees north and forty degrees north of the equator. This is the hard core of unreached people who live in an oblong shaped window. This window includes the Muslim, Hindu, and the Buddhist bloc.

The Church must focus our efforts toward evangelism. The need for bringing the message of Christianity to this vast window of opportunity is overwhelming. It is there that the Church must combine its forces relating to seven important realities: *first*, the historical and biblical reality; *second*, the unevangelized people and countries; *third*, Islam; *fourth*, three main religious blocks; *fifth*, the poor; *sixth*, the quality of life; and *seventh*, the citadel of Satan. Here there are two billion unreached people, many of whom have never heard of Jesus as Savior, and many who are not within reach of Christians among their own people. The 10/40 window is where two-thirds of the people of the world live and in only one-third of the total habitable land area. In addition, 97 percent of the three billion people who live in the fifty-five most unevangelized countries live in this window.

In 1995 the Billy Graham Global Mission successfully reached into the 10/40 window with the satellite network. Therefore evangelist Luis Palau boldly held meetings in

Egypt. Many experienced a conversion in Christ. As Christians in local areas, can we also witness verbally for our loving Christ?

We need to consider the mandate of Christ to preach the gospel to every person, to make disciples of all nations, and to be His witnesses to the four corners of the earth.[2] Many are being martyrs for Christ. Are you a Soldier of the Cross, fighting on the winning side?

Ministry and Spiritual Gifts

Two points should be made. First, God is sovereign in the granting of all His gifts; and the gifts of evangelists, pastors, and teachers are sufficient for the perfecting of the saints today. Speaking in tongues not learned and the working of miracles gradually ceased as the New Testament Scriptures were completed and their authority became established. By the second century, church leaders wrote that no one then living had seen such miracles *(I Corinthians 12:4-11; II Corinthians 12:12; Ephesians 4:7-16; II Corinthians 12:12).* "My grace is sufficient for you, for my power is made perfect in weakness."

Secondly, God does hear and answer the prayer of the faithful, according to His will, on behalf of the sick and afflicted *(John 15:7; I John 5:14, 15).*

Spiritual Gifts to the Grace Believer

"Now, there are diversities of gifts, but the same Spirit... For to one is given by the Spirit, the word of wisdom; to another, the word of knowledge by the same Spirit; to another faith by the same Spirit; to another, the gifts of healing by the same Spirit; to another, the working of miracles; to another, prophecy; to another, discerning of spirits; to another, diverse kinds of languages not learned; to another, in-other, diverse kinds of languages not learned; to another, interpretation of languages not learned; but all these work that one and the selfsame Spirit, dividing to every man severally as He will *(I Corinthians 12:4, 8-11)*. All of the above gifts edify and nurture the body of Christ.

Is the spiritual gift greater when it edifies you, the Church, or God? Which are more fruitful? Search the scriptures. This does not mean that God cannot give these gifts today, but, rather, that He does not generally give them because He has given us His Spirit and His word. Study *I Corinthians 14:1-40; I Corinthians 12:9,30; Acts 28:3-10; II Corinthians 4:13-18;* and *Mark 3:13-15.*

Note that believers are not commanded to exercise particular spiritual gifts, either to obtain salvation, or to prove their salvation. They are given salvation when filled with the Spirit that saves them through the transformed grace of Christ. Those He heals internally never die. It is a blessing of regeneration far beyond the temporary exercise of any single gift. Use the gift to glorify God.

On Tongues and Healing

Christ performed miracles, such as healing the sick and raising the dead. He bestowed upon His apostles unknown languages they had not learned, gifts of healing, and even raising the dead. These were important in the early church as a testimony of God's power, and the vindication of His message, as given by the apostles. But, to say that these gifts have ceased does not limit God's power. We do believe that God is omnipotent, and that He can do whatever He pleases *(Jeremiah. 32:27)*.

> *Jeremiah 32:27*
> *Behold, I am the Lord, the God of all flesh: is there anything too hard for me?*

If God wills to heal in answer to prayer, He is certainly able! Therefore, we may pray for the healing of the sick, but we must always say, "Not my will, but Yours be done." Even Jesus prayed this way *(I John 5:14-15; Matthew 21:22; Mark 14:35-36; Luke 6:19; Note James 5:15-18)*.

Paul said, "I speak with tongues more than you all; yet in the church I had rather speak five words with my understanding, that, by my voice, I might teach others also, rather than ten thousand words in an unknown language *(I Corinthians 14:18, 19)*." Ask God for the gifts that will help the Church *(I Corinthians 14)*. Paul did exercise the gift of speaking in an unknown language. The entire fourteenth chapter of *I Corinthians* should be carefully studied in regard to this lesser gift.

God also uses Other Means

God has endued skilled physicians with wisdom and an understanding of the human body, so that a person can be, by the means of His (Christ's) hand, healed of sickness and disease. He has given other skilled persons wisdom to discover wonderful drugs and medicines. When these are applied, we can pray that God will bless the means for His glory. But we must also remember that it is not always God's will that a person should be healed. God did not heal Daniel *(Daniel 8:27)*, Elisha *(II Kings 13:14)*, Timothy *(I Timothy 5:23)*, Trophimus *(II Timothy 4:20)*, and Paul *(II Corinthians 12:7-10)*. Some must endure a life of suffering, while God takes some out of life at an early age.

Fannie Crosby, who gave us some of our greatest hymns, was blind and remained so until death. Notice what Paul wrote about one of his friends. "Trophimus have I left at Miletum sick *(II Timothy 4:20)*." Paul had, undoubtedly, seen many people healed through his prayers, but this man was left sick. Another time, he wrote to Timothy that he should drink a little wine for his stomach ailment. Contrast, also, Peter's healing of Aeneas *(Acts 9:33-35)* with his raising of Tabitha through his prayer to God *(Acts 9:40-42).*

Gifts of Talented Men

"But, unto every one of us is given grace according to the measure of the gift of Christ..." In the early churches, "He gave some apostles ; and some, prophets ; and some, evangelists, and some, pastors and teachers for the perfecting of the saints, for the work of the ministry, for the edifying of the body of Christ *(Ephesians 4:7, 11, 12)*."

I Corinthians 12 speaks of God's bestowing spiritual gifts upon individual believers. *Ephesians 4* speaks of God's gift to the church of gifted men. Apostles, prophets, evangelists, and pastor-teachers are men whom God equips, and calls to be His gift to the church, which is the body of Christ. The express purpose of their ministry is the equipping of the saints, that is, all Christians, so that they can do the work of serving the Lord, and building up the body of Christ. Christians are a priesthood of grace believers who use their abilities and gifts for the glory of God. We are a chosen generation, a royal priesthood *(I Peter 2:5-12).*

Women are to be used in the ministry as long as they do not exercise authority over men *(I Timothy 2:11-13; I Corinthians 14:34; Ephesians 5:22; Colossians 3:18; I Peter 4:10 II Peter 1:3; Jam. 1:17).* If a called man is not available, a women is to preach and teach the full counsel of God. Her gift is then deserving of respect. Gifts from all saints need to be beneficial and appropriate to the whole Church.

Legacy of the Church

A number of points need to be made regarding the Legacy of the Church in this present age:

1. The church, which is the body and espoused bride of

Christ, is a spiritual organism made up of all born-again persons of this present age *(Ephesians 1:22,23; 5:25-27; I Corinthians 12:12-14; II. Corinthians 11:2).*

2. The establishment and continuance of local churches is clearly taught and defined in the New Testament Scriptures *(Acts 14:27; 20:17, 28-32; I Timothy 3:1-13; Titus 1:5-11).*

3. There is autonomy in the indigenous church. Freedom from external authority and control is taught by Jesus Christ to His disciples, with a minimum ritual, but well organized for the glory and worship of God *(John 13:1-17).* Study also *Acts 13:1-4; 15:19-31; 20:28; Romans 16:1, 4; I Corinthians 3:9, 16; 5:4-7, 13;* and *I Peter 5:1-4.*

4. The ordinance of spiritual baptism is given in the Scriptures *(Acts 1:4-5; 11:15-18; Matthew 3:11; John 1:26-36).* Ephesians stresses one Lord, one faith, one baptism, one God, one body, one Spirit, one hope, in outlining the mystery (something hidden in the past) of the Church *(Ephesians 4:3-6).* Baptism signifies public identification with Christ. John the Baptist baptized in water *(Acts 1:4-5; 11:15-18),* which is an outward, symbolic sign of an inward change by the Holy Spirit.

Man has made this topic complex and explosive in regard to the mode of baptism. John informs his audience that he baptized in water, but Christ, who is *preferred* before me, baptizes with the Holy Spirit. Water baptism modes are traditionally used in the Visible Church distinctive to keep alive the practice of baptism identification *(Romans 6:3; Galatians 3:27-28).*

Peter, in *Acts 2:38-39,* teaches us to repent and be baptized (buried - *Sunthapto*) in the name of Jesus Christ for the forgiveness of sins *(Matthew 3:16).* Then you will receive the free gift of the Holy Spirit. This promise is for you, the members of your family, and for all people God Almighty will call and save.

Paul, in *Romans 6:4-8*, does not contradict Peter. Paul is saying that in our sinful condition, we were buried, or immersed, into His death.[3, 4, 5] We are united with Christ visibly before others, and declared as grace believers, simply believing by faith, in Christ, in His death on the cross, physical resurrection, and ascension to heaven. No religious leader can claim the death, resurrection and ascension. Only God has the sovereign capability of doing this, for the Father and the Son are One *(John 10:11-30)*.

The Holy Spirit fills and dwells in the believing sinner, and identifies him with His Savior, Jesus Christ! (Study *Colossians 2:10-15* carefully and prayerfully.) If the believer wants to be immersed, or any other mode of baptism, do it! It is not the mode of baptism, but the spirit of the baptism given.

Matthew 28:19 offers the most reasonable interpretation. Make disciples of depraved sinners who have received the Holy Spirit *(Acts 2:38)*. Then, if you will, water-baptize the disciple. *Romans 6:4-5; I Corinthians 12:13; II Corinthians 5:21* and *Ephesians 1:6; 2:18* suggests Holy Spirit baptism at conversion.[6]

Water baptism is a symbol and public testimony to the world that the disciple-believer is united to Jesus Christ by faith alone in His death and resurrection.[7] It is the devine saving power of the Holy Spirit who enters, indwells and reigns in the born-again believer. Then the Holy Spirit comforts, teaches and leads him through all adversity and prosperity. Read *Acts 10:38-48; Romans 6:4-5;* and *Matthew 28:18-20*.

Differences in view on water baptism have divided Christians and created persecution. The Devil and the flesh have allowed that adversity to be propagated into heresy for centuries. The word "baptism" has been transliterated from the Greek word *Baptismos* (verb *baptizo*).[8] Further Biblical sources must be studied carefully to break down the misconceptions of baptism (see *Acts 2:38-42; 8:12, 38; 10:47-48; I*

Corinthians 12:13). The critic must be prayerful when he studies these Scriptures. He should have a uniform love and testimony for the brethren. Study *I Corinthians 1:10; 11:18-19;* and *Romans 16:17.*

5. In remembrance of Him, the Lord's Supper signifies a Christian testimony for the church age of grace *(Acts 2:42-47; I Corinthians 11:23-34).* This dispensation conveys the true origin of the supper. The bread is Jesus' body. The body is broken for the sins of the world. The cup represents the new Covenant (Testament) and is symbolic of Christ's blood.

When one partakes of the elements, that is, to say, the bread, which signifies Jesus' body, and the cup, which signifies Jesus' blood, one personally proclaims the Lord Jesus Christ's death and resurrection until He returns for the invisible, or true, body of Christ (the Church). God's judgment is upon any Christian who unworthily takes the elements without the confession of their sins. Study *Luke 22,* where the Last Supper institutes the promised New Covenant. Also *Matthew 26:26-29; Mark 14:22-25;* and *John, chapters 13-16,* informs us of what was said there.[9, 10]

6. Jesus instructed His disciples with a very simple lesson in foot-washing. Why? Because the climate was hot and dusty, and foot-washing was comforting to the receiver. No, the lesson has far more depth than would appear. Jesus told them they were not all clean. But they did not understand the purpose of the foot-washing.

Later some of them did. He, as servant, washed their feet, though some objected. Jesus explained, "If I don't wash your feet, you have no part with Me. Do you really know what I have done to you? You call me all sorts of names. Teacher, Lord, Master, Good, etc. I washed your feet; surely, you also, ought to wash one another's feet."

This is a lesson in submission, that we should humbly serve others.[11] The Lord Jesus Christ rendered the lowly act of a servant *(John 13:1-20).* The sovereign Jesus knew of their hypocrisy. He knew of their failure to serve the weak, the poor, and the handicapped.

Paul describes this lesson *(I Corinthians 1:10* and *Romans 16:17)*; also John gives an account of Jesus relating to the act of foot-washing. Local congregations today are caught up in quarrels and divisions not only concerning baptism, but also foot-washing. Note *I Corinthians 11:18-19*. There are parties in the Church that approve, by examination, testing, and knowledge, what Jesus taught. The believer should study the issue if it concerns him, and then follow the Lord's teaching. The majority of churches have refused to follow the example our Savior taught.

Humility is never learned, in service and in love, unless Christ indwells in you as you walk with Him. Does the Holy Spirit live inside you? Judge for yourself. How do you express your love to others—especially the stranger? Should this lesson be practiced in the body of Christ? Apparently many churches ignore this cardinal lesson.

In summary, we may say:

a. Holy Spirit baptism occurs immediately upon believing. The Holy Spirit does the converting.

b. Water baptism is an outer identification and testimony to the world that you are a child of God.

c. There are several ways that the gospel, the death, and the resurrection of Jesus is declared:

1) by preaching the full counsel of God

2) by living a life that is a witness to others

3) by abiding in the ordinances Christ taught us to use while He reigns as our great High Priest in Heaven, with the Father, before His return for the true church.

The Church as Christ's body

"And has put all things under His feet, and gave Him to

be the head over all things to the church, which is His body, the fullness of Him that fills all in all *(Ephesians 1:22, 23)."*

"As our bodies have many members and all these members make up the body, so likewise the church of Jesus Christ, which is called His body, has many members. As in our physical bodies, some members are invisible, while others are visible. All members of the body of Christ are not known to us, but to God, they are known. As all members of our bodies have their special functions to perform, so, likewise, all members of the body of Christ have their special functions *(I Corinthians 12:12-31)."*

Known only to God are the effectual prayers that live in the hearts of the believers, whose intercession makes successful the work of the ministry.

Christ Loves His Church

"Husbands, love your wives, even as Christ, also, loved the church, and gave Himself for it; that He might sanctify and cleanse it with the washing of water by the Word, that He might present it to Himself a glorious church, not having spot, or wrinkle, or any such thing; but that it should be holy and without blemish *(Ephesians 5:25-27)."*

By His death, Christ made it possible to have a glorious Church. Some day, His heavenly Church will be presented to Him without blemish. In due time God will claim an earthly church among the Jewish nations. God's process of removing the spiritual spots, wrinkles, and blemishes is through the water of the Word of God. As we read and study the Word, it cleanses us. How important, therefore, to apply ourselves to meditate on the Word of God daily!

But for those who do not apply themselves to reading the Word of God, and therefore do not receive the cleansing power of the Word, there will be a more severe process of cleansing at Christ's coming, that of fire. Thus, they will suffer the loss of rewards. Christ's bride will be spotless, and without blemish. For further study, read *I Corinthians 3:12-17*.

One Body, many Members

"For as the body is one, and has many members, and all the members of that one body, being many, are one body; so, also, is Christ. For, in one Spirit are we all baptized into one body... whether we be bond, or free; and have been all made to drink into one Spirit. For the body is not one member, but many *(I Corinthians 12:12-14)*."

Christ's church is made up of persons who have experienced a true conversion. It makes no difference of what nationality, color, or race they are. People often confuse the Church of Jesus Christ with a denomination, or the building in which they worship. The true members of the Church of Jesus Christ are those who know Him as their personal Savior, together termed the Invisible Church *(IHebrews 12:23-24)*.

Our churches are not energetically battling for righteousness and the proclamation of the full counsel of God. We need a spiritual awakening to change each of our hearts and lives by giving sacrificially as servants to the glorious gospel of our Lord Jesus Christ *(II Peter 3:18)*.

The Visible, local Church

God alone sees and knows the Invisible Church. Does any of us have an excuse for not believing the Father? Not really! Study *Romans 1:18-20; Colossians 1:15-19;* and *I Timothy 15-17*. We also recognize the Visible Church, more commonly referred to as the "local church." Read and interpret *Matthew, chapter 13*.

"And when they were come, and had gathered the church

(local congregation) together, they rehearsed all that God had done with them... *(Acts 14:27)*."

"From Miletus, he sent to Ephesus, and called the elders of the (local) church.... He said unto them... Take heed therefore unto yourselves, and to all the flock, over which the Holy Spirit has made you overseers, to feed the church of God, which He has purchased with His own blood *(Acts 20:17, 18,28)*." Merrill F. Unger states, "The book of *Romans* teaches that no one will attain eternal life, except persons who have been justified (declared righteous) by God Himself *(3:21-5:11)*. Such a declaration results not from possessing some supposed personal righteousness, based on self-effort or good deeds, but from having God's own righteousness imputed to the believing sinner who puts his entire trust in Christ's completed work of redemption."[37]

Officers of the local Church

Elders and deacons, along with pastors, are the officers ordained by God to oversee the work of the local church. Study *I Timothy 3:1-16* and *Titus 1:5-9.*

Christ's church is made up of persons who have been born again. It makes no difference of what nationality, color, or race they are. People often confuse the Church of Jesus Christ with a denomination, organization, or the building in which they worship. The true members of the Church of Jesus Christ are those who know Him as their personal Savior—collectively, they are a living organism.

The diagrams on pages 94 and 95 describe the biblical transformation of human nature, showing how the Spirit of God regenerates the soul, spirit, and body of man with His divine nature. Thus concludes the Bible Doctrine establishing the believer's two natures, his separation from the world and its apostasy, the great commission for souls, and the legacies of Spiritual gifts and the Church.

State of Unsaved

Body - World Consciousness
Soul - Self Consciousness
Spirit - God Consciousness

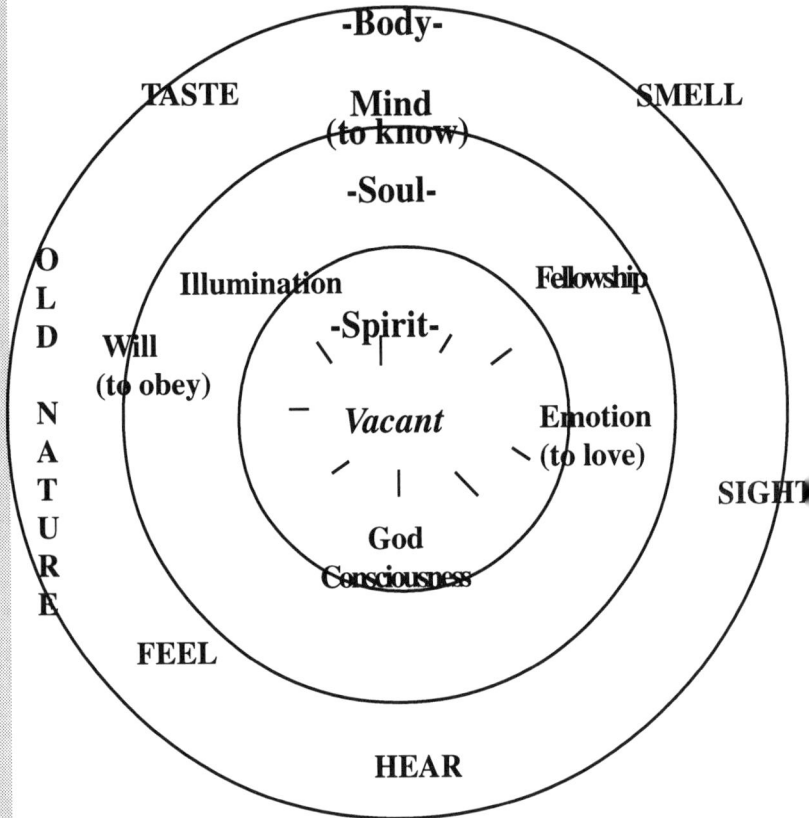

-Body-

TASTE

SMELL

Mind
(to know)

-Soul-

O
L
D

Illumination

Fellowship

N
A
T
U
R
E

Will
(to obey)

-Spirit-

Vacant

Emotion
(to love)

SIGHT

God
Consciousness

FEEL

HEAR

Satan
World System
Attacking from
without through
the body

State of Unsaved
Body - slave to sin
Soul - depraved
Spirit - dead

State of Saved

Body - World Consciousness
Soul - Self Consciousness
Sprit - God Consciousness

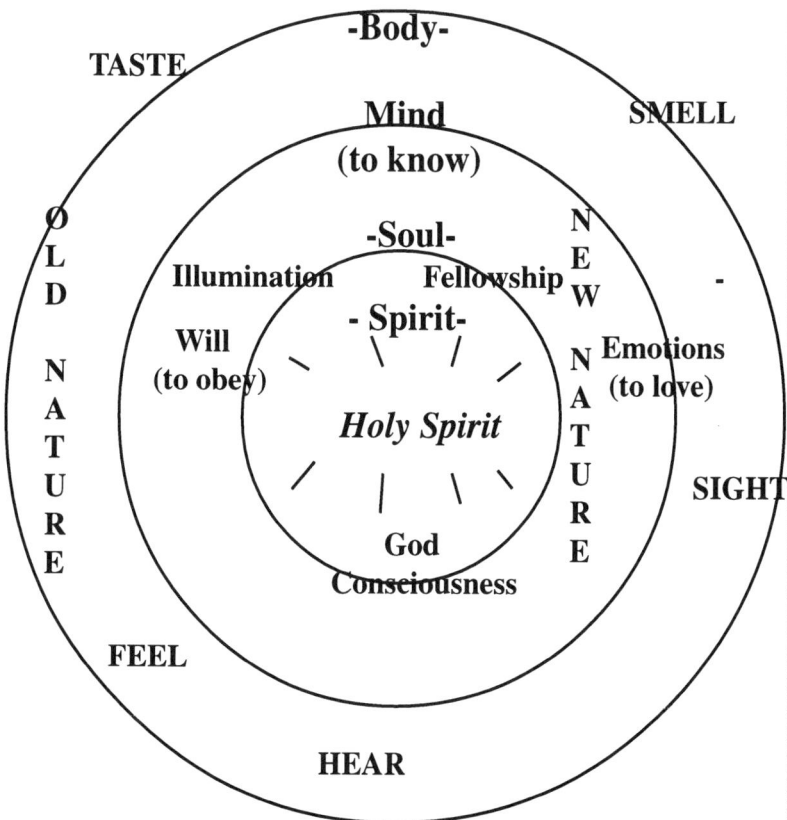

TASTE

-Body-

SMELL

Mind
(to know)

-Soul-

Illumination   Fellowship

- Spirit -

Will
(to obey)

Holy Spirit

Emotions
(to love)

Ø
L
D

N
A
T
U
R
E

N
E
W

N
A
T
U
R
E

God
Consciousness

SIGHT

FEEL

HEAR

Satan
World System
Attacking from
Without through
The body

State of Saved -
Body - instrument
unto righteousness
Soul - energized
by the Spirit
Spirit - alive unto
God

95

ENDNOTES

[1] Enns, Paul. *The Moody Handbook of Theology*. Chicago, IL: Moody Press, 1989, p. 481.

[2] Bush, Luis. *Focusing on The 10/40 Window*, "Dallas Insider." Winter Issue, 1991, Vol. 14, No. 1, Part I; Spring Issue, 1991, Vol. 14, No. 2, Part II.

[3] Worrell, A. S. *The New Testament Revised and Translated*. Philadelphia, PA: American Baptist Publication Society, 1904, p. 218.

[4] Enns; pp. 362-365.

[5] *The Life Application Bible*. The Living Bible. Wheaton, IL: Tyndale House Publishers, Inc. and Youth For Christ/USA, 1988, p.1710.

[6] Chafer, Lewis Sperry. *Major Bible Themes*. Findlay, OH: Dunham Publishing Co., 1926 & 1953, pp. 92-95.

[7] Enns, *op. cit.*, pp. 362-363.

[8] *Ibid.*, pp. 362-363.

[9] *Ibid.*, p. 360.

[10] Tidwell, Josiah Blake. *The Bible, Period By Period*. Nashville, TN: Broadman Press, 1923, pp. 293-294.

[11] Worrell, *op. cit.*, p. 149.

CHAPTER SIX: The Meaning of Marriage

Marriage, Divorce & Remarriage

Marriage was instituted by God at the dawn of history, and He created man and woman in every culture and society. He then commanded that man should leave his father and mother and be united with his wife, and they would have a oneness, a relationship of one body, as long as they both should live. Study carefully *Genesis 2:18-3:20* wherein God's plan was made known to His people.

God ordered that man should be created in His own image *(Genesis 1:27)*, and commanded him to be fruitful, to establish a family *(Genesis 4:1)*, and to be its master. God further ordered that there be but one man and one woman within the confines of a lawful marriage *(Proverbs 18:22; Genesis 2:24)*.

Paul stresses that a man ought to love his wife as he loves his own body *(Ephesians 5:21-32)*. Just as Christ loved His true Church and gave Himself for it, the sanctity of marriage is God inspired and must not be tampered with or defiled *(Hebrews 13:4)*.

> Hebrews 13:4
> Marriage is honourable in all, and the bed undefiled: but whore mongers and adulterers God will judge.

Two present-day expositors have made interpretations in regard to what the Scriptures say about the marriage commitment. Their analyses of a successful marriage profile bear careful attention.

A. Paul Van Gorder[1] asserts that specific core values are taught by the Apostle Paul. In *I Corinthians 7:1-16*, the Apostle Paul taught that:

1. Only monogamy is practical *(I Corinthians 7:1-2; Genesis 2:24)*.

2. The relationship must be mutual *(I Corinthians 7:3-5)*.

3. The wife may not depart nor shall the husband put away his wife *(I Corinthians 7:10-11)*.

4. The unbeliever, likewise, shall not be left behind nor put away *(I Corinthians 7:12-13)*.

5. The unbeliever may depart, and a brother or sister is not under bondage in such cases *(I Corinthians 7:15-16)*.

B. David Egner[2] has expressed clearly what the Scripture teaches for a sustained marriage. His outline for a God-centered marriage has these criteria:

1. The most vital ingredient is that husband and wife live *Christ-centered lives.* They must share a spiritual companionship with Jesus Christ *(Ephesians 5:25-28)* in their daily lives.

2. *A lifetime commitment* is expected unless one spouse should die. Then the marriage contract ends. The other person may then remarry. Our Lord Jesus Christ taught this lesson in *Matthew 19:4-9.* Because of man's depravity, Jesus continued the commandment that Moses brought down from the mount.

An annulment, or a judicial declaring that a marriage is invalid, is forbidden in the Bible. Sexual immorality is the only reason a divorce would be permitted. An innocent party would be allowed to remarry.

Today, our court system permits many reasons for a person to gain a divorce. Most of these reasons are contrary to Biblical teaching *(Matthew 5:31-32)*. Christians and nonbelievers continue to break vows to God, and they will be held accountable in the Day of Judgment. A vow is a promise not to be broken. Study *Ecclesiastes 5:4-7*.

3. *A marriage is a union bonded by God.* People need to learn how to deal with the world while maintaining the guidelines for marriage established by God. The world has uncertainties, injustices, and unpredictables. But God bestows blessings and the relationships that are inherent in a family, which ought to strengthen the bonds the couple established in their union. Study *Genesis 2:23-24*.

In a valid marriage, oneness is established in the eyes of God. Each person in the marriage must compliment the other rather than merely contract to coexist. Prayfully and spiritually each person must work together with the other in the trials of life. The backgrounds of the couple will vary; such as their habits, personalities, emotional hurts, etc. A couple may be as different as two maple leaves. Only God can foster a mutual oneness so that the couple can minister to each other, and so that they, as a family unit, can offer aid to others. Involvement in church activities, when one is given the opportunity, will assist the couple to grow closer to each other. How does this happen? By together helping others with their problems. If a marriage is blemished, there is little to build upon which would make the marriage fruitful.

The Genesis account advocates that lives be joined in a fulfillment of service to others. Sharing goals with your mate helps you to respect and understand one another. Friendships are established when you are involved jointly in caring and sharing with others who are less fortunate than you. Exhibiting such concern for others results in a caring Christian life for you and your children. When you believe, and walk with Christ in your marriage, unbelief and skepticism gradually disappear. Remember, Christ has graciously put you together, as one, and has given you a whole new life. Unbelief will be erased when Christ is the center of a marriage.

4. *Each Christian couple is committed in marriage to a vow of faithfulness.* When a couple has total faith in God *(Matthew 5:33)* and in each other, the vow is upheld. Temptation, flirtation, and fantasies flee, and a spiritual companionship thrives when a couple engages together in committed prayer-life and Bible study. Their desire then is to minister to each other and to any other persons who also need love and attention.

5. *Husband and wife ought to live consistently in well-defined roles according to God's plan.* The uncertainties, injustices, false values and unpredictabilities of society and the world can taint a marriage. According to current modes, the wife has the same rights as her husband. She does not have to submit to him or anybody. Likewise, the husband is independent of the wife.

When we make our own rules and rights, however, we are out-of-sync with God's teachings. The structure of a marriage begins with well-defined roles in God's Biblical plan, including an obligatory harmony. Study carefully the following Bible passages: *I Corinthians 11:3; Ephesians 5:23.* God wants to direct your life away from self-centered, sinful tendencies and desires *(Romans 7:15-25).* Sequentially, the head of every man is Christ; the head of every woman is man; and the head of Christ is Almighty God.

> *I Corinthians 11:3 But I would have you know, that the head of every man is Christ; and the head of the woman is the man; and the head of Christ is God.*

If you possess a mind-set of unbelief you will continue to strive against God, His plan for the Church, and His plan for marriage. Man's role is that of a spiritual leader and companion. He is to be a non-dictatorial, presiding head of his family. According to God's plan, the husband:

a. *Provides* love to his spouse above his love of himself *(Ephesians 5:25; Colossians 3:19)*.

b. *Follows* Christ's love for the Church *(Ephesians 5:25)*.

c. *Administers* understanding *(I Peter 3:7)* and honor in living and prayer. A more definitive life of equality is sustained for each other.

d. *Lives* in love with an absence of bitterness and vindictiveness in his marriage and family relationships *(Colossians 3:19-20)*. The husband lives a life endeavoring to remove unnecessary pressures and demands on the wife, for they are all one in Christ Jesus *(Galatians 3:28)*.

From the beginning, the woman's role has also been established. The wife is to submit to the leadership of her husband. Study carefully *Ephesians 5:22-24; Colossians 3:18; I Peter 3:1;* and *Titus 2:4, 5.* Marriage is spiritual, happy, and successful when both husband and wife accept their roles *(Philippians 4:1-19)*. God and His Son are one *(John 10:30)*. Christ is the perfect example of submission. Husband and wife need to learn this first lesson of submission in their own marriage.

6. *Unconditional love* is constantly given and cultivated by the Holy Spirit in the lives of the married couple. In better or worse conditions, the couple ought to be content in a relationship of oneness. Though love may be unappreciated, it is always there, because Christ and the Holy Spirit are in the lives of those who took the vow before God to love and take care of each other.

The husband and wife obviously are not perfect. With unconditional love, in their walk through faith in Christ, God will not forsake or leave them. One partner *must* not reprimand the other unkindly when anxiety comes into their lives. The real test of stability is often revealed in matters of money, unemployment, a wayward child, or a terminal disease, etc. *(John 4:27).*

Be contented or satisfied in Christ for Almighty God loves, looks over, and will never leave you. Always manage your problems together, with dialogue and openness, praying to God and waiting patiently for Him to resolve your problems in His time and in His way. The Christian must be satisfied with God's decisions and purposes. Your problems and your successes are never solved simply by your own reason.

God wants you to pray to Him and seek His will in your life. Always maintain an unreserved love for God and for each other, and God will surely bless you in His time and way. He will direct, chastise, and teach you in growing in His truth and obedience. Remember that twisted human logic and rationalization may appear fine in your minds, but God's thoughts and ways are not our thoughts and ways *(Isaiah 55:6-9; Matthew 6:25-34).*

7. *Married couples should love each other in tender respect.* They should fortify each other with trust, security, confidence, and with sincere communication. The Lord cautions the husband not to deal treacherously with the wife of his youth. She is your lifetime companion. You have made a covenant with her before God.

God hates divorce and renders severe penalties when marital infidelities happen. The Old Testament teaches that the guilty party was put to death. Today as in the past, couples have willfully disobeyed God. They think they are wiser than God. With the criteria expressed in this section, the couple needs to learn to work through marital strife in tune with the Word of God. Study *Malachi 2:14-16; Deuteronomy 24:1-5; Matthew 5:31-32; II Samuel 11:1-26; 12:1-14; Hebrews 13:4-6;* and *I Corinthians 7:1-17.*

8. *One of the most difficult tasks in marriage is the ability to communicate with each other.* The couple ought to take time for open dialogue with each other. This is a problem of

great magnitude in many marriages. One of the partners may assume certain things about the other partner, often confronting and manipulating the other spouse with his or her own self-centered interests. Unwise management of money may also cause mistrust, hostility, and even a spirit of "getting even" to sever communications.

Unless Christ is the center of the marriage, all sorts of selfish, unkind reactions can spew out of the marriage relationship. We must listen to each other. Talk about it. Do something about it.

Try to please your mate. He or she is your lifetime companion and friend. Have you forgotten your promises, in Christ, or were they just words, with no action in mind and spirit? In marriage there must be a great deal of bending, called *submission*, to please the other.

There may not always be a 50/50 balance of responsibility in the marriage. It may be 20/80 sometimes, especially when one or the other comes home from the hospital. Man, can you prepare a meal, clean house, wait on your wife, write letters or call friends and relatives? Woman, can you keep a clean house with the help of your husband and children, balance the checkbook, etc?

Even social activities can cause you to neglect your marital responsibilities and overextend your time and energies. Do you then murmur, argue, or nag your partner? To be well balanced and temperate in all affairs is difficult to do. The ego is always getting in the way.

God does not promise us tomorrow. Trials will arise. You do not know what problems or decisions you must make or how you are going to react. But God knows how you will react, especially when the Spirit of God is working within you *(II Corinthians 3:5)*.

Be yourself as the Spirit leads

> *II Corinthians 3:5 Not that we are sufficient of ourselves; but our sufficiency is of God...*

you, though you have limitations. You must get your ego out of the way; then the Holy Spirit can do the leading in your life. Prayer and Bible study will enrich your life decisions, so you will be doing God's will in this life. Live not by a philosophy or by humanistic reasoning, but by God alone. It is God's victory in your lives which ought to catch hold of you at your work place, in your marriage, and in your affairs with other people.

Can you be content in all your affairs in life? If you cannot be content with what God offers you, then something is radically wrong. You need to reflect carefully without allowing your ego to get in the way of your life with God.

Are you doing something that is constantly against the will of God? Perhaps there is a void in your life. You escape into drugs, alcohol, sexual affairs, other marriages, or even into more mundane distractions, for example, large shopping sprees.

If such is the case, pray, search the Scriptures, and get involved with other people and their problems. Perhaps your body is suffering or is addicted. Then eat a balance of the right kind of food. Sleep and rest are important too. Give your physical body a chance to work for God

The Christian life is not easy. You have a wife, friend, and prayer partner; God will bless you even though persecution and tribulation are all around you. God will not forsake you. His precious promises are always there.

Establishing and retaining values and a successful work ethic are an enormous responsibility in marriage. Play and engage in work activities with your children such as home projects, camping, games, art, music, even homework. There are 168 hours in a week, and a managerial balance can be aggressively pursued.

When money is behind most activities, the world becomes an infirmary of sorrow and speed. Contrary to the ways of the world, the true Christian needs to share his faith, wealth, and good fortune with others. Realistically, the Christian must be careful not to overextend himself, which is a problem with some brethren. God expects us to accept our own limitations and to create a balance in our lives.

9. *Mutual submission is required as the Spirit guides each of us in obeying God.* Study *Ephesians 5:18-21; Philippians 1:5-7; James 4:7;* and *Romans 6:13-14.*

Submission and love are elements that grow together. Recall that Christ always loves us and He went to the Cross in great humiliation and submission *(Philippians 2:5-8).* If we do not live also in submission, according to His will for us, we do not believe what He has done.

Christ has always loved us while we have not always loved Him. Christ died for our sins to provide everlasting life for us. Again, if we do not live in Christ, we do not believe Him. A Christian marriage will flourish if a couple will love and obey God and if they will possess an intimate "mind in Christ" *(I Corinthians 2:14-16; Philippians 2:3-5; I John 4:4-6; II Corinthians 6:14).*

Our mind controls what goes into our life. Sin divides our mind. Therefore, when in the Spirit, we will not want to carry out the desires of the flesh. As soon as a sinful thought enters our minds, we must dismiss it before it becomes a problem. If we should entertain or consider such a thought, Satan will cunningly get us, quickly or gradually. Therefore, we must prepare our minds in all readiness in Christ *(I Peter 1:13).*

The Lord is the greater power in you, so fill your thoughts with ways above and do not aim for worldliness *(Colossians 3:1-2; James 3:13-18).* He will handle all your inadequacies. Set your mind in Christ. The Spirit will help you sort out the truth. As soon as you

> *I Peter 1:13*
> *Wherefore gird up the loins of your mind, be sober, and hope to the end for the grace that is to be brought unto you at the revelation of Jesus Christ.*

allow an unholy thought to go further in your thinking, the devil will sift and defeat you. He will get you to distort the truth, to lie, to cheat, to be greedy, etc. The devil and his advocates are determined then to defeat you by tempting you through your human weaknesses and thereby preventing you from knowing God's will for your life *(I John 4:1-6)*.

Paul counters this idea, however, in *II Corinthians 3:5* and *II Corinthians 10:4-5*, saying God has given us weapons to destroy the enemy's stronghold. Therefore, you must use the weapons that are different from those of the world. You must overcome disputes that are contrary to the knowledge of God. God gives us authority to reject temptation by living in the Spirit, in prayer, and in the Word of truth.

Mutual submission in marriage is a protective intimacy reserved for one another.[3] In it we must give freely from your heart. Egner has made an analysis that:

a. Marriage is a balance of give and take.

b. Marriage cannot be a struggle of the wills.

c. Marriage is overcoming your self-centeredness.

d. Marriage is serving another just as God serves you.

e. Marriage is rejoicing in doing favorable and unfavorable tasks to please your partner as you glorify God.

f. You must, therefore, serve God as the true Church.

10. The final criterion that cements a spiritual, social, physical, mental, and emotional relationship is *sexual intimacy and fulfillment (Genesis 2:24-25)*.

Marriage faces daunting challenges, as expressed in the above analysis. Much emphasis is placed on sex in our society that is difficult to withstand so that we may live and function correctly. God bestows His blessings upon us in a sexual union only within the confines of marriage.

> *Genesis 2:24-25*
> *...they shall be one flesh. And they were both naked, the man and his wife, and were not ashamed.*

It is usually the man that is

pulling away from God's institution of marriage. At present there is a national movement aboard called the *Promise Keepers*, a Christian body of men, also women, who seek to strengthen our witness in Christ and the strengthening of family relationships. We recognize the need for many to reach out to other persons who are in need of fellowship and help in order to reach those goals.

Each needs to reach the goal and secure the prize for which God calls a person to a life in Christ *(Philippians 3:14)*. Study also *Jeremiah 18:1-6*. God can shape you in the center of His will, if you allow Him.

One breaks down the protective intimacy of husband or wife by contriving to judge, by our own insights and self-righteousness, our partner in a marriage. Unfaith-

> *Philippians 3:14 I press toward the mark for the prize of the high calling of God in Christ Jesus.*

fulness is the only Scriptural writ for divorce. Divorce is expressly denied for the immediate purpose of marrying someone else *(Mark 10:11-12)*.

Today, divorce can be obtained for many reasons other than marital infidelity. Both the innocent or offended person is allowed, though not required, to obtain a divorce. The devastation is compounded by the fact that divorce is expensive, hurting both parties and the children involved. According to the Bible, only the offended mate may marry again *(Deuteronomy 24:1-4)*.

If an unsaved husband or wife refuses to continue to live with his or her mate, the believer may agree to a separation. But if the unbeliever departs, let him or her leave, and the Christian mate is free. Under those circumstances of separation divorce may result. The innocent mate may then remain single or remarry *(Matthew 5:31-32, 10:4; I Corinthians 7:10-16)*.

Still church members judge harshly those who divorce

and then remarry. This is unwarranted. All forms of sin may flourish within a marriage. However, conditions were often no different centuries ago. Marriage is not entered into seriously as a sacred mandate, and many are indifferent to God's blessing or displeasure *(Matthew 7:14; Proverbs 30:12)*.

> *Matthew 7:14*
> *Because strait is the gate, and narrow is the way, which leadeth unto life, and few here be that find it*

Many say we should replace Christianity with atheism, human secularism or even New Age concepts. They say we do not need Judeo-Christian principles of God, marriage, family values, etc.

What a "great entrapment" we are experiencing! Reeducating our spirituality, redefining our goals and revamping our religion will never achieve a lasting satisfaction. We should observe what happens when God and His legacy are erased from our lives.

When God is in the center of our daily lives, marriage and family values are pertinent to the will of God. Many in today's world are avoiding God's designed plan of marriage which offers us strength to resist the temptations we encounter. In that plan:

a. Marriage is protective *(I Corinthians 7:2)*.

b. Marriage is enjoyable *(Proverbs 5:15-19)*.

c. Marriage has reasonable expectations *(I Corinthians 7:3-5)*.

Society emphasizes lust, escape, fantasy, etc. If you are in tune only with the world and your old nature, they will exploit and destroy your marriage. Sin, unbelief, and a strong self will gradually and inevitably destroy you. The addiction of sin and unbelief is so unassuming that you will unconsciously become immune to the will of God. God will then be totally erased from your life. You will have allowed your life to be consumed by the mentality of this world.

Still, Christ made the final assessment. When sexual infidelity is practiced, grounds for divorce is granted. In review, divorce gives the right for remarriage to the innocent spouse *(Matthew 19:8-9)*.

11. The final point in Egner's analysis is that the *homosexual community is not to be recognized as a family.* Biblically and historically the family has been defined as a mother (female) and a father (male) with children. In America and Europe of today's world homosexual couples are demanding recognition as a family unit with the right to adopt children. Permissive adoption agencies have been instrumental in allowing this.

The homosexual union is to be considered an abominable act of disobedience to God's designed plan concerning marriage. The public anxiety in regard to homosexuality is a serious social and spiritual concern.

Why should we also be concerned? Because vulnerable children are then nurtured into the mindset of abnormal homosexual behavioral. Such influence will then turn children away from God and ingrain into them homosexual behavior as an approved behavior for their lives.

Homosexual partnerships should not be biblically and psychologically recognized as a moral equivalent of marriage. Such undermining practices cloud the minds of youth and are contrary to God's marriage plan. What has stood up to the test of time? Yes, God's designed marriage. In contrast, man's reprobate mind has contrived homosexual partnerships. These have harbored disharmony and disease among people who refuse to obey God. People do matter to God. Study the literature[4] concerning homosexual acts over the centuries. Read also in the Bible for what God has commanded *(Leviticus 18:21-30; Leviticus 20:13-24; Ezra 9:11; Romans 1:22-32)*.

Concerning Divorce and Remarriage

God teaches that unfaithfulness and death terminate a

marriage. After death of one partner, a spouse may remarry *(Romans 7:2; I Corinthians 7:39)*. Also the innocent party in marriage wrecked by adultery may remarry another person who *never* married, or was never caught in the adultery net of sin. Study *Matthew 19:1-15; Matthew 5:31-32; Mark 10:2-12; Luke 16:18; Romans 7:1-25; 8:12-16; I Corinthians 5:1-13, 7:1-39; Ephesians 5:21-6:4; Colossians 2:16-23; 3:1-25; I Timothy 2:1-15;* and *I Peter 3:1-22.*

> *I Corinthians 7:39 The wife is bound by the law as long as her husband liveth; but if her husband is dead, she is at liberty to be married to whom she will; only in the Lord.*

Many of the passages mentioned will offer insight and wisdom from God as the Spirit guides your daily life.

Bruce Dunn[5] provides a sharper interpretation of *Matthew 19:9* in regard to the remarriage of the innocent spouse. *Matthew 19:9* says, "And I say unto you, Whosoever shall divorce his wife, except it be for unfaithfulness, and shall marry another, committeth adultery; and whoso marrieth her which is divorced doth commit adultery." Dunn says, "Read that verse the other way around, because if one is true the other is also."

Therefore, if a man put away a woman for unfaithfulness, and marries another, he does not commit adultery. God has established attainable standards through Christ that enables man to be happy and successful in his marriage, or remarriage, without guilt.

Some couples may attend Christian enrichment marriage seminars with a Biblical orientation. There may be some merit in working out differences with each other prior to taking the marriage vows.There are a variety of personality and temperament tests that can be used for analysis and guidance in resolving some of these differences. God's will for mankind, however, is that a believer and an unbeliever should not marry under any circumstances *(II Corinthians 6:14-7:1)*.

Both the Old and the New Testament recognize circumstances allowing remarriage. Jesus takes a passage in *Deuteronomy 24:1-4, Matthew 5:31-32, 19:3-12* and *Mark 10:2-12* which indicate that removing or putting away a wife dissolves the marriage and allows remarriage. Jesus is consistent on the nature of divorce. He makes it very clear, concerning all rationalizations for divorce, that only the innocent party, whose former marriage was rescinded by divorce, may remarry without guilt.

Remarriage on grounds of desertion alone is not permitted. According to *I Corinthians 7:11*: "But and if she depart, let her remain unmarried, or be reconciled to her husband: and let not the husband put away his wife." In other words, if the unbelieving deserting party is not deceased and does not remarry, neither should the one who has been deserted remarry.

When two unbelievers have been divorced and one is subsequently converted, and neither has remarried, the Christian should attempt to restore the marriage. If the non-Christian refuses, this makes the marriage the same as the kind described in *I Corinthians 7:15*, quoted above.

Persons who are divorced, or divorced and remarried on Scriptural grounds, are entitled to the full privileges of fellowship and Church membership. The Church has no authority to judge, ignore, or legalistically dismiss persons who have endured the divorce and remarriage experience. God, Who knows everything, will do the final judging of every situation in our lives. Remember, the grace of God in our Lord Jesus Christ forgives all sin. So how can one judge another? Is he judging in the flesh or in the Lord? God forbids the former and reserves the latter unto Himself alone.

Marriage Vows and Celebration

The gift that God created for man is a woman to be his companion, helper and wife, and to make him complete. For marriage to last for a lifetime, it must be built upon *agape* love, which is Christian love such as is accompanied by the Eucharistic celebration. In the thirteenth chapter of Corinthians, the apostle Paul offers a description of *agape* love, as should be practiced in the home: "Love is patient; love is kind and envies no one. Love is not quick to take offense. Love keeps no score of wrong or blame, does not gloat over other mens' sins, but delights in the truth rather than the legalistic grid. There is nothing love cannot face; there is no limit to its faith, hope, and its endurance" (adapted from *I Corinthians 13:4-7*).

Love such as this can bring honor and glory to God. In the early days of creation, God looked at Adam alone in the Garden of Eden and declared, "It is not good that man should be alone." So God created woman to be his companion, and the first marriage relationship was established. God took the initiative in the formation of the institution of marriage because he realized our need as human beings for a deep and supportive relationship. Since the first union in the Garden of Eden, couples have sought love, acceptance and companionship in the marriage.

A marriage should be celebrated. For each, according to his own heartfelt commitment and to the commandments of God that he expects to fulfill, vows should be celebrated. Those vows can be personal, or they can prescribed by a minister, in accordance with Scriptural laws and promises.

For example:

Today, we have gathered to celebrate the union of Ralph and Pauline in Christian marriage. In one sense, this is a very personal and sensitive moment that belongs only to them. But this event is also a service of thanksgiving and celebra-

112

tion that should speak clearly to each of us. During these moments together, we should each breathe a prayer of thanksgiving to God Almighty for His blessings in our lives. Renew your own marriage vows and allegiance to your family and to the Lord. And for Ralph and Pauline, it is my fervent prayer that your marriage will always be blessed with Christ in the center of your living.

Vows: Ralph to Pauline

I believe that God has chosen to make me complete by providing you to be my wife and companion-helper in life.

In order to receive you as a gift from God, I shall accept three main responsibilities. First, in the same way that Christ loved the Church, so will I love you: realistically, in spite of all our weaknesses; sacrificially, no matter what the cost; purposefully, that you may be made holy and blameless before God; willfully, regardless of the presence or absence of motivation; and absolutely and unconditionally, without limitations or reservations.

The second responsibility deals with leadership. Christ is the head of the church. Likewise, God has placed the husband as the head of the wife. As your husband, I promise to lead you in love, affection and cheer, to provide security in maintaining open and honest communication, and to encourage spiritual growth and maturity in our home.

My third responsibility concerns the realization that our marriage involves a lifetime commitment to Christ. For as long as we both shall live, I will be your husband, and I will love and lead you as God directs me.

I recognize that my own strength is insufficient for these vows, and I will rely on the Spirit of God to enable me to keep my word and promises to you and give myself only and always to you until death parts us.

Vows: Pauline to Ralph

Believing that God has chosen you to lead me, I accept your leadership. I will be obedient to you, trusting that God will enable you to lead me according to His will. The Lord has opened my heart to you, and I come to you with admiration and trust; I will honor you.

The Lord has strengthened my trust in you, and I come to you prayerfully, in peace and delight. I come to you with my whole self; I will love you. Recognizing that my own strength is insufficient for these vows, I will rely on the Spirit of God to enable me to keep my word and my promises to you and to give myself only and always to you until death parts us.

Parenting

King David grieved and wept over the loss of his beloved son Absalom. He desired that God would have taken him instead *(II Samuel 18:33)*.

Then there was the prodigal son, whose compassionate father ran to him, embraced and kissed him. With a forgiving spirit, the father rejoiced in his son's return. "Let us celebrate and give thanks to the Lord. God has forgiven you and so do I," said his father.

The elder brother was angered by his father's actions. That son had faithfully carried out the chores of his father's estate. Was there partiality present? It must be remembered that the father said unto his eldest, "Son, thou art ever with me, and all that I have is thine *(Luke 15:31)*.

Why didn't the brother appreciate his father's love and understanding of the prodigal? Perhaps the father had neglected to show him that love in similar ways, for he loved both sons. It is difficult to determine in this parable if the prodigal son's father was a good parent. Likewise, a father exhibited favoritism when Jacob chose Joseph over all his sons, who then sold him into Egypt *(Genesis 37:28)*. In these instances, we learn very little about the responsibilities of fathers in reference to their children. Reflecting on Biblical history, many of the kings, including David, were never very credible dads either. Fortunately, the Scriptures inform us in other ways.

In the present day the father is often the major wage earner while mother is employed both inside and outside the home. Without commitments within the home, he may not be neither a good husband nor a good father. With wild selfish sensual drives, the adult male may even father a child out of wedlock. The young, or not so young male may then feel he is caught in a quagmire of circumstances. He is then unfaithful in the family unit and an abomination to God. Finally, the mother may be abused and/or abandoned by the husband.

In contrast, a godly father is a pacesetter, protector, provider and spiritual leader to his wife and children. He participates faithfully in the activities and interests of his children. With a father or other male relative to establish and maintain a male image, a bonding and a meaning for their lives, a mother can reinforce the building of character, the example of submission, a respect for other people, and a love of God in their children.

The lessons and counsel emanating from a home where God is the head are many. Fear God, for that is the genesis of wisdom. Respect the government. Know sound Bible doctrine to reinforce a believer's life-style. Learn to relate to others even when you are critical, and be thoroughly equipped to deal with the onslaught of humanistic and New Age philosophies.

Children should be given responsibility they can manage according to their ability, learning rate and maturity. Mothers and fathers must complement each other if the children are to excel or enjoy music, art, sports, etc. No time should be spent viewing and listening to violence, sexual innuendo, nudity and murder as created by the film industry.

Mentoring the young in moral and spiritual values requires stable parents who reinforce each other in the child-rearing process—something the Promise Keepers currently are trying to carry out. Neither parent can be overly protective but must use discretion in allowing each child independence in accordance with his ability and emotional maturity, encouraging each toward confident preparation for an enjoyable vocation and a responsible adulthood. Such nurturing enables the child to relate well with his peers and with adults at school, at church, and in other social groups.

Male presence throughout a child's developmental years provides a figure of authority, a guidance in love, and his own loving care. This productive relationship with sons and daughters results in a parental bonding which will then be passed on to their children.

President Theodore Roosevelt in his writings revealed a fine parental modeling. T. R. would disrupt a foreign diplomatic meeting in order to participate in game activities with his children. Those who are consistently supportive but not overly protective of their childrens' affairs will find the experience rewarding for all. When we train up a child in the way that he should go, he will not depart from it *(Proverbs 22:5-9)*.

The experience of prayer, selected Bible stories, and the application of the Scriptures to life situations in the early years can provide a great influence upon one's life. What an awesome legacy to pass on to one's own children. Many biographies bear this out.

As a parental example to children, numerous guideposts could be suggested. Still, you wonder if your child will continue to live in the grace of God after leaving your home. Some suggested guideposts follow:

1. Strive to be good examples in your homes *(I Peter 5:13)*.
2. Instill life consecration to glorify the Godhead.
3. Love God, your neighbors, and the nature of the universe.
4. Be doers of the Word and not hearers only *(James 1:22)*.

116

5. Obey the Ten Commandments.
6. Possess a spirit of forgiveness.
7. Retain the fruits of the Spirit *(Galatians 5:16-26)*.
8. Remove self from false pride.
9. Uphold Godliness for we brought nothing into the world and surely will carry nothing out. Therefore be content with your work ethic and with such things as you have *(I Timothy 6:6-8; Hebrews 13:5; Philippians 4:11-13)*.
10. Living here is temporary. The cherished everlasting life of joy for the believer is with the Father, Son and Holy Spirit *(Isaiah 61:7: John 3:36; Hebrews 13:20; I John 5:11-21)*.
11. Sustain loyal and regular attendance in the local church.
12. Contribute offerings and talents to the local church.
13. Avoid prejudice and the discriminative practices of the world.
14. Worship God and respect human life as sacred.

The above are just some of the suggested legacies to pass on to your children. Perhaps you have others to offer.

An Addendum

I would like to address youth in regard to marriage and to warn them not to turn their lives into turmoil and regret. Biblical common sense in regard to sexual purity prior to marriage is God's call to each of us *(Ephesians 5:29-32)*. One can see in the marriage, divorce and remarriage of many how the devil, the flesh, and worldly entrapments strangle people's lives, especially those who do not honor and obey God from the beginning.

It is admirable to observe teenage abstinence movements are growing in the country, for example, among the *Promise Keepers*. These groups request a vow of chastity, asking their members to pledge not to have sex until marriage. The Bible teaches that God wants us to remain sexually pure. Therefore, some people, young and old, do make a commitment to God to maintain purity and virtue. The commitment is not only to God, but also to family and friends. This is not always easily done. This is one reason why God instigated a plan called marriage.

Presently marriages are failing, and divorce and remarriage are common. Sixty-four percent of the marriages in North America fail. The Church, with all its entrapments, has not been capable of maintaining God's institution of marriage. That is why so many would set standards for the conduct in this area other than the authority of the Bible. Their standards may be in accordance with Bible standards, but they should also be strengthened by reference to Biblical teaching.

ENDNOTES

[1]. Van Gorder, Paul R. *The Church Stands Corrected: A Solution For Today's Church Problems.* Wheaton, IL: Victor Books, 1967, chapter 5.
[2]. Egner, David. *What Will Make My Marriage Work?*; Grand Rapids, MI: Radio Bible Class, 1986.
[3]. *Ibid.,* p. 8.
[4]. "Morality And Homosexuality." *The Wall Street Journal*; Thursday; Feb. 24, 1994; Section A, p. 18.
[5] Dunn, Bruce; *Divorce And Remarriage*. Peoria, IL: #45: The Grace Worship Hour, p. 8.

CHAPTER SEVEN: The Dispensations

Doctrinal Statements

There is abroad an extreme teaching known as "hyper-dispensationalism," which would oppose either the Lord's table or water baptism as Scriptural means of testimony for this present church age. The dispensational view of Bible interpretation rejects that position and its rationale, and its implicit rejection of Biblical directives *(Matthew 28: 19, 20; Acts 22: 41, 42; 18:8: I Corinthians 11:23-26)*. There is a large amount of literature on the question.

Such authors desire to contribute a fresh look upon Christendom by involving other writers in issues that are philosophical in thought and theory rather than holding to the inerrancy of the inspired Word of God. In criticism of such Ronald H. Nash claims, "If evangelicalism does seem 'new' to any people, it only proves how far they have drifted away from the moorings of Reformation theology (and the Scriptures) into the dismal morass of dispensationalism." [1]

One needs to return immediately to the inspired teaching of Jesus Christ. Christ is fundamental. Christ is evangelical. Was Christ a dispensationalist? Terms such as *fundamen-*

> *James 5:7 Be patient therefore, brethren, unto the coming of the Lord. Behold, the husbandman waiteth for the precious fruit of the earth, and hath long patience for it, until he receive the early and latter rain.*

tal, evangelical, dispensational, need to be carefully defined so the semantic structure of any context may not be misinterpreted.

God's Word—the Bible—is the seed that is cast upon the good tilled soil. The quality of soil is discussed in *James 5:7; Matthew 13: 1-9*. The soil is the world, not the church. Now, if the soil is impregnated with the seed (the Word of God), God allows the Christian, in weakness, to sow seed in good soil. Then he is productive, for his sufficiency is in the Father *(II Corinthians 3:5, 12:10)*. God offers the right conditions in soil nutrients, water, and climatic conditions, for God does give the increase, and gathers the harvest.

We, as the body of Christ, are the living organism, growing as we search out the fundamental truths of the Bible—the seed. Jesus Christ taught us to execute the Great Commission, which is to evangelize the world. As Christians, we study the Scriptures, where God distinctly, and naturally divided into age periods, which are term dispensations, in His divine plan. Recognizing the age periods, or dispensation divisions of the Bible, enables us to better comprehend God's plan for the ages.

In the dispensation in which we are living, Christians are not carrying out the act of witnessing locally to the world for a variety of reasons. Fear, intimidation, embarrassment, persecution, apathy and martyrdom are common ones.

Fundamentally, we are to search the Scriptures daily. *Acts 17:11-14* describes Paul's and Silas's fellowship with the noble Bereans. These Christians searched the Old Testament Scriptures daily, and tested whether the things Paul was proclaiming concerning Christ were true. They were ready of mind and spirit, ready to receive the truth from the inerrancy of God's inspired Word. They were *fundamental*, submitting to God's revealed truth and accepting God's judgmental values for their daily living.

The Bereans searched the Scriptures, and shared and cared for the salvation of others. They rightly divide the Word of Truth *(II Timothy 2:15)*? Did they quench the Spirit?

When Paul preached to this great fellowship, the unbelieving Jews, the flesh and Satan, stirred up the people. Why? Because Paul was preaching the fundamental truth laid down by God's divine plan.

> *II Timothy 2:15   Study to shew thyself approved unto God, a workman that needeth not to be ashamed, rightly dividing the word of truth.*

Paul was not preaching salvation by law, ceremony, asceticism, mysticism, or Gnostic concepts. Nor was he preaching anti-dispensationalism, twentieth century orthodox new-evangelism or even salvation by good deeds. God forbid that he might today have taught the worship of angels in this day of contemporary cults—the New Age Movement.

Paul had performed enough grievous blunders before his conversion. In *Acts 2-:22-24*, Paul, with his afflictions, did not know what would happen to him. But the Holy Spirit witnessed through him in every city. He was elected, and called by the Lord. Not being concerned about his aches and pains, he suffered only for the cause of Christ. As soon as the unbelieving Jews in Thessalonica discovered Paul was teaching in Berea, they came there and stirred up and troubled the crowds *(Acts 17:12-15)*. They were unbelieving and under the influence of Satan, and his experience with them must have been harrowing. But he did expect to finish his course with joy, testifying and bringing the Gospel to lost souls. It was the grace of God that allowed Paul to continue this ministerial course.

There are many who are called today, as was Paul, but few are chosen to witness for the Lord and His plan to the world. As predicted in *Acts 19:20*, the Word of God has grown mightily, and Christendom has prevailed even in the war years of more modern times. The biography of C. T. Studd[2] tells about a celebrated athlete and missionary; who was raised up and used by God Almighty as a faithful ambassador to the lost world.

The autobiography of Charles W. Singer, another faithful witness, tells of his experiences as a worker under persecution during the German-Russian wars. Pastor Singer's life is another Spirit-directed ministry, which flourished under duress in Latvia and the surrounding countries. His autobiography[3] tells of his work among refugees in Europe. Reading it, you will be challenged and enriched. Mr. Singer is another example of a man raised up by God to evangelize the fundamental truths of the Bible, which were so carefully laid out in the Dispensation of Grace.

Joseph Aldrich[4] is another who has chronicled his evangelical ministry. He concludes, "Evangelism is expressing what I possess in Christ... evangelism is displaying the universals of God's character—His love, His righteousness, His justice, and His faithfulness—through the particulars of my everyday life… Evangelism is what Christ does through the activity of His children as they are involved in (1) proclamation, (2) fellowship, and (3) service." Evangelism is that act whereby we testify and win people by the regenerative power of Christ. It is the Holy Spirit that does the actual converting of depraved sinners to new creatures *(John 16:8-16; 3:8)*.

Understanding Dispensations

The following explication is taken from H. A. Ironside's *Wrongly Dividing the Word of Truth:*[5]

"The word "dispensation" is discovered in the English-American Bible. The translated Greek word "*oikonomea*" means house order, stewardship.

In the various ages, God gives faithful men and women certain responsibilities. In one era, God deals with man under the law. Then, in another period of time, God deals, manages and tests mankind under an unmerited favor called grace. God's orders were different under the rule of law, a perfect law that Israel was unable to keep. Under grace, believers are saved entirely through grace *(Ephesians 3:2; I Corinthians 9:17; Colossians 1:25)*. The Christian life is not easy in the sorrows of this world, but God offers eternal life to *all* grace believers, though the temptation is strong to turn from it *(I Corinthians 10:11-15)*. Here we have the hope, faith, and love that only a good God can bestow upon us.

Dr. C. I. Scofield,[6] in his booklet, *Rightly Dividing the Word of Truth*, has an enlightening chapter on the seven generally accepted dispensations. He says,

"These periods are marked off in Scripture by some change in God's method of dealing with mankind, or a portion of mankind, in respect to two fundamental questions, which are sin and man's responsibility. Each of the dispensations may be regarded as a new test for the natural man, and each ends in a judgment, marking his utter failure in every dispensation."

The Sequential Dispensations

Lewis Sperry Chafer has written concerning the seven dispensations[7] that can be distinguished in the Scriptures. Bible scholars have concurred with this interpretation of these dispensational periods.[8] Spirit-led students can discover this harmony in the Scriptures without compromise or contention. Men may bicker and make war with words and swords, but a general understanding prevails concerning these divisions:

1. *Dispensation of innocence*

Time: from the creation of Adam to his expulsion from paradise. During this period, man was innocent of sin. This dispensation ended in judgment, because of man's disobedience to God. Adam and Eve were driven out of their beautiful abode into a world now cursed by sin *(Genesis 1:28 to 3:22)*.

2. *Dispensation of conscience*—Before the Flood.

Time: From man's expulsion from paradise to the flood. Because of sin, the human race was now conscious of both right and wrong. This dispensation ended in judgment because of ungodly living. All mankind was destroyed by the flood, except righteous Noah and his family *(Genesis 3:22 to 7:23)*.

3. *Dispensation of human authority* —Government

Time: From the end of the flood to the confusion of language. After the flood, God said to Noah: "And the fear of you and the dread of you shall be upon every beast of the earth, and upon every fowl of the air, upon all that moves upon the earth, and upon all the fishes of the sea: into your hand are they delivered *(Genesis 9:2)*."

This dispensation ended in judgment because of man's disobedience, in not wanting to spread over the whole earth as God had commanded. The people stayed in the land of Shinar, and started to build a huge tower to make a name for themselves. But God came in judgment and confused their language, thus forcing them to spread over the earth. This was the beginning of the different races *(Genesis 8:20, 11:9; Numbers 25:3; James. 3:7, 6:25-30; I Kings 16:31; 18:18; II Kings 9:3)*.

4. *Dispensation of man under promise*

Time: From the confusion of their language to the giving of the law. God now sought out one man, Abram, with whom He made a covenant. In this covenant, the promises were gracious and unconditional. God has kept all of them and, since some of them are eternal, He is still keeping them.

To receive the blessings of the covenant, the Israelites were to obey God, particularly in regard to staying in the land of Canaan. But they repeatedly disobeyed God, and this dispensation ended in judgment. They were in Egypt for 400 years, the latter part in bondage *(Genesis 12:1 to Exodus. 19:8).*

5. *Dispensation of man under law*

Time: From the giving of the Mosaic law to the death of Christ. While the Israelites were in the wilderness, God proposed a covenant of law. If they had been wise, they should have pleaded to remain under His former covenant of grace, *Genesis 14:18-20; Hebrews 7:1-20*, but instead they said arrogantly, "All that the Lord has spoken we will do *(Exodus 19:4-10)*." They did not understand their inability to keep the Mosiac law, they broke it in every respect.

This dispensation has even more years to run. It will commence again when God takes the Church to be with Himself at the rapture, when the Tribulation period begins. Thus, this dispensation of law also ends in judgment: The Great Tribulation, which is also called the "time of Jacob's trouble" *(Jeremiah. 30:7; Daniel 9:23-27).*

6. *Dispensation of man under grace*

Time: From the death of Christ until His future return for the Church. We are now living in this dispensation. It is called "grace" (unmerited favor) because God's grace offers the sinner free salvation through Jesus Christ. This age will also end in judgment when an apostate world will be left to endure the seven years of tribulation during the reign of the Antichrist, after the Church has been raptured or removed from this world.

7. *Dispensation of man under the personal reign of Christ*[9, 10]

Time: a thousand years, from the time of the victory at

the battle of Armageddon to the judgment of the Great White Throne *(Deuteronomy 28:13; Revelation 20:4-9).*

8. *An added, eighth dispensation*

Larkin[11] views the eighth dispensation as the fullness of times *(Ephesians 1:9-10).* In it God creates new heavens and a new Earth *(Isaiah 65:17; Revelation 21:1),* and the first heaven and earth will pass away. This will be the time of the new Jerusalem, a holy city of God, where saved nations shall walk in the light of it and the leaders of this new earth bring their glory and honor into it. Study *Revelation: chapters 21 and 22.*

> *Deuteronomy 28:13 And the Lord shall make thee the head, and not the tail; and thou shalt be above only, and thou shalt not be beneath; if that thou hearken unto the command-ments of the Lord thy God, which I command thee this day, to observe and to do them*

The Personality of Satan

Satan is a person, the author of sin, and the cause of the fall. He is the open and declared enemy of God and man, and he shall be eternally punished in the lake of fire *(Job 1:6,7; Isaiah. 14:12-17; Matthew 4:2-11; 25:41; Revelation 20:10; 19:20).*

> *Revelation 20:10 And the devil that deceived them was cast into the lake of fire and brimstone, where the beast and the false prophet are, and shall be tormented day and night for ever and ever.*

Satan's Character.

Satan has great power; he is the god of this earth. He is far more powerful than man, but he is not omnipotent (all powerful). Only God is omnipotent. Satan is wise, far beyond the wisdom of man, but he is not omniscient (knowing everything). Omniscience belongs to God alone. Satan is very active, but he is not omnipresent (everywhere present). Only God is present everywhere.

The Bible often speaks of demons. (In a number of places in the Bible, the term *devils* is used, but this should be *demons*). There is only one devil, but there are innumerable demons. The multitude of demons is employed by Satan to carry out his diabolical plan against God. Because of this vast host of helpers, it *seems* as though Satan is unlimited in power, in wisdom, and in presence; but, in reality, he, himself, is not omnipotent, omniscient, or omnipresent.

Scripture reveals that several wicked characters made attempts to exterminate the line of David. The devil attempted to destroy the royal genealogy that lead directly to the birth of the Lord Jesus Christ. Down through the dispensations, the devil has tried to eliminate the Jews. Moses and the Jews were allowed to leave Egypt. Haman in the book of Esther made radical decisions to do away with the Jews. Athaliah also , in her wickedness and struggle to retain leadership and power, failed to destroy the line of David.

Therefore, God will always preserve His plan in every dispensation *(II Kings 11:1)*. Almighty God is still in charge, for He is the sovereign King of Kings and is accountable to no being. Why God allows Satan to exert so much power over men and nations is incomprehensible to us, but it fits in with God's holy purpose—to ultimately exalt Christ and crush Satan under His feet *(Psalm 2)*.

Satan's Origin

From God's Word, we learn that Satan, at one time, was a perfect being, created by God. "Your heart was proud and lifted up, because of your beauty; you corrupted your wisdom by reason of your splendor *(Ezekiel. 28:17)*." See also *Isaiah 14:12-14.*

"You were perfect in your ways from the day that you were created, till iniquity was found in you *(Ezekiel. 28:11)*." See also *Ezekiel 28:15-19*. God allows sin and Satan's activity for His sovereign purposes.

Satan's Fall

"How are you fallen from Heaven, O Lucifer, son of the morning! How are you cut down to the ground, which did weaken the nations! For you have said in your heart, I will ascend into heaven. I will exalt my throne above the stars of God, I will sit also upon the mount of the congregation, in the sides of the north. I will ascend above the heights of the clouds. I will be like the most High *(Isaiah. 14:1-14)*."

Satan's downfall was because of his pride. Given free will, Satan sought to exalt himself to be equal, and above God. Why did God allow Satan to corrupt himself with pride? Why did God allow Satan to exalt himself and attempt to be equal to God? A mystery.

Many angels fell with him

"For, if God spared not the angels that sinned, but cast them down to Hell, and delivered them into chains of darkness, to be reserved unto judgment... *(II Peter 2:4)*." See also *Matthew 25:41*. One of these scriptures poses the question, the other tells not why, but *what* he did.

> *Matthew 25:41   Then shall he say also unto them on the left hand, Depart from me, ye cursed, into everlasting fire, prepared for the devil and his angels...*

Our Lord Jesus affirms the reality of hell. Study *Mark 9:43-48* carefully. If your hand offends you, cut it off. It is better for you to enter into life damaged, than possess two hands and go straight to hell, into the fire that never dies. Other examples are offered in the passage. The other option is to enter into the kingdom of God with the loss of an eye, foot, hand, etc., rather than have two eyes and be cast into hell fire.

Jesus Christ warns the scribes and pharisees with a blunt question, "How will you escape the damnation of hell?" Hell was prepared for the devil, his angels, and the children of wrath, which are those lost in unbelief and separated from God. The final judgment, which is hell, will open up and receive a population that will enter an everlasting torment *(Revelation 20:12-15)*. Hell is a waste heap where the fire never burns out.

In *Luke 16,* a rich man was in eternity without God. His memory was very good, and he asked for Lazarus to warn his brothers. Hell is a place of torment and loneliness. Today, some unsaved will say, "I want to be where my friends are." The story of the rich man would be meaningless to them. Study *Matthew 23:15, 33; 25:41, 46; Revelation 20:11-15; 21:8.*

The Scriptures, however, are explicit. "And the angels which kept not their first estate, but left their own habitation, He has reserved in everlasting chains, under darkness, unto the judgment of the Great Day *(Jude 6)*."

"Then shall He say also unto them on the left hand, 'Depart from me, you cursed, into everlasting fire, prepared for the devil and his angels *(Matthew 25:41)*.'"It is evident the demons must have fallen with Satan *(Matthew 8:28-34; Luke 8:30-40)*.

Satan's Power

"For we wrestle not against flesh and blood, but against principalities, against powers, against the rulers of the darkness of this world, against spiritual wickedness in high places *(Ephesians 6:12)*."

"In time past, you walked as aliens according to the

course of this world, according to the prince of the power of the air *(Ephesians 2:2-3)*."

We see that Satan has great power and a highly organized kingdom. The demons have their appointed places and positions. He undoubtedly planned his kingdom after God's plan. But Satan's kingdom leads to destruction, while God's kingdom leads to eternal life.

Satan's working

"You are of your father, the devil... He was a murderer from the beginning (murdering spiritual souls for eternity)... when he speaks a lie, he speaks of his own; for he is a liar, and the father of it *(John 8:44)*."

He works through lying and deceit, and men and women everywhere believe his lies and are deceived for eternity. He is a real being *(Matthew 4:1-11)*. He never was good, loving, merciful, kind, gentle, patient and pitiful. He was a sinner from the beginning *(I John 3:8)*. He lures men to commit sin. It is impossible for him to attack God. But he attacks and alienates God's creation, which is man. The Bible reports Satan as.:

1. lying *(John 8:44; II Corinthians 11:3)*
2. robbing *(Matthew 13:19)*
3. tempting *(Matthew 4:1)*
4. harassing *(Job 1 and 2; II Corinthians 12:7)*
5. hindering *(Ephesians 6:12; I Thessalonians. 2:8; Zechariah. 3:1)*
6. sifting *(Luke 22:31)*
7. copying *(II Corinthians 11:14,15; Matthew 13:25)*
8. accusing *(Revelation 12:9,10)*
9. tainting with disease *(Luke 13;16; I Corinthians 5:5)*
10. possessing *(John 13:27)*
11. killing and devouring *(John 8:44; I Peter 5:8)*

In some of his approaches, Satan is as fierce as a lion.

Such is the case in many heathen lands, where he works in horrible ways. He works and manipulates people in the home and church. Satan is cunning and tactful. He can draw anyone or anything under his power, except for the sovereignty of God. BEWARE!

He also makes his appearances in beautiful ways, even in the fashion of liberal preachers, and fine-sounding cults and sects. Beware of his wiles and his deceitful ways! "And no marvel; for Satan himself is transformed into an angel of light *(II Corinthians 11:14)*."

"Be sober, be vigilant, because your adversary, the devil, as a roaring lion, walks about, seeking whom he may devour *(I Peter 5:8)*."

"The accuser of our brethren is cast down, who accused them before our God day and night *(Revelation 12:10)*."

He is the great accuser of Christians. Only the advocacy of Christ can reconcile and protect us *(II Thessalonians 2:1-12; I John 3:4-8: Corinthians 5:14-21)*.

The story of Job brings this out very clearly. Read *Job 1:6-12*. We can relate to Job, a contemporary of Abraham. Bildad chides and reprimands Job severely *(Job: chapter 18)*.

Job responds: "Why do you pursue me as God does? Have you not hurt me enough, Bildad? My desire is to have my words carved into lead or even stone. I know my Redeemer lives, and He will stand upon the earth in the end of time. My body will be destroyed. Still, I will see God with my own eyes and my heart wants this to happen *(Job 19:22-27)*." What positive consolation Job offers each of us today who has a strong faith and belief.

Satan's Destiny

In *Isaiah 14:12*, we learn that Satan was "cut down to the ground." Although he still has access to God (see *Job 1:6,7)*, his domain is now that of the "prince of the power of

> Ephesians 2:2
> Wherein in time past ye walked according to the course of this world, according to the prince of the power of the air, the spirit that now worketh in the children of disobedience...

the air *(Ephesians 2:2)." John 12:31* says, "Now, is the judgment of this world; now, shall the prince of this world be cast out." Jesus said, "The prince of this world is judged *(John 16:11)."* Therefore, the judgment of Satan, which had been predicted in *Genesis 3:15,* took place at the cross. As we trace Satan through history to the day of judgment, we note others fell also *(II Peter 2:4)*, such as angels and men. Here are some Biblical scenes:

1. Satan is in heaven *(Luke 10:18; Isaiah 14:12)*. No time is given in these scenes *(Ezekiel. 28:14)*.

2. Satan travels to the Garden of Eden and expresses himself in the form of a deceitful serpent *(Genesis 3: 1-15; Ezekiel. 28:13)*, tempting man and woman into sin.

3. Satan then has access to heaven and earth *(Job 1:6, 7; 2:1, 2; Ephesians 2:2; 6:12)*. He is running to and fro as the Prince of the Power of the air, attempting to create turmoil!

4. Satan hones in on earth as an Antichrist during the seven tribulation years, deceiving many. The true church has been snapped away by the Lord before this frontal attack by Satan takes place *(Revelation 9:1; 12:9, 10, 12, 13)*.

5. Finally Satan and his angels will be cast into the depths of Sheol, called the abyss. See *Romans 10:6-8*, also *Deuteronomy 30:13. Luke 8:31* describes it as the lower regions as a habitat where demons will be loosed at a later time period. Satan rebels with his armies and attempts to interfere with God's plans. Then out of heaven a fire from God will devour the armies of Satan, and he will be thrown into the lake of fire *(Revelation 7-10)* to be tormented forever.

Job was from Uz. This man was blameless, upright, feared God and abstained and avoided evil. He had seven sons and three daughters. With immense wealth and material goods, Job was the richest man in the area. The family had festive banquets. During those good days, Job offered sacrifices for the sins of his sons whom he feared might possibly have sinned and renounced God.

Then a day arrived when the sons of God presented themselves to God. Also Satan came with them. And God addressed Satan, "From where did you come?" he answered that he was walking throughout the earth.

Then God asked Satan if he had noticed his servant, Job, who is blameless, perfect, an upright example of a man who is God fearing and resisting evil! Satan, the accusor, answered God, saying, "Does Job really fear God for nothing? You have built a hedge about him and his temporal goods. You have blessed Job's work and increased his goods in the land. You have extended your hand now and influence all that he has, but suppose you remove anything Job has. Surely he will denounce and despised you to your face."

The Lord God Almighty responded to Satan, "Everything he has is in your power. But the man Job, do not lay a hand upon him." We all remember the trials and tribulations that were then visited upon him through the malice of Satan *(Job 1:1-12)*.

How shall we meet Satan?

"Put on the whole armor of God that we may be able to stand against the wiles of the devil *(Ephesians 4:27, 6:11-18)*."

"Whom (Satan) resist steadfast in faith *(I Peter 5:8-9)*."

"Submit yourselves therefore, to God. Resist the devil, and he will flee from you. Draw near to God, and he will draw near to you *(James 4:7,8)*." Jesus explains the parable of the Sower. The Sower scatters the Word. As soon as people hear it, Satan instantly snatches away the Word which has been dispersed in them. Satan cunningly will divide their minds. Believers are responsible for what they hear *(Mark 4:12-20; I Corinthians 2:10-16, 10:11-13; II Timothy 3:15-17.).* All Scripture is written for us, but not all Scripture is written to us.

We are to be clad with the whole armor of God. We cannot move against Satan's power in our own strength. By God's grace He has given us a divine nature and the strength to resist Satan.

Satan's eternal punishment

"And the devil that deceived them was cast into the lake of fire and brimstone... and shall be tormented day and night forever *(Revelation 20:10)*."

Return of Christ for His Own

The believer looks forward to the blessed hope, the personal, imminent, re-tribulation, pre-millennial return of Christ for His redeemed saints, called the true, and universal Church to establish His millennial kingdom *(I Thessalonians. 4:13-18; Zechariah. 14:4-11; Revelation 19:11-16; 20:1-6; I Thessalonians. 1:10; 5:9; Revelation 3:10).*

We use the word "rapture" *(parousia)* to describe this wonderful event. The word means "caught up." The idea is clearly given in this verse, and others: *I Corinthians 15:52.* Two distinct things will happen: all the dead in Christ (who, of course, are believers) will be raised from the dead, and the believers who are alive at the time will be changed so that both groups, with

I Corinthians 15:52   In a moment, in the twinkling of an eye, at the last trump: for the trumpet shall sound, and the dead shall be raised incorruptible, and we shall be changed.

bodies made like the resurrection body of Christ, will be caught up to be with the Lord in the air. Only as much time as it takes for the twinkling of an eye will be needed for the whole process *(I Thessalonians. 4:13-5:11)*.

Let us continue to encourage one another to eagerly look forward to this great journey. Even as we face death we can rejoice in the victory we have in our Lord Jesus Christ *(I Corinthians 15:54-58)*.

Events between the rapture and revelation

1. Judgment of believers' works

"Every man's work shall be made manifest; for the day (at His coming) shall declare it, because it shall be revealed by fire; and the fire shall try every man's work of what sort it is... If any man's work shall be burned, he shall suffer loss (of his reward); but he himself shall be saved; yet so as by fire *(I Corinthians 3:13,15)*."

"For we must all appear before the judgment seat of Christ; that every one may receive the things done in his body, according to that he has done, whether it be good or bad *(II Corinthians 5:10)*."

And behold, I come quickly; and my reward is with me, to give every man according as his work shall be *(Revelation 22:1)*."

Rewards are earned,[12] salvation is free, God offers several crowns to His children at the judgment The Spirit bears witness to the truth and is truth *(I John 5:6-8)*; He gives joy and righteousness *(Romans 14:17)*; He supplies comfort, righteousness and truth *(John 16:7-14)*. How faithfully He assists the grace believer!

a. The *incorruptible crown*

Every man must strive for control in his life by being temperate in all his affairs *(I Corinthians 9:24-25; 15:42-45;*

Acts 13:35-37). The believer will never attain this by self control, but by the leading and controlling of the Spirit. We are forewarned in Scripture of losing our crown *(Revelation 3:11).*

b. The crown of *joy and rejoicing* of our Lord Jesus Christ at His coming *(I Thessalonians. 2:19).*

c. The crown of *righteousness (II Timothy 4:8)* is awarded to those who complete their course of life here, and look eagerly for Christ's appearing. *Stephanos* (Greek) denotes a victor's crown in completing life's plan according to God's will and direction.

d. The crown of *glory (Proverbs 14:18; I Peter 5:4; Revelation 2:10)* . The crown must be carefully guarded. "Hold on to what you have, and let no man remove your crown *(Revelation 3:11).*"

e. The crown of *life (James 1:12; Revelation 2:10;3:11).* This glorious crown is awarded to believers who endure testings with an unfailing faith to the end.

2. The Marriage of Christ and His Church

Let all grace believers rejoice, be happy and give God the glory! For the marriage of the Son of God to His bride (the church) is in readiness. The church has been given her fine linen, bright and pure such is the character of God's righteous deeds of the saints. They are called and blessed unto the marriage supper of the Lamb. These are the true words of God *(Revelation 9:7-9).*

Glossary of Terms

Dispensation: Orderly periods of events by divine Providence necessary to visualize the scope and sequence of God's plan. God dealt differently with man in each dispensation, according to His perfect changeless plan.

Divine Unction: *John 2:20* - The gift of the Spirit in aiding Biblical truth, keeping one's understanding of the truth Christ taught that glorified Him *(John 16:14-15)* in whom the complete unveiling of God is bestowed. Christians are a chosen body of holy and royal priests *(I Peter 2:1-10)*.

Evangelism: Spreading the Gospel or good news of Jesus Christ

Exposition: The act of communicating literally the context in historical and present day application in written or verbal expression.

First Resurrection of Christians: Same as Rapture

Fundamental: Essential, basic foundational root are literally true

Hermeneutics: Interpreting the Word of God by investigating the grammatical language and laws of thought in context. Scripture is truthfully explaining meaning of the historical and literary context.

Imminent: Possible at any time

Inerrant: Without error

Millennium: 1000 year reign of Christ's Pre-Tribulation: After the seven year tribulation

Pre-millennial: Before the 1000 years of Christ's reign on this earth

The Rapture: The invisible church is taken up to meet Christ and be with Him. *(I Thessalonians 4:16-17)*

ENDNOTES

1. Nash, Ronald H. *The New Evangelicalism.* Grand Rapids, MI: Zondervan Publishing House, 1963. Preface and p. 176.

2. Grubb, Norman. *C. T. Studd, Cricketer and Pioneer.* Washington, PA: Christian Literature Crusade, 1985.

3. Singer, Charles W. *A Testimony of God's Grace and Faithfulness.* Los Angeles, CA: The International Refugee Mission, Inc., pp. 1-154.

4. Aldrich, Joseph C.*Lifestyle Evangelism*; Portland, OR: Multnomah Press, 4th Printing, 1983, p. 29.

5. Ironside, H. A. *Wrongly Dividing the Word of Truth - Ultra-Dispensationalism Examined in The Light of Holy Scripture.* New York, N.Y: Loizeaux Brothers, Inc., 1938.

6. Scofield, C. I. *Rightly Dividing The Word of Truth.* Neptune, NJ: Loizeaux Brothers,1896 & 1986, pp. 13-16.

7. Chafer, Lewis Sperry. *Major Bible Themes.* Findlay, OH: Dunham Publishing Co., 1926 & 1953, pp. 96-102.

8. Zuck, Roy B. *Basic Bible Interpretation.* Wheaton, IL: Victor Books; Scripture Press Publishing, Inc., 1991, pp. 235-241, 284.

9. Chafer, *op. cit.,* pp. 96-102.

10. Scofield, *op. cit.,* pp. 13-16.

11. Larkin, Clarence. *Dispensational Truth.* Philadelphia, PA: Publisher Rev. Clarence Larkin, 1924; pp. 17-18, plus Dispensational Chart.

12. Thiessen, Henry Clarence. *Introductory Lectures in Systematic Theology.* Grand Rapids, MI: Eerdmans Publ. Co., 1949, p. 458.

CHAPTER EIGHT: Biblical Illiteracy

Justification for the Study

Bible literacy among the masses will be the question considered in this section. With a question so important, how can we assume that those who profess to know the Bible so well, which presumably directs their lives, actually do understand its teachings? How can we neglect to investigate whether the Bible study we urge so heartily is effective?

Assessing that effectiveness has been the goal of an experimental study, carried out with precision over a period of time, which will be reviewed here.

First, however, let us review the justification for a life of dedicated Bible study.

The application and improvement of Bible study in one's daily living has come to be considered a continuous developmental process. When we meditate day and night on God's Words *(Joshua 1:8-9)*, God tells us that He will make our way prosperous. Do you thank God for life, for the fruits of the Spirit, and for your talents? You have one life to live, many fruits of the Spirit, and at least one talent or gift. But what about the Word of God? Do you know the Word of God?

God is the one foundation that will never crumble. Listen to Joshua's lesson that is current and practical in our daily living *(Joshua 24:14-23)*. Honor and obey God and no other gods or idols. Make a true acknowledgment personally to serve the Lord God.

Daily Bible study needs to be expanded and refined at each successive level of maturity. God chastens those whom He loves. It is God who is taking you through these successive levels of spiritual refinement.

Study the Berean account in the book of Acts. They were more noble than those residing in Thessalonica. The Bereans possessed a readiness in receiving and studying the Word of God carefully and thoroughly and applying it each day of their lives.

The faithful searched the Scriptures daily, verifying those things that were true *(Acts 17:11)*. Dr. Luke expounds the principle of Scriptural study. Jesus thoroughly interpreted to the disciples all the Scriptures concerning Himself. The disciples reacted one to another as Jesus made the Scriptures lucid unto them *(Luke 24:25-3)*.

Therefore, search the Scriptures carefully in regard to eternal things. Know the Scriptures so you may testify of Jesus *(John 5:39)*. The Scriptures were written for our learning and for applying the lessons to all life experiences. When we have patience and comfort in Scriptures, we have hope *(Romans. 15:4; II Timothy 2:15; II Timothy 3:14-17; James 3:17; James 1:21; I John 5:1; Hebrews 6:1)*. Therefore glorify God in your body and your spirit which belongs to God *(1 Corinthians 6:20)*.

> *Hebrews 6:1*
> *Therefore leaving the principles of the doctrine of Christ, let us go on unto perfection; not laying again the foundation of repentance from dead works, and of faith toward God...*

The Nature of the Research

The study is confined to a 1215 selected population of volunteer, evangelical, fundamental, believing Christians in the United States. The study is being expressed in an inventory survey of twenty assorted true and false statements gleaned from Old and New Testament Scriptures. The Bible Literacy Inventory (BLI) survey items were screened by an editorial board for clarity and semantic composition. This survey purports to reveal the literacy level of persons studying the Bible.

A few assemblies among the seminaries recognized as EFBC (Evangelical Fundamental Believing Christians) were evasive, threatened, and doubtful of the benefits of a literacy Bible survey. Some people responded to the survey negatively.

Their Comments:

1. Cannot answer it in seven minutes.

2. Theology and doctrine would not be able to give simple true or false answers to certain statements.

3. Some church workers stated they would give the survey, but they were not people of their word. A follow-up indicated they had not done it.

4. Some church leaders said they were not interested in doing the survey.

5. While some seminary leaders snubbed the survey, they suggested Bible colleges.

6. One vice president of a seminary did not see his way clear to offer the survey to any of the school's students, saying that their students are extremely busy. This was a seminary that wants you to contribute money, make a charitable trust, and purchase its publications; but it could not offer seven minutes for a survey. Consideration of worthy goals of others was lacking in some EFBC institutions.

Positively, forty assemblies composed of 1215 volunteers, who claim to study the Bible, graciously submitted to the seven-minute Bible literacy survey.

The study embraced:

1. Two Christian Oregon secondary schools.

2. Four Oregon Bible colleges and a college in Virginia

3. A Church summer camp in Oregon

4. A missionary group in Arizona

5. A Kansas newspaper staff

6. Two radio staffs from California and Texas

7. Five Bible classes from Oregon and Washington

8. Thirty individual persons in Oregon

9. Twenty-three congregations of varying denominations and non-denominations from Oregon, Texas, Virginia, Washington and New Jersey.

The EFBC sample sizes ranged from 5 to 148 participants, contained in forty (40) participating assemblies from Arizona, Kansas, New Jersey, Oregon, Texas, Virginia and Washington.

The Problem

A. To determine to what extent Bible knowledge has been acquired by the aggregate of EFBC bodies, with comparisons made of certain areas.

B. To determine the literacy level acquired by EFBC bodies in order to assess the aggregate and make comparisons.

C. To offer ministers and teachers a spiritual perception of the limited Bible knowledge and understanding of their specific surveyed group.

D. To determine what criteria may be used to improve the spiritual life of persons taking the BLI Survey.

Limitations of the Study

A. Only scattered samples outside of the states of Oregon and Washington were given.

B. The study only measured the acquisition of Bible knowledge in particular areas of Old and New Testament scripture.

C. Factors impossible to measure were not included:

142

1. An overall index level of human spirituality such as conversion experience.

2. Faith, trust and belief elements

D. No opportunity was set for observing the groups ahead of time

Procedure:

Over a one-year period, EFBC representatives administered the BLI. It was composed by the investigator and an eight member study committee. All twenty survey inventory items were composed, reworded, and selected for validity and understanding of certain Bible statements. The statements varied in content and were gleaned from Old and New Testament passages of the Bible.

The BLI was administered exclusively to EFBC assemblies. The survey was offered to persons of all ages and backgrounds without a reading or language problem. The survey was administered in seven minutes without former announcement or planning.

The confidential data was collected, scored, and returned to the group leader for his use and discretion. All persons received the same instructions. The survey procedure was rigidly controlled for time, quiet, and identical BLI forms.

The following instruction sheet was given to all leaders administering the BLI for standardization purposes.

Dear Sir:

Enclosed is a Bible Literacy Inventory. The inventory is a personal research study with the assistance of other ministers, teachers and friends. I would appreciate your careful participation in this study.

1. Please *duplicate* the inventory for the number of persons taking it.

2. The purpose is to have your congregation, church

school, or Bible class *complete the form in seven (7) minutes*, without pondering on the facts and concepts. This literacy inventory on Bible knowledge is being administered in this country.

3. The *purpose* is to offer the minister/teacher a spiritual perception of limited Bible knowledge and understanding of your specific surveyed group.

4. This is *only an indicator* for the people taking the survey. It is not a test. No name or group is placed on the form. The minister or teacher returns the forms to RALPH CATER for scoring and interpretation. *Remember* to forward your name and address so the results of the study can be returned to you.

5. *The inventory is administered to people who can read and do not possess a reading skills or language barrier problem.*

6. The results are confidential and are only returned to the person allowing the survey.

7. The inventory offers the leader confidential data on the people in his group.

8. The study is limited to a small number of inventory statements of understandings and misconceptions. It does not measure faith belief of any individual.

Thank you for providing the time, interest, effort and kindness for supplying any size sample for this study. *Philippians 2:13*

Sincerely in Christ,
Ralph Cater

The BLI was critiqued by an eight-member study committee composed of:

1. A software engineer
2. Two evangelical ministers
3. Two music teachers
4. A construction contractor

5. An English teacher

6. A seminary professor of Bible Exposition

The structured statements attempted to provide established, semantically correct, and non-compromising ideas from the reader. Statements were chosen to conform to possible, reasonable answers by the writers of the inventory, according to the following criteria:

1. Are the arguments valid, or invalid, as the reader might conceptualize and/or reconceptualize them from his recall of Biblical knowledge and interpretive value judgments?

2. What is each statement confirming to you that would suggest or reaffirm a truth, or counter a truth, as it might be found in the Bible?

3. Can you react to each statement critically, in context, for interpretative judgments in accordance to Biblical standards and values?

INFORMAL BIBLE INVENTORY

An attendant will supervise the taking of this informal inventory on Biblical literacy. Since this is a confidential review, no group or personal name is necessary. Respond to each statement quickly by answering it as accurately as you can. CIRCLE T (true) or F (false).

1. The names of the first five books of the Bible are *Genesis, Exodus, Leviticus, Numbers* and *Deuteronomy*.   T   F
2. The angel of Jehovah appeared to Moses
   at the burning bush.   T   F

3. The Apostle John turned water into wine.   T   F
4. Jeremiah was highly successful in the ministry.   T   F
5. The hymns of the Old Testament are the Psalms.   T   F
6. The Battle of Armageddon will be fought
   in the future.   T   F

7. Babylon is located in present day Iraq	T	F
8. Everyone will be resurrected someday.	T	F
9. The Bible has one covenant.	T	F
10. Jesus Christ is perfect.	T	F
11. By God's law no flesh shall be justified.	T	F
12. Sadducees believed in the resurrection.	T	F
13. Paul, a Pharisee, committed murder before his conversion	T	F
14. Abraham was the principal author of the Old Testament.	T	F
15. Melchizedek "King of Salem" was a type of Christ.	T	F
16. John was the first martyr of the church.	T	F
17. Baptism offers a person eternal life.	T	F
18. Jesus sent demons into a herd of pigs	T	F
19. Revelation was written by John the Baptist	T	F
20. There is no limit of God's grace.	T	F

You can take the Bible Literacy Inventory without help in seven minutes. Then score your survey statement. The answers follow in Section VI. Do the BLI now. Now compare your score of the number of right answers with others who took the survey. Then read on and see how the answers were Biblically interpreted. The format for the survey statements administered should consider these questions:

1. Why are the arguments valid or invalid for each BLI. statement. The believer should conceptualize or reconceptualize their ideas from the criteria they deem truthful, accurate, for each statement. Each statement is valid if it is scrupulously scrutinized in accordance with Biblical context.

2. What is the context saying to the reader? To relate to this question the believer must constantly review the

factual, conceptual, and inferential material from the Bible.

3. What is the context able to do for you? The answer would be to discover the literal or figurative interpretation of the statement again in accordance with scriptural passages that substantiates or refutes the levity of each statement.

One must be able to evaluate and structure his personal explorations of the context necessary to institute probing inquiry into those relationships of personal, unbiased thought, values in harmony with Bible truth. A passage is randomly taken from Scripture to prove the correctness of a statement.

Example one: Was Jeremiah successful in the ministry? According to man's reasoning, Jeremiah was not successful. He did not reach a high level of satisfaction or worldly prosperity. Did he obtain wealth, recognition from his good deeds as the world would view him? True success is knowing and obeying God according to the standards of God's wisdom and calling.

Analysis of each inventory item

1. The names of the first five books of the
Bible are   *Genesis, Exodus, Leviticus,*
Numbers, and *Deuteronomy.*   [T] F
Illustrates rote memory sequence of the first five books of the Bible—the ability to recall information.

2. The angel of Jehovah appeared to Moses
at the burning bush.   [T] F
Exodus 3:2 teaches us the angel of Jehovah appeared to Moses at the burning bush. The statement is interpretive in nature *(Mark 12:26).*

3. The Apostle John turned water into wine

T [F]

Jesus Christ turned water into wine is a factual memory item *(John 2:1-10)*. The reader has the ability to remember and understand a factual narrative.

4. Jeremiah was highly successful
in the ministry.   [T] F

Jeremiah was chosen by God. He was credible and available before he was formed, sanctified and ordained as a prophet-teacher to all nations *(Jeremiah 1:5-10)*. Such a prophet was called, commanded, and used by Almighty God. Jeremiah had a broken heart. He was called the weeping prophet, a chosen vessel through the Word of the Lord. The Lord used Jeremiah to warn. He was rejected by his people *(Jeremiah11:18-21; 12:5-6)*. The people did threaten, harass, persecute, and imprison God's vessel *(20:1-3; 37:1-21)*. His message was God's message.

Was Jeremiah successful? Yes! He did *obey God's ways and carried out God's Will* by warning the people not to reject Jehovah and rear their *own gods. (chapters 2-3)*. We read of the destruction of Jerusalem and the people caught up in captivity in Babylonia. Jeremiah obeyed God and therefore was highly successful in God's ministry. No one would listen, but he carried out God's instructions. *This item is interpretive and evaluative* in nature: to truly understand how God used him and how man abused him. The analogy is: Jesus was very successful, but few believed He was the Son of God, the Savior of the World.

5. The hymns of the Old Testament
are the *Psalms*.   [T] F

The *Psalms* is a collection of poem-song-hymns of praise and worship in the temple. This item is definitional in nature.

The *Psalms* can be really understood and appreciated when you study them and hear them sung in the Jewish Temple service. The *Psalms* are coauthored. They convey celebration, judgement, thanksgiving, and deliverance. Some express with musical instruments *(Psalm 150)*.

6. The Battle of Armageddon will be
fought in the future.   [T] F

The Battle of Armageddon will be literally fought in the future *(Ezekiel 39:17-22; Daniel 2:34,35; Revelation 16:13-21; Zechariah 14:1-4)*. The item is sequential prophetic information and factual final conflict. The battle of the great day of a sovereign and intimate God. This item has a high degree of content validity. Content validity is inherently connected to Bible Study in groups and on an individual basis.

7. Babylon is located in present day Iraq.   [T] F

Babylon is located geographically in present day Iraq. The news media and secular history supports this city. An item of fact and the skill of locating the city on the map. This type of item permits one to choose the correct location based on study, travel, and media news exchange. Similarities and differences of categorize countries that are identified through confrontations in war, economics and natural resources, etc. Leaders, government types and activities, plus historical events classify this objective inventory item to a designated location. Babylon, a city in present day Iraq, or Armageddon will be fought after a series of events at Mount Megiddo *(Revelation 16:13-16)*.

8. Everyone will be resurrected someday.   [T] F

The righteous and unrighteous will be judged in the future *(Acts 24:14-16; I Corinthians 15:22; Daniel 12:1-2; John 5:28-29; Revelation. 20:6-15)*. This is a scriptural position; teaching the concept that the just as well as the unjust will be brought forth that sleep in the dust of the earth. Some shall awaken to everlasting life and others to shame and everlasting contempt and torment. The good or just shall be resurrected to life; the evil or unjust will be resurrected, judged, and tormented.

9. The Bible has one covenant.   T   [F]

The Bible has two basic covenants called the Old Testament and New Testament *(Genesis 9:16; II Samuel 23:5; Isaiah 24:5)* an everlasting Covenant. Then I will make a new covenant with Israel and Judah *(Jeremiah 31:31; Matthew 26:28; Romans 11:27; Hebrews 8:7-9:28; Hebrews. 12:24)*.

A covenant is a concept item. It is an arrangement or pledge between two parties with a meeting of minds. God promised to bless those who obey him by following his laws. The covenant then has written or verbal conditions that are obeyed. A marriage or mortgage today apply this concept of a covenant.

10. Jesus Christ is perfect.   [T]   F

Jesus Christ has divine perfection. The item is a precept-concept statement. It connotes Christ is complete and perfect. *(Deuteronomy 32:4; Psalms 18:30; Hebrews 5:8; II Corinthians 5:21; Hebrews 7:26; I Peter 2:22)*. Christ is God-man. Through the virgin birth, He was not born into sin or contaminated with sin, but literally and tacitly imposed upon Himself the sins of the world in all dispensational periods of time. His blood was shed once on the Cross for all the sins of humanity. What a sacrifice He made for humanity! Jesus, God's obedient servant, pleased the Father because His death for us upheld the justice of God while allowing God to be merciful to sinners. No one is able to keep God's perfect Law. We are not perfect, therefore we cannot obey God's Law perfectly. Our very best efforts are insufficient, so trusting in our own works is futile. Even Job was justified by faith, not works.

11. By God's law no flesh shall be justified. [T] F

By God's perfect law one is unable to keep the law. We are not perfect, therefore the works of the law are insufficient by trusting in our own works. The Law can condemn and judge. If you break one of God's laws you break all of them *(James 2:10; Galatians 3:10).* We are incapable of measuring up to the perfect law.

If we attempt to be justified by keeping God's Law, we fall far short of God's standard, and we fall from grace *(Galatians 5:4).* We have knowledge from God's Word that man is not justified by the works of the Law, but by the faith of Jesus Christ. Paul warns us in *Galatians 2:16* that absolutely no flesh will be saved by obeying or observing the Law, but it is by the Law that we become conscious of sin *(Romans 3:20).*

This item is conceptual in its meaning. One must know what the Law is unable to do for us. The concept that Jesus Christ has given us a finished work we can accept by faith. By believing in Him, He can cleanse us and continues to cleanse us of our sins. His grace (unmerited favor) is sufficient though we are so imperfect now *(Revelation 22:21, Titus 3:4,5).*

12. Sadducees believed in the resurrection   T   [F]

This is a factual and doctrinal item. The Sadducees did not believe in the resurrection while the Pharisees believed and taught the resurrection. In *I Thessalonians 4:13-18* the grace believers during the church age are caught up before the Tribulation. Old Testament and Tribulation believers are raptured or caught up after the Tribulation *(Revelation 20:4).* We read in *Revelation. 20:11-15,* unbelievers *(Romans 9:18;14:23),* are raised at the end of the millennium reign of Jesus Christ. They are hurled into the lake of fire and tormented day and night forever. No language can surpass Scripture to describe the excruciating psychological infliction that never stops. It is definitely the largest suffering, infinitely beyond any earthly pain and distress.

13. Paul, a Pharisee, committed murder
before his conversion.   [T]   F

The item reports Paul committed murder. This is not a trick statement. It is a statement requiring information, interpretative understanding of contextual clues discovered in Scripture. The context must not be twisted to minimize the felony Paul committed prior to his conversion. The statement is both factual and inferential. *Acts 22:4,* "I persecuted this Way unto death." In *verses 22:19-20,* "I was imprisoning and beating those that believe on Jesus Christ. When you imprison and beat, surely the weak die." Not all, not always. Paul was merciless in his zeal.

Paul's anger is also described. Note *Acts 9:1* and *8:1-3,* breathing threats and murder to the disciples of the Lord. He ravaged the Church physically and in his heart. The inference is anger. *Acts 26:11*: "I punished them often in every synagogue, and compelled them to blaspheme; and being exceedingly mad against them, I *(Paul)* persecuted them even unto strange cities."

Paul, known as Saul before his conversion, was a zealot for the legal law. When he persecuted the Church, the high priests and the Jewish Sanhedrin were eye-witnesses to his activities. Paul arrested, punished, and murdered. He was an accomplice in felonies toward Jewish brethren.

14. Abraham was the principal author
of the Old Testament.   T   [F]

This is a factual item. Moses was the principal author of the Old Testament. Records prove Moses wrote the first five books of the Bible under the inspiration of God like all other authors of the Scriptures.

15. Melchizedek "King of Salem" was
a type of Christ.   [T]   F
Hebrews 7:1, 11-15-17, Melchizedek "King of Salem" was a type of Christ. He appears out of the pages with no origin expressed *(Genesis 14:18; Psalms 110:4)*. Melchizedek was king and priest of God the Highest, a priesthood forever a better, more perfect type, like Christ, that lives and reigns with the Father without end *(Hebrews 5:5-10; 6:20; 7:1-28)*. Christ is the media of a superior covenant, which has been legislated upon superior promises to Israel and Judah.

Question 15 warrants a sequential understanding of the Levitical earthly priesthood for Jews and the Melchizedek spiritual priesthood for all believers forever with Christ. Christians are a priesthood of believers *(I Peter :5,9; Revelation 1:6; 5:10)*. Therefore the Lord Jesus Christ is our great high priest without end.

16. John was the first martyr of the church.   T   [F]
John was not the first martyr of the Church. In *Acts 6-7,* we are offered an account how rapidly the church grew. This item is a biblical fact recorded of Stephen's miracles among the people.

Certain opposers of his activities stirred up the people. Stephen is arrested on false accusations. Stephen defends his position and recounts the historical account of Israel to the Sanhedrin (Council of Elders). Stephen recounts of Israel before the Council fell on deaf ears. The Holy Spirit comforted Stephen while the masses cast him out of the city and stoned him. Stephen is considered the first martyr of the early Church *(Acts 7:56-60)*.

17. Baptism offers a person eternal life.   T   [F]
Water baptism, regardless of the mode has no power to save a person from their sins and offer eternal life. Only Jesus

Christ has the ability to offer the free gift of everlasting life. The following six requirements of salvation are:

A. Recognize and *acknowledge* your sins; your depravity or fallen condition, and your separation from God.

B. *Repent* of your sins.

C. *Believe* Christ died for your sins by shedding His blood on the Cross.

D. Christ *paid the final price* through His blood for the remission of your sins.

E. *Christ offers the free gift of eternal life.*

F. By your faith—trust in Christ alone. You are assured of your salvation only in Christ *(John 3:36).*

Water baptism is symbolic of a verbal testimony of your conversion. If your conversion is 100% true, then you are automatically baptized in Christ with the Holy Spirit living within you *(John 1:25-33).* See *Matthew 3:5-16; Acts 1:8; Luke 3:21-22; Mark 1:9-11; Acts 2:38.*

Christ declares His divine nature by identifying himself with the Father. Believers in faith follow Christ. Christ gives eternal life and no one can take it away. The concept is collectively termed the invisible Church. Only the Godhead knows this. The Father is greater than all and no man has the capability to take them out of the Father's possession—not even self.

This is a precious promise in faith for all grace believers. Remember Christ and the Father are one. Christ became a priest after His ascension and sent another entity called the Holy Spirit to every believing child of God *(John 10:25-42).* The Scriptures cannot be broken. God has sanctified His Son to do the will of the Father. Therefore, by faith belief, the works you do really confirm your trust in God, His Son, and

God's Holy Spirit in each of us.

The Godhead (three persons in one) refuses to neglect us. The Holy Spirit will live in each of us *(John 14:17-20; 15:26-16:1-17; Ezekiel 36:27; Romans 8:9; John 10:1-40; I John 2:27-29; I Corinthians 3:16; John 2:28; Matthew 3:11).* God will never lie for He is all truth.

Study the above passages carefully for understanding. A good translation will read: "I will not leave you comfortless or helpless, for I promise to return to you in and through the Holy Spirit. Shortly the world will not see me anymore, but grace believers will see me. I live; you, too, shall live.

You will understand that Christ is in His Father, and you are in Me, and I am really in you. Remember the rejected world has lost Him, but we have gained Him."

The statement is conceptual in nature. The study and comprehension of the water baptism that John administered, and the baptism of the Holy Spirit Jesus offers to the true repentive, steadfast grace believer two different concepts.

Water baptism will not save. Water baptism symbolically means you are buried with Christ. It is your testimony that you believe by faith Jesus Christ is your Savior. By faith trust you are saved. Immediately, by taking the step by faith the baptism of the Holy Spirit comes and reigns within you.

18. Jesus sent demons into a herd of pigs.   [T]   F

This is a narrative demonstrating Christ's dominion over unclean spirits. Christ gave them leave from Legion (many evil spirits) and permitted them to enter the pigs *(Mark 5:9-15; Luke 8:30-34).*

19. *Revelation* was written by
John the Baptist.   T   [F]

Revelation was written by the Apostle John. The authorship is accepted by most scholars who accept the book as divinely inspired by God. This is a factual statement.

20. There is no limit of God's grace.   [T]   F

God's grace is discovered in *Nehemiah 9:17; 29-31; Genesis. 18:26; Genesis 19:16; Ezra 9:13; Psalms 103:11.*

II Corinthians 6:1—you receive not the grace of God in vain. *Romans 3:24*—being justified freely by his grace. *II Corinthians 9:8*—God is able to make all grace abound. *Ephesians 3:7*—according to the gift of the grace of God. *Philippians 1:7*—you are all partakers of my grace. *I Peter 5:12*—true grace of God wherein you stand. Grace is unmerited favor—*I Corinthians 15:10; Romans 4:16).*

By the grace of God, I am what I am, and His grace which was bestowed upon me was not in vain; but I labored more abundantly than all of them; yet not I, but the grace of God which was with me. "I have set before you an open door *(Revelation 3:8-10)*." With the grace of God in you, your depth of knowledge and wisdom makes you lax in your human reason. *Ephesians 4:7*— Christians are given unmerited favor according to the measure of the gift from Jesus Christ.

How does God deal with an alien like Paul, or even myself? There is a proliferation of false teachers, movements, racial and psychological war and devastation which are all sin-linked.

Paul addresses this question. Each person must face up to his sins, transgressions, hang-ups, problem. Everyone has problems in our physical body, sins we must acknowledge. If we did not have problems, we would not be physically alive. We dare not acknowledge that we have spiritual problems because we are spiritually blind. We by our nature are sinners from birth. For that reason we are not perfect *(I Corinthians 3:16-20; II Corinthians 4:4; Ephesians 4:18; I Peter 1:9; I Corinthians 2:10-16).* Therefore we are sinners by birth and nature. Paul counters each question, carefully, again and again—*I Corinthians 15:9-26.*

What does the grace of God mean? God displays favor

by expressing his love, mercy, strength and kindness toward all sinners *(II Corinthians 8:9; Titus 2:11)*. God is all knowing and therefore will express this grace only after sin is judged. No human merit has an influence upon the bestowal of divine grace. Grace is given only to the man who acknowledges Christ died on the cross for his sins. Read *Ephesians 2:8-9*.

The Lord God proclaims and maintains pity (mercy) to millions, forgiving all expressions of sin. Repentance is imperative. The Lord will not clear the guilty *(Exodus 34:6-7)*. It is like when an earthly father has pity for his children. Our heavenly Father pities all them that fear him *(Psalm 103:13-14)*.

Benefits of this Survey Study:

A. To offer a committed Christian scored results of Bible knowledge and understanding.

B. To encourage Christian leaders to build or reconstruct a better study approach. Bible knowledge and understanding is constantly needed to enrich grace believers who are willing to pray and study Scriptures carefully for daily living as the Spirit directs.

C. It is the author's prayer that you will learn to discern clearly what the Bible literally teaches.

Striking Facts in the Study

The BLI survey was administered to 1215 people from various homogeneous and heterogenous groups, and a *serious deficiency of Bible knowledge and understanding was discovered.* Much time, effort, and expense were made in completing the coded results of the survey analysis. There emerged a question as to whether groups of people which were studying the Bible as a text, with Bible quarterlies and commentaries, were learning to be good examples and to gain right attitudes from the spiritual wisdom of God.

Donald S. Whitney[1] concurs that professing Christians may lack Bible knowledge and understanding. His experience as pastor supports the author's survey.

From the data reported, there is some evidence that EFBC groups were falling short in encouraging effective Bible-centered study. At the very least, there were calls for improvement. For years Sunday School materials and Bible correspondence courses have been used. The survey results suggest that such study should have resulted in better understanding.

Satellite groups such as Vacation Bible School, AWANA, and Child Evangelism Fellowship definitely encourage an infrastructure to nurture human character, spiritual values, and the salvation of souls, as urged by the Scriptures *(Hebrews. 6:10)*. *Proverbs 22:6* expressed it clearly: "Train up a child in the way he should go and he will not depart from it."

> *Hebrews 6:10 For God is not unrighteous to forget your work and labour of love, which ye have shewed toward his name, in that ye have ministered to the saints, and do minister.*

Through the Bible Radio, Dr. J. Vernon McGee has presented a meticulous nontechnical study of the Bible in a five-year sequence, which has been repeated, in numerous languages, over the years.

The person caught up in viewing television for hours may not be aware of the McGee's Bible-Centered Study. Free outlines as well as informal commentaries are used to help the radio listener. Write and request the free Bible outlines:

Through the Bible Radio
P. O. Box 7100
Pasadena, California 91109-7100

Few Christians study the Bible daily for eternal answers for daily living. They have other interests in their lives that they give more importance.

BLI Tabulations For 1215 People

Schools	State	N*	AM**
High School I	OR	109	14.0
Paul's High School II	OR	51	13.5
College I	OR	17	16.4
College II	OR	13	16.7
College III	OR	148	16.0
College IV	VA	60	18.7
	Total	398	15.9
Bible Study Group I	OR	11	17.5
Bible Study Group II	OR	1	15.0
Bible Study Group III	OR	13	17.7
Bible Study Group IV	WA	15	17.2
Bible Study Group V	WA	18	17.3
	Total	65	16.9
Individuals not in a group per se	OR	30	15.0
	Total	30	15.0
Miscellaneous Groups			
Radio Staff	CA	5	17.2
Radio Staff	TX	10	18.4
Newspaper Staff	KS	19	15.5
Church Camp	OR	39	15.0
Missionary	AR	10	14.5
	Total	83	16.1

*N = Number of People given the BLI in the group
**AM = Arithmetical mean or average score for the group given twenty Bible statements

BLI Tabulations

Churches	Location	N	A.M.
A	OR	8	15.3
B	OR	104	15.0
C	OR	10	15.9
D	OR	45	16.2
E	OR	15	16.5
F	OR	5	15.6
G	OR	16	15.8
H	OR	15	16.5
I	OR	36	13.3
J	WA	8	14.8
K	WA	26	16.5
L	NJ	27	12.6
M	OR	33	16.5
N	OR	55	14.9
O	OR	12	15.0
P	OR	12	15.3
Q	OR	25	13.9
R	OR	27	16.0
S	TX	22	14.2
T	OR	30	16.5
U	OR	24	11.5
V	OR	44	15.2
W	OR	40	14.1
Total		639	15.1

Interpretation of the BLI Survey

1. College scores were higher than high school scores.

2. A few church groups did as well as the college groups. However, church samples large or small did not do as well as the college groups, but they did better than the high school groups with few exceptions of earning lower scores. We can say in this analysis, the high school and college groups were more homogeneous by age, receiving formal Bible study.

3. Individuals that volunteered to take the survey did as

well or better than some church groups, one Bible study group, and one church camp group. The heterogeneous individuals varied in age from 12 to 93 years of age. Some attended church, studied their Bible periodically, and came from various cultural-ethnic backgrounds claiming to be Christians in Spirit and truth. This group did as well as the church groups but were below other target groups.

4. In the miscellaneous groups, radio staffs did as well or better than Bible study groups and college IV. It is quite probably that staff members have studied Bible in schools, continuously writing and editing Bible materials in the broadcasting field, and studying Bible among their particular group, as well as hearing a great deal of teaching while program monitoring.

5. The Church camp is a heterogeneous random selection of people representing a number of heterogeneous churches from Oregon and Washington. Therefore, their average performance is reflected in the overall average of the 23 churches represented in the study.

6. The mission field in Arizona did almost as well as the established church groups! There are no missionary groups to compare with this small sample.

7. The newspaper staff in Kansas did as well as some of the churches and individual volunteers taking the survey.

It is of interest to note in the data analysis of 1215 people who have taken the BLI that forty-nine persons received a perfect score which is 4% of the total representation of survey statements.

In studying the Bible Literacy Inventory, the researcher is only reporting data and not judging the performances of the groups in the confines of 1215 people. No judgmental cutoff standard was set up in advance. The goal was to urge a deliberate study of Bible facts, concepts and understandings. Such an approach will award every person, through the Spirit, a life that permits him to glorify God.

161

As you grow in the Grace of God through Our Lord Jesus Christ you will ward off the temptations of the gods of this world. You will not allow others to corrupt, deceive, distort, or even make merchandise out of His Word *(Matthew 13:19-23; II Timothy 3:1-17; II Timothy 2:15),* but give the Word in season and out of season even though you will be persecuted *(II Corinthians 4:8-12).*

False teachers and doctrines will come and go. Many people are like waves in the ocean. They will be tossed to and fro. The protection from such entrapments is building a solid foundation upon the chief cornerstone (Jesus Christ) that will never be shaken by the winds of false teachings *(Ephesians 4:17-32).* The Spirit will deliver a heart of knowledge far beyond the scope of head knowledge.

A Systematic Approach to Bible Study

Now is the time for all good men to come to the aid of their Spiritual knowledge and understanding of the Bible. Teachers, ministers and students can augment their reading powers by integrating a few simple techniques. One of the greatest obstacles in Bible study is the apathy among teachers to teach reading as a skill to their students. Many colleges and public schools assume that their students know how to read and study.

With computer, video, and internet learning sources on the market, people cling to media for the acquisition of knowledge and understanding. It has a spoon-feeding effect upon one's mind as long as electricity fills the circuit. Its methods of communicating information channel one's thinking quickly, *creating both the question and the answer,* tasks which emanate from the realm of artificial intelligence.

Such sources of information may or may not be of advantage to the student who wishes to improve his reading skills or to process his own inquiries into the Bible. The learner is not challenged to use his own hierarchy of mental processes, because the media gratifies ones thinking quickly.

There is now much media information available for Bible study on the video, the internet, and for processing on the computer. There will undoubtedly be more. The question most pertinent will always be *who* is producing the material and *what* do they want you to believe or understand. It will be, of course, their own interpretation of what the Bible says. It may be a very worldly interpretation, an entrapment of our hearts, minds, and souls.

Media sources of communication are much in demand in the business and industrial world. Brilliant programs are available that structure the thinking of the person using them. Much creative thought in graphic design and planning is required to produce such programs. People who know precisely what information they want or what they desire to communicate can make effective use of such media sources.

If one exercises judgment concerning biblical information and its source, a Bible student can acquire much knowledge and wisdom from God. There is so much to be learned, and so much that needs to be retained!

A computer processes, stores and retrieves information at a moment's notice. The learner can be interactive with instructional programs in the form of CDs, disks, videos, and the Internet. These formats are efficient information sources which are more social and more ego-directed than the traditional reading from a book. They do allow the student to reflect and socialize about ideas, but they also can become addictive.

Remember, however, those ideas were formulated by someone. As those sources become more and more sophisticated, look carefully into the possibility that some will emanate from sects and religions capable of managing large amounts of money which they extract from their adherants to ensnare our minds. They may offer free Bibles when their real goal is to forward their own agenda.

Computers can solve easy and difficult problems quickly. People cannot compete with them. Scholars can use them for proficiency sources in every discipline in which knowledge can be stored. Small battery-charged computers, like books, also have the capability of being used in isolated locales such as at the beach, air flight, and the cemetery, etc.

Computers can understand simple language, process images, and help manufacture products. They can even learn from examples. Recognized programs can be learned, therefore, which produce superior results to human specialization. We have common knowledge that computers can do numerous things that require intelligence.[2] We know, however, that knowledge which produces changes in the spirit, the heart, and one's salvation is impossible to measure objectively.

In the reading act, much time is spent separating out and synthesizing from the context what are new and different facts. Precepts, concepts and value judgments must be understood in depth. Students of all ages struggle with unfamiliar vocabulary, poor adjustive reading rates, and low comprehension. Some read so slowly that they lose continuity of thought. They may be tested on facts, which have no relevance to them, without gaining any understanding of their true meaning in a context.

However, many Christians have the ability to read words and do a Bible assignment, but they lack the realization that time, skill, experience, insight, and spiritual maturity are vital factors in a Spirit-controlled life. Reading and thinking, at whatever level, are necessary factors on the road to that maturity and spirituality.

In order to interpret words and phrases into facts, ideas and concepts, one must analyze the sequential procedure in the reading process. To determine definite purposes in the reading act, the writer has analyzed that procedure and has developed a program to enhance Bible study. It has been called the PQ3RO technique (meaning Preview,Question, Rapid-Read/Study-Read/Review and Outline).

To utilize the PQ3RO technique[3] of studying a specific Bible passage thoroughly, the individual must pray and ask God's Holy Spirit to open the Scriptures to his mind and heart in oneness with the Lord. This factor is often missing in guiding instructional and reading processes.

CATER'S DIAGNOSTIC READING COMPREHENSION AND VOCABULARY DEVELOPMENT PROFILE

BIBLE STUDY SCHEDULE

Herein is outlined the PQ3RO Procedure in the reading-meditating stages of Bible study. First, select a Bible passage. Here are the steps by which you must read it, meditate, and gain a greater depth comprehension and understanding of God's Wisdom.

STEP 1. You must first preview it, observe the many specifics and discern the overall purpose. *Preview* means to skim 10-20 verses or less in a passage from a study Bible— *observe* for 30-60 seconds special names, terms, numbers, dates, amounts, pictures, locations, footnotes, author, etc.— *the purpose* is to obtain the gist of what the author is trying to say.

Then write down on paper items for memorization you have selected from your previewing without looking back at the portion of context just previewed. Try to recall as many names, terms, numbers, etc. in sequence as you can with speed and accuracy.

STEP 2. *Pose the question(s)* from the title of the passage, as well as from topical or side heading of the portion of context just previewed. Step 2 and 3 function together in the initial reading.

STEP 3. *Rapid-read* the 10-20 verses just previewed by posing questions taken from the title, topical, and side headings. *Rapid-reading is reading a little faster than you ordinarily would read.* The questions posed will help the reader communicate with the author, keep his interest high, concentrate better, and hold onto what the author is saying. Read just for those questions and main ideas. This is an *assimilative process. Underline words you do not know as you rapid read in your Study Bible.*

STEP 4. *Vocabulary development*—use dictionary aids such as a lexicon and concordance of Biblical words. Define the words you do not know; a word you have already underlined in the rapid-read step. Write the definition in your notebook or write the definition in your Bible for study and review.

STEP 5. *Study-Read* —is rereading that portion of the text that you have already previewed and rapid-read. Read for main ideas, again read for details, critically read for technical or personal reasons. Reread certain portions not completely understood to gain depth and substance of what the author is driving at. *Underline as you Study-Read the passage in context.*

STEP 6. *Review materials* already underlined or outlined.

STEP 7. *Outline or take notes* on pertinent facts, concepts, etc. for study and review purposes. (Optional steps depend on the content of the material and how the outline will be used).

STEP 8. *Test yourself* carefully on the content of the information by taking a paper and pencil test or a review session with your peers, etc. Note that 75% or better in understanding is a level you must attain if your reading is to be meaningful and have a spiritual impact.

An adaptation of the PQ3R0 for studying the Bible has been tried over a controlled period of two years with 1,177 secular college freshmen (545 in 1958 and 632 in 1960). All classes contained homogeneous groups of 35 to 40 subjects. Students were carefully orientated in the writer's PQ3RO (Preview,Question, Rapid-Read/Study-Read/Review and Outline) technique of studying reading matter for purposeful reading, interrogation and sensitive interpretation.

Using the PQ3RO method of study, the student can make Bible study meaningful. Only when the student places the demand on himself with plenty of accompanying prayer will his knowledge of the wisdom of God's Word grow in his human and spiritual life. One will see more than a gain in literacy rate from a Bible survey. He will grow in grace as the Lord opens up new understanding from the Scriptures.

Roy B. Zuck[4] describes the fabulous features which are to be found in Scripture. Discovering the patterns, styles and forms helps one to interpret and comprehend. The Bible presents characters as real, live people. One reads of heroes such as David, Moses, Joseph, Daniel, Ruth and Queen Esther. The Bible describes many human experiences—involving emotions, joy, conflict, disappointment and other human, literary and spiritual qualities—which ought to entice and strengthen the reading process.

Summary

The BLI was a series of survey statements submitted to certain EFBC groups. Deficiencies were discovered; however, each person has the ability to read and comprehend. The study consists of a sample of 1215 people. The BLI has been scored and interpreted.

Purposes of the study are here reviewed:

A. To discover the literacy condition of each group surveyed.

B. To compare Christian bodies with schools that formally include Bible in their curriculum.

C. To suggest a systematic approach to Bible Study.

Also reviewed and described in this chapter was the method of reading comprehension designed by the writer called the PQ3RO. At one point in the study students were asked to select a portion of scripture to study using the PQ3RO method. They were asked to fill out the following forms. The reader is invited to do the same. One must do something with scripture. Create your own exit test.

1. Apply it to your heart, mind and life.

2. Teach or preach it.

3. Witness to the Christian and the infidel.

Day _____   Date _____

Scripture

_____

Verse for today

_____
_____
_____

1. What is the main subject or who is the main person?

_____

2. What do I learn from this passage about this subject or person?

_____

_____

3. Is there an example that I should follow?

_____

_____

_____

4. Is there any warning?

_____

_____

5. Is there any prayer arising from this passage, or how does it help me to pray?

_____

_____

ENDNOTES

[1]. Whitney, Donald S. *Spiritual Disciplines for the Christian Life*. Colorado Springs, CO: NavPress, 1991, pp. 24-25.

[2]. Winston, Patrick Henry. *Artificial Intelligence*; Second edition. Reading MA: Addison Wesley Publishing Co., 1984, pp. 6-17.

[3]. Cater, Ralph F. "A Systematic Approach in Student Reading," *Improving College and University Teaching*. International Quarterly Journal. Corvallis, OR: Oregon State University, Autumn, 1962, pp. 190-192.

[4]. Zuck, Roy B. *Basic Bible Interpretation*. Wheaton, IL: Victor Books, A Division of Scripture Press Publications, Inc., 1991; pp. 10-26, 124-142.

CHAPTER NINE: Worldly Entrapments

Has man forgotten or neglected God? We read constantly of a world engulfed in sin and the entrapments of man's own construction. Was this always the case? Has there ever been a time when man was obedient and walked humbly and prayerfully before his Lord?

It may have always been so. In the major and minor prophets of the Bible, numerous examples of the willful disobedience of the Hebrew tribes in following the Word of their most merciful loving God are evident.

The Jews, like us today, walked prudently away from God *(Ephesians 4:17; 5:15, 16)*. They did not really know God in their hearts. They claimed to know God, but they did not glorify Him. They were thankless, selfish, ungrateful, and evil in their own imaginations. We can derive from the Scriptures examples of sin, disobedience, and failure of Old and New Testament people, entrapments paralleling the snares that are evident today.

People are everywhere engulfed and entrapped by the idols of this world. They may be wise, intellectual, and worldly, but many

Romans 1:22 Professing themselves to be wise, they became fools.

171

are living in spiritual darkness *(Romans 1: 19-26)*. Social change and the influence of human development theories seem to touch the lives of people of all age levels. Everywhere we are influenced by what everyone else is saying and doing. Media influence and advertising struggle to make us one, with identical learning environments and behavior patterns—but with God divorced from our will and thinking.

Listen, readers, the sad dilemma is that we are worshipping idols we have made with our own hands rather than to worship and understand the living God. This can be applied to anyone's efforts and works. Near the end of his life, Michaelangelo lamented that he had made art his idol, instead of worshipping the One who died for him.

As a result of man's fallen nature and unbelief, God is going to shake heaven and this war-torn world to its very senses *(Hebrews 12:26-29)*. God is a consuming fire *(Deuteronomy 4:24)*. Everything that is transitory will be taken away, such as all ritual and human systems that are alien to Christ. Wherefore, receive

> **Deuteronomy 4:24**
> *For the Lord thy God is a consuming fire, even a jealous God.*

God's kingdom, the unshakable reality. With grace given from God, let us serve Him acceptably with repentance, wisdom and Godly fear. Scriptures abound which allude to the shaking of heaven and earth, and the destroying of the kingdoms of the heathen *(Joel 2:12-13;3:16; Haggai 2:21-22)*. What an awakening awaits!

Imagine what would happen if we were to give God the reverence and glory that the Bible exhorts us to give! No earthly show, by even the most recognized players on the stage of life, can promote peace, harmony and hope without God's grace. No efforts to eliminate war, poverty, crime or violence in any part of the world can be effective, permanently, without the infinite love of God working in the minds and hearts of all people.

Why? Because the untamed fallen nature, and the prince of power of this world, which is Satan, are the leading powers. People may attempt to spread the message of peace by working with large world organizations, but their power is only available to their partners in power.

Manipulations of power are alien to Christ, who is the Prince of Peace. People cannot understand that the will of God will come to pass, so preoccupied are they with their goals. They strive for recognition and peace without God.

Genesis through the Revelation in the Bible teaches us how fragile mankind is. How useless and temporal are his inadequacies and activity. The idea that man is basically good is a fallacy.

Crimes and Punishment

Present-day behavior patterns have not changed. History keeps being repeated; sin has not changed; it still corrupts and destroys.

In each of the following situations we recognize sin in its rampant manifestations. The cases in these briefs are real, and have been tabulated partly from the writer's experience on the Grand Jury. We shudder to think of them.

As we look, let us say a prayer to God, Who loved all people, and would reach out to them with His saving grace.:

In Case #1 A depraved man, divorced with children, gainfully employed, teaching a Bible class, attending church, was living intimately with a woman during the week. The woman was having a relationship with a neighbor also. The first man became jealous and angry, so he murdered her. This is clearly a case of fornication far beyond a redeemable relationship.

Case #2 A grandson stole money and a video recorder when his grandmother was on vacation.

Case #3 A professor who would receive sexual favors

from his students.

Case #4 A sixty-year-old grandfather fondled his granddaughters and forced them to touch his secret parts.

Case #5 A gang of white men challenged, pushed and fought innocent black men. There was a stabbing.

Case #6 A woman in a minority group possessed, manufactured, and marketed a controlled substance in a local park. The subject had $900 with her when arrested. The transaction took place 100 feet from a school.

Some of the following cases feature acts that are considered crimes: a misdemeanor with a year's prison term and a felony with a minimum term of imprisonment of at least one year.

Case #7 A person exhibits himself or herself, commits a crime of public indecency. This is a Class A misdemeanor.

Case #8 A person commits the crime of abandonment of a child under 15 years of age. The parents, guardian or person who deserts this child commits a Class C felony.

Case #9 A woman takes her elderly mother's checkbook and forges her mother's name on a number of checks before the arm of the law intervenes. Forgery is a Class A misdemeanor.

Case #10 A large masked man enters a convenience store early in the morning. The person commits a crime of robbery in the first degree. He is armed with a deadly weapon. He attempts to use the dangerous weapon but no physical injury was incurred. This is classified as robbery in the first degree, a Class A felony.

Case #11 Two children sixteen years of age possess burglar's tools. They knowingly intended to use the tools to forcibly enter a home. This is a Class A misdemeanor.

Case #12 A middle-aged man commits the crime of arson in the first degree. He intentionally starts a fire that produces an explosion, therefore damaging private and public protected property. This person endangers another person's life. This is termed a Class A felony. If it was proven reckless burning, the judgment would have been a Class A misdemeanor.

Case #13 This case involves a person entering and remaining unlawfully in or upon a premise at a time when it was not open to the public. The person is not licensed or privileged to be there. The law condemns and interprets the act as burglary that does not include theft.

Case #14 An angry, profane man barricades himself inside the house he occupies, which prevents peace officers from executing a court order of eviction from the property. Neighboring families are threatened by his hoax that he possessed explosives, would level the area, and do away with himself. Incarcerating the man and relocating the neighbors in a safe setting cost the taxpayers over $40,000. But this jailed, rabid and confused man wants his freedom in society now.

Case #15 A young adult with mental problems is allowed to leave his parents' home to visit someone near midnight. The man travels to a remote area, smashes in a door of a home. The intruder lunges toward the owner who is armed. Two bullets of warning are given. Then six lethal bullets enter the man's body. He is dead.

Case #16 A fiend not only stole the canine, in a fenced backyard, but removed the dog's canine teeth. The motive was to use the animal as a sparring animal for fighting other dogs. The victim dog is usually chewed to death. The law enforcement agent would call this a Class C felony, and the people attending the fight could be charged with a Class A misdemeanor.

Restitution

In these cases we see some of the evils of our society, and we see also some of the forms of punishment that are

175

exacted. Punishment, however, does not constitute restitution. Fines and time served do not make restitution to the victims of crime.

Restitution [1] is essential to justice. The Word of God spells out very carefully that restitution in some form of settlement is required. *(Exodus 22:1-17; Leviticus 6:1-7)*. Restitution is essential to righteousness. Restitution is essential to forgiveness *(Numbers 5:5-10; Luke 19:1-10)*.

Criminal Justice

A boy-man is raised up by his mother. With gangs & crimes about him, his mother had a strong influence in guiding him in early life. His mother did the best she could in a fatherless home. This young man worked hard to earn the honor of induction into the football Hall of Fame.

Did anyone ever witness to O. J. Simpson about the plan of salvation? We do know OJ grew in stature, money, and influence. He was well recognized because of his skills and personality. He was widely respected as a football commentator and his fame extended into an acting career. He always had people, money, and business success, and the world visualized Simpson as the good guy.

As far as the public knew, he treated people with respect and dignity. Later it became known that he was subject to extreme anger and depravity. But did O. J. Simpson ever turn to God in the good and bad times of his life?

People perceived him blindly as the greatest on the field and off the field. Recently, however, the world was confused, frustrated, and shocked by the allegation that he had murdered his former wife. The question remained, after one of the biggest criminal investigations in history, was he guilty of the crime for which he was acquitted? The restitution he was finally made to pay indicates there were serious doubts and a preponderance of evidence that he was guilty.

What does this have to tell us about the power of money and the courts? The mindset of the world is blind. The criminal justice system has become tainted and twisted. Justice can never be correctly administered according to the Judeo-Christian principles that were once the foundation of the American justice system.

It is now flesh against flesh, rights against rights, liberals against conservatives, homosexuals against heterosexuals. Children are disorderly to parents and teachers; youths are out of control; and public servants, who themselves are without God to guide them, are creating a war *(Galatians 5:17-18 and 6:8-9)*. The society is torn asunder in its diversity of life-styles, value judgments, and morals.

Who is right? We have turned away from God. The rights of the deviate, the premeditated murderer, and the rapist protect them from execution and long-term punishment. The attorneys and court strategists find ambiguity in the statutes to free a criminal or to liberalize punishment by plea bargaining. Even liberal parole boards have the power to reduce the justice or jury decision.

The taxpayer is victimized, and the defendant is protected. Detestable acts are tolerated that only God will truly judge some day.

A Salem, Oregon newspaper invited readers to express their position on the merits of capital punishment. Of 48 written responses, 42 supported execution.[2] Their questions included:

1. Are we supporting the rights of murderers?

2. Why not do away with death-row persons?

3. Should religious and legal bodies (ACLU) usurp the decision of the state and federal courts?

4. Why fatten up the killer prior to the execution?

5. Have executions over the centuries been a successful system?

6. Is capital punishment reasonable and does it act as a

deterrent to further crimes?

7. Does execution protect the innocent by removing the killer from the world?

8. Does the state and nation save money by retaining lawyers and criminals from grandstanding with all appeals?

9. Why does the world need to know when someone is being executed? Are abortions publicized?

10. Is capital punishment an example for would-be criminals and criminals in society?

11. Does crime pay when punishments are not rendered? Does crime pay when inmates in crowded prisons are merely guests of the taxpayer.

12. Does capital punishment make it easier on law enforcement agencies?

13. Who sets the rules for human conduct?

14. Are there two alternative methods—God's, or man's?

15. Does God teach capital punishment as expressed in *Genesis 9:6*?

16. Is *Genesis 9:6* a valid guide for today's world? Is the phrase that man was made in the image of God as true today as in the beginning?

Genesis 9:6 Whoso sheddeth man's blood, by man shall his blood be shed: for in the image of God made he man.

17. Was *Genesis 9:6* established before the Ten Commandments?

18. Why shouldn't a person who deliberately takes the life of another have to forfeit his own?

19. Does it cost four times more to support a life termer than educating a student?

20. Is it possible a murderer may be released by a liberal parole board and vindictively kill again?

Questions submitted to readers of the *Statesman Journal* could also be considered by the readers of this study. Remember, however, the above open-ended questions would require the reader, or believer, to study the Bible in regard to God's will concerning the problem of murder. The following verses would be applicable: Genesis 9:6; Exodus 20:13; 21:12,14; Leviticus 24:17; Numbers 35:16,31; Deuteronomy 19:11-12; Proverbs 28:17; Matthew 19:18; Romans 13:9; I Peter 4:15; and I John 3:15.

Presently we have federal and state laws with liberal courts, but the citizenry has the ability to change laws by their voting power. The law is able to condemn, fine or punish criminal behavior by reducing one's freedom. The law of the land is not capable, however, of correcting, rehabilitating or even changing the morals and value judgments of persons. The law of the land can condemn and punish, but it is not likely to change the attitudes of people. Only God's grace can do that *(Matthew 5:3-12; 6:33, Romans 9:1-3).*

The Problem of Sin

Sin is defined as unrighteousness and disobedience against God. Sin is any universal fault, misdemeanor, or breaking of moral principle through a willful act. Presently, man refuses to recognize his departure from God into sin. If he has lived a life separate from God, he is then at war with God. Only through *true repentance,* which means to turn by changing one's mind, can he find his way back into God's grace *(Luke 13:3-5; 24:47; Ezekiel 14:6; 18:30).* [3]

Through confession of sin we are *redeemed*, set free, delivered from our sins instantly by being washed continuously by the *blood* of Jesus Christ. Christ's blood and death allow us to live in Him *(Hebrews 9:11-14; 10:19-25; Matthew 26:28; I John 1:6, 2:2).* Then he gives you, and me, the *free* gift of salvation and eternal life. Study *Deuteronomy 21:8; Jeremiah 15:21;* and *Hosea 7:13).* Therefore, confession and repentance are indispensable to salvation *(Ephesians 2:4-10).* God is faithful and just to forgive us our sins immediately.

179

> *Galatians 3:22 But the scripture hath concluded all under sin, that the promise by faith of Jesus Christ might be given to them that believe.*

We are sinners from the beginning. We are born with a sinful, fallen nature *(I Corinthians 2:13-16)*. Seldom do people recognize they are committing sin. One will sin, unknowingly, until physical death *(Galatians 3:22; Romans 3:9-12)*, referring to the sinner who refuses to understand and seek after God. People go their own way and are enslaved by their own efforts, activities and works. They compare themselves with others. Sin is not a concern to them when their understanding is clouded by irrational human judgments.

When you really believe you are all right, are you also trying to find out what God thinks of you? Are you, therefore, vile with your life, your understandings and your education from a university? What is your ambition in this life? Do you have a real purpose?

Perhaps you are recognized as a speaker and author, and you are rich. Maybe you are a minister, a church member, a choir director or an usher, but you are still living with your secret sins—such as a profane tongue, temper, pornography, masturbation, smut etc., though heaven forbid! Perhaps you simply have a void in your life. You may be covetous or moving from one dissatisfaction to another, never reaching contentment. What has God to say about this *(Hebrews 13:5)*?

> *Hebrews 13:5 Let your conversation be without covetousness; and be content with such things as ye have: for he hath said, I will never leave thee, nor forsake thee.*

Every area of the media world and every advocate for the social betterment of mankind avoids discussing sin. We live in spiritual poverty. But does the Church also dismiss the question of sin?

Most people ignore sin. Jesus corrected the rich man about what is good; for no one is good except God. The rich man claimed he did all the right acts. Jesus required that the man sell his riches, give to the poor, and, said Jesus, "I will give you treasures in heaven. Then follow Me. You will lack nothing." The man responded in amazement *(Matthew 19:16-22)*.

This is a most difficult lesson to learn from the Lord Jesus Christ. Man's will is depraved, alienated, defiant and blind. It is part of the sinfulness that resists the precious blood of Jesus, which alone can redeem him. Jesus Christ forgives him with a love mankind is unable to grasp. No wonder it is so hard to enter the kingdom of God.

Study carefully *Mark 10:17-44; Matthew 19:16-30;* and *Luke 18:18-30.* Self-ambition continually stands in the way of repentance and salvation. A man might live for many years and one day discover "when all is gained how little then is won! And to gain that little how much is lost."[4] He cannot even tolerate others witnessing to him about God. He calls them religious squares, Bible thumpers, extremists. :He is very comfortable until he receives AIDS, cancer, or some other terminal condition. You name it and this world has it. Still his mind is clouded with sin.[5][6]

Homosexuality

In the sports world, many athletic performers strive for recognition, success and money. It is a precarious world, and some achieve the ultimate recognition; much time, money and training, however, are invested in every Olympic medalist. Yet boxers end up with brain injuries, and ball players are traded off because of money or age.

One of the greats among athletic performers was purposed to have a concealed sexual orientation. It was an incredible burden, and so there was no openness in his life except for his performance. He had bouts of depression, along with suicide attempts and little or no support from his father—until some Olympic awards were earned.

His mother was always supportive, however. Early in life, this athlete recognized that he was homosexual. He had a close associate who took his money, exploited him sexually, and made him feel inferior. Even school peers called him disparaging names. Others termed him mentally retarded. He had difficulty learning to read, and in segments of his life he was subject to abuse.

Now he is an American hero, who is openly gay, but with HIV. It is tragic.

One might question whether the exploitation, the abuse or the discrimination had anything to do with his choices. We might question whether the effect of being a hero, and therefore being openly gay, had anything to do with his downfall.

Perhaps no one, in all his associations, ever introduced him to the saving power of Jesus Christ. Homosexuality is condemned in Scripture, and it is not a legitimate lifestyle to teach children to accept or practice. Evangelical churches and Christian organizations, however, are termed extremist if they try to help keep those with a twisted sexual orientation from destroying themselves, by leading them to the truth and love that only Jesus Christ can offer.

Out of Bondage

One of the most memorable stories of the Bible is the deliverance of the Jews from their bondage in Egypt. The Israelites had sinned against Almighty God and are still sinning to this day, as are all of mankind. They were thankless, selfish, self-centered and deceitful.

After God removed them from bondage in Egypt, what did the Israelites do? They returned to serving, worshipping and idolizing other gods like the heathen nations. Then God deported the Israelites to Assyria to this day *(II Kings 17:1-23)*.

Gentiles are no exception. Inner anger is a turmoil in people because of their sinful nature and their personal separation from a sovereign God. There are many levels of frustration among mankind due to their ignorance, spiritual blindness, and strong will that disassociate them from God. Such a separation Gentiles experience, for those who have no law are a law unto themselves (Romans 2:14). For a majority of humanity there exists this heritage of sin.

The Answer to Sin

God invites you to do something in regard to your condition. The best route God has for you is the free gift of eternity and the necessity to deny ourselves.

There is much conflict and violence in the world that man is not designed to handle. He sees the surface issues. He struggles blindly *in the flesh* to work out difficulties through education, reform and compromise. Sometimes the motive behind his thwarted behavior is greed, pride, envy, selfishness, etc.

Where are we going in these fleshly bodies we possess? Some believe that whatever you do, make it fun, for life is full of tricks. So you make fun out of it. When there are issues to solve, man breaks down and can't agree with other men. They may try to make changes, but they cannot agree on how to correct what they perceive as social ills.

Men may express themselves as blatant liberals, rigid conservative, or warped-minded doers of nothing. God tells us to sit up and listen to Him, not to expect compromise to solve his problems *(Matthew 6:33)*. Glorify God in whatever you do. "For those who honor Me *(Christ)* I will honor *(I Samuel 2:30)*." We need to invest the precious time given to

> *Matthew 6:33 But seek ye first the kingdom of God, and his righteousness; and all these things shall be added unto you.*

us studying God's word and living it. All else will be added unto us.

We are so caught up with activities and issues we begrudge the time involved in seeking God's will for our lives. By nature we resist allowing God to challenge our pattern of beliefs and behavioral systems. We do not reflect carefully on how we spend our time.

Time is life, however, in God's network. Wise choices in life depend upon your learning how to live. A priority listing of God's agenda is to pray, study, witness, worship, serve others and then offer your monetary exchange and talent to glorify the Lamb of God. Does this make you uncomfortable? By your nature, you refuse to allow God to shatter your beliefs.

> *Ephesians 5:16 Redeeming the time, because the days are evil.*

You can gain much insight by Old and New Testament readings. By taking time to pray, study, witness and worship, you will never again doubt things, for you are enduring evil all day long *(Ephesians 5:16).*

Are you ready for life? Life is not always fair. You have problems and so does the other person. But our gracious God encourages us to press on toward the goal. The Father has given us Godly hope; and God always comes when you thought He wouldn't, because He has a better plan than yours. Paul claims the prize is in the high calling in

> *Philippians 3:14 I press toward the mark for the prize of the high calling of God in Christ Jesus.*

Christ Jesus *(Philippians 3:14).*

The Power of Politics

Times have changed! Prayer and Bible teaching has been removed from the home, school, and business place. A very small segment of real Christians are litigating to place Bible teaching and prayer freedoms back into the schools. This struggle requires courage, tenacity and great expense in terms of time and money.

Meanwhile, abortion and homosexual practices are being condoned as personal rights and freedoms. The undertow is taking us further away from God's teaching. The media reflects the scope of worldly reality and distortion.

"Politicians tell people what they want to hear, and people like to be told they are really *good.*" So speech lines [which compliment the voters and scourge their enemies] are surefire applause-getters. But good politics can make bad theology; and when we begin to believe our own press release we become victims of our own delusions."[7]

There is little an individual Christian can do in a depraved world to influence political process. His vote—and a lobby of persons with similar motives—is his only power.

On the positive side, the Christian experiences little persecution in this country. Times are rapidly changing, however. We will be persecuted more and more for the cause of Christ. What are you personally doing to glorify God? What will you be prepared to do in the future? Study *Jeremiah 17:9-14; Matthew 5:16-20.*

The Christian Life

The Spirit-led believer is a daily adherent of Christ. In his life-style and behavior he also faces trials, as Christ did. Christ offers us grace, love, joy and peace. He will certainly sustain us, His servants, in persecution, pain, sufferings, trials, tribulations, diseases, *and finally, physical death.* Remember, the Savior suffered and died on the cross for all our sins and for all of those committed in this world. Therefore, trust in the Lord, Who will take care of you.

Some small groups of witnessing believers in Europe, Asia and Africa live under extreme tension with constant threats, betrayals, slanders, denials, beatings, imprisonment and martyrdom. When they are successful in bringing one to Christ, the new convert's greatest danger is his own family, who will often turn against him. People in Hindu and Islam territory who express any form of allegiance to the gospel of Christ are persecuted.

Regardless of circumstances in some of these foreign countries, the Church there is strong. Bible groups praise the Lord in prayer and song, visiting and helping the poor and sick in need. Evangelism is active in homes and other low key-settings as the Lord directs His ministry through His ambassadors. It is only through the Spirit of God that the motivation to risk their lives for Christ is ongoing.

Remember Paul, who relates at the end of his life to Timothy: "I have fought a good fight, I have finished my course, I have kept the faith *(II Timothy 4:7)*." He had preached the Word of God to all the lands. He had reproved, rebuked, and exhorted with all long-suffering and doctrine. His work was done.

In *II Thessalonians 3:1-7*, Paul urged prayer, that the Word of the Lord might have free course. Herein Paul again warns the brethren against walking according to the ways of this world. This letter of Paul's, written under the inspiration of God, also embodies Paul's study, observation and experience with the churches. He urged them to discover from the Holy Scriptures truths old and new to them for

> *II Thessalonians 3:1*
> *Finally, brethren, pray for us, that the word of the Lord may have free course, and be glorified, even as it is with you...*

their daily living.

The Pagan Life

When government leaders endorse, legalize and permit sinful behavior we observe 1) children recruited into a homosexual life-style; 2) alcoholism, uncontrolled usage of drugs, etc. running rampant while tobacco is destroying 400,000 people annually; 3) abortion and euthanasia being superimposed upon a pagan people who would rather serve the creature than the Creator *(Ecclesiastes 12:1-8)*.

What are the grace believers doing in the midst of these occurrences? Where are those who strive to live according to Biblical principles *(Psalm 37:22-27)*? God sees the total picture and He forsaketh not His saints.

Our nation has fallen away from the Bible. Thanksgiving and Christmas are perfect examples. Earlier in the century, these days were set aside to give thanks to God and to worship and celebrate the holy birth of Christ. Today most Americans are celebrating days of hedonistic escape and indulgence in the appetites. Such idols of addiction as sex, gambling and drugs are the form of worship and preoccupation. Mood-altering drugs elevate levels of dopamine in the brain. The addict finds the reality of the mind is changed.

So many pockets of society are indifferent to God's ways. With riots, murders, mobs and bombings of helpless victims, they are on the verge of anarchy.

Are state and federal laws correcting our crime? In some cases they are allowing it in the form of sinful occupations. But people need to honor the leaders of the country if they are in God's will and submit to the laws of the land. Study *(Ezra 7:26; Proverbs 24:21; Matthew 22:21; Romans 13:1; Titus 3:1; 1 Peter 2:13-14 & 17; Exodus 22:28; Ecclesiastes 10:20; Acts 23:5; Proverbs 14:34; Proverbs 16:12)*. May God grant that we have leaders who are worthy of honor.

187

Common Distractions

The breakdown of values in contemporary life has been led by powerful distractions. For years television personalities have become comfortable role models for establishing a philosophy and life-style for daily living. We imagine that they are good because everyone around them seems pleased and happy, or at least winning, in a controlled display of crime and violence.

New Age teachings have crept into the society. The New Age movement has even infiltrated the Visible Church, where people have been made to feel backward and trapped in an outmoded theology.

Attitudes have become tainted in every segment of society. Here are some marked value changes which have blinded people to the established Church:

1. People have learned to murder others through every conceivable psychological means.

2. People have established a rigid mindset that man can work toward being good through believing in himself and perhaps others, rather than God. Such mindsets emanate from the New Age Movement, for example, the Universal Brotherhood of Mankind. The Promise Keepers, so far, appear to be placing their faith in God.

3. People have learned to preoccupy themselves with physical and mental game activities.

4. People have become dependent upon on-line Internet technologies to access information, inspiration and companionship, and to add to their comfort, desires and appetites. Some of these desires might be:

- to live in an earthquake-free structure.
- to receive another organ so life might be extended.
- to receive a cosmetic facelift or tummy tuck.
- to travel quickly to another area of the world scene.
- to be relieved of pain and death through the help of

medicine and physician assistance.

- to experience perverted sex, to fantasize love affairs.

Most people are aware of innovations constantly being introduced in all forms of auditory and visual media. The forms of exchange available through media hookups may involve 1) people with small minds, gossiping about each other (a totally unproductive use of time), 2) people with mindsets ready to discuss events and subject areas that might have productive results, and 3) access to the minds of great thinkers, as they wrestle with precepts, concepts, and ideas, using deductive and inductive reasoning.

Good News

Jesus Christ taught with authority from God. He taught lessons about all kinds of people, of wise and foolish men in *Matthew 7:24-28*. Beyond that, He called upon people to spread the Good News, to become also fishers of men. Some people, including those who say they are Christians, attempt to do this, but they are disorganized, undisciplined and reluctant to accept suggestions from others.

You may be a leader who boosts morale and possesses a great sense of humor. You always look on the positive side of most issues. You feel you must perceive an issue with realism. When you do, then the positive and negative points of view must be assessed. There is no sense in skirting the issue with your rational human thoughts. You are ever learning, but you may never be coming to the knowledge of truth. God is truth *(Isaiah 55:6-11; John 14:6,17; 8:31; Daniel 10:21)*.

The Christian is persecuted when witnessing the Good News. Christians, living in an unbelieving world, are engaged in unpopular, but constitutionally protected expressions and religious associations. But it is not protected speech for the individual in the classroom to organize Christian groups and tell the Good News of Christ. Christians do not promote violence, but violence occurs against the person doing the witnessing for Christ's sake, for the Cross is an offense.

Others may witness in schools and public forums in regard to sex education, abortion, starvation, HIV and AIDS, and funding is available for research for all of these. There is no persecution against those who promote things the world has condoned.

While some people have lost control of their well-being and appear to be agents of the devil, God calls us to model our faith in the life of Christ, not in works of ourselves *(Philippians 1:12-30)*.

Fatal Attractions

There are many temptations in the world. The prince of this world makes them so attractive that one finds it more convenient to take up an attraction rather than to forego it.

Listed are just a few of the sins and attractions that drag people down. One must identify his own among them:

1) false pride and conceit
2) white, gray, black lies (distortion of the truth)
3) prejudice of all sorts
4) harassment
5) discrimination
6) hate
7) deceit
8) revenge
9) belittlement
10) hostilities
11) boastfulness
12) designer of schemes
13) vanity
14) cunning, plea bargaining
15) covetousness
16) selfishness
17) thanklessness
18) envy
19) ingratitude
20) anger

Popular Remedies

There is probably a telephone number a person can call for any sort of problem he may have, either near him locally or toll-free from anywhere in the United States. He may be able to listen to a tape or converse with a person about the problem. The prevalence of sin is such that every person may need help with the many distractions in his life somewhere along the way. The question is, where should he go for help?

It is possible, when led by the Holy Spirit, to live a careful, reconciled life, in peace with all people *(Romans 14:19; Hebrews 12:14-17)*. The Christian's defense against temptation beyond his own will is God. He will not permit you to suffer or allow Satan to hinder you beyond what you can bear. Our Father has provided an escape from the snare of destruction. God's Spirit within you

> Romans 14:19 Let us therefore follow after the things which make for peace, and things wherewith one may edify another.

works harmoniously with the Word of God and prayer in helping you resist, in faith, satanic evil. Satan will flee from you. Draw near to God and He will draw to you *(I Corinthians 10:13; I Peter 5:8-9; Ephesians 6:11-18; James 4:7-8; II Timothy 2:26)*.

Yes, a true believer, constantly fed by the Holy Spirit in prayer and the washing of the Word will resolve bias attitudes, resentments, tantrums, hang-ups, anger, turmoil, frightening guilt, etc. It is possible to control these disruptive behaviors when the Spirit is constantly comforting and teaching in daily life. Still, the old nature will never go away and one must live with it, not excuse it. The disruptive behavior will come and go as the two natures struggle within. We must let our behavior be guided by the Spirit, and we will seldom gratify those fleshly desires. Study *Galatians 5*.

Fads and Fancies

We may be distracted also by fads and fancies which

seem innocuous when we encounter them, especially when they appear in the context of the church:

A. More hunger for physical food than spiritual food.

B. Entrapments to attract the unchurched, for example, sports, position in the church service, etc.

C. Music with a generational rhythm and style. Hymn book singing with a good message may be omitted.

D. Celebrations and performances by professional singers instead of worship services.

E. Gossiping newsletters delivered to the home of church members.

F. Inventive gimmicks to hold the interest of the people.

G. More psychological principles are being taught and used among church followers than Biblical precepts.

H. Playing favorites among the church members. People in leadership positions not treating others with equality.

I. A great deal of joking and telling yarns. This is interesting to some people whose minds are easily amused, but these should not distract from the Word of God.

J. Profane and blasphemous utterances in the field and work place, harassing others with frustration and madness.

The Media and Social Ills

When injustices occur within the context of the secular world, the public occasionally hears about it. Kay Kusumoto, a business reporter at the *Statesman Journal* newspaper in Salem, Oregon, wrote a column on racial discrimination, harassment, and hate:

"The man in line behind me at the bank in Portland stood waiting like everybody else. Except for his dark skin and thick, black mustache, he stood out no more than any other customer, there presumably to take care of financial matters. Because I grew up in a suburb of Los Angeles where more than a third of the neighborhood was Latino,

I barely noticed him. But someone else did. Another customer, an older man, probably in his fifties and old enough to know better, took one look at the man behind me, managed a disapproving grunt and said clearly under his breath, but loud enough for the man to hear: "Why don't you go back to your own country?" To my surprise, the man behind me was not so silent. Before I could replay the words in my head, the man behind me exploded. "You want me to go back to my own country. I'm from San Francisco, California. That is where I'm from. I'm tired of being called a wetback, being told to go back to my own country. I'm tired of being hassled. Can't anyone just say 'Good morning?' I cannot change. I am what I am: Mexican American."[8]

The Kusumoto commentary is about racial hatred, harassment, and hostility. The book *Black Like Me*,[9] similarly, reveals distressing acts against a white man who impersonates a black man in a black community to observe discrimination.

Another example of strong media coverage concerned a rabid, disgruntled and unemployed individual who fired upon and killed innocent home-bound passengers on the Long Island Railroad at Garden City, New York. Briefly, the reasons were racism, hatred, revenge, discrimination, etc.

The news media has revealed many other cases where there were acts of sin in a depraved, unbelieving person. In the city of Liverpool, England, two eleven year old boys kidnapped a two year old. The boys committed the heinous crime of taking the life of the toddler.

What went wrong? One could say the same thing in regard to the Biblical story: "Why did Cain kill Abel?" The experts search for answers. Some believe the parents are to be blamed. A child behavioral counselor believes children are not born evil and need to be educated.

Reeducation sounds good on the surface, but it is not

foolproof. Mixing children socially and training them in the right way is a community ideal that is difficult to achieve. People with all kinds of values and ideas have remedies, but they are not the same values and ideals.

Suppose they could agree. Still, the love of God and Biblical character building is not in the plan. Neither is the teaching of God's ethics and morals.

People in Liverpool are struggling to find solutions in order to raise their children to respect each other. Unless the teaching of Jesus Christ enters into the solution, however, parents will disagree over their man-made perspectives, and they will vary widely.

God is able to focus directly upon the depravity of all humans regardless of age, environment, background or cultural spectrum. Every generation refuses to learn the wisdom of God. People continue to war, murder, lie, and steal. Whoever would create a solution must use God's love to make a difference in the hearts of the perpetrators.

People continue to talk about educating the whole person. We are not doing it! We deny evasively that we have sin in our lives. If wrongdoers do not confess, renounce sin and then go forward with repentance and forgiveness, we will continue to repeat history, and every generation will repeat the same patterns.

Sin is observed in all people, the wealthy and the poor, in every country and culture, from birth to death. We see evidence in the fact that there are homeless people in every culture and setting. God says all have sinned and lack God's glory. Only God can make people right by His free gift of grace *(Romans 3:23-24)*.

Therefore, continually train, guide, and encourage a child in the way God wants him to go, in hope and in faith that he will not depart from it *(Proverbs 22:6)*.

Godly parents have a tremendous responsibility beyond propagating the human race. *Joel 1:3* informs us to instruct our children about these things, and urge your children to instruct their children and your grandchildren to instruct their children. God has spoken. Parents have allowed the training of children to go out of style. That is why children of wrath are increasing by the day.

> Proverbs 22:6   Train up a child in the way he should go: and when he is old, he will not depart from it.

No wonder Jeremiah spoke out that the heart and mind is deceitful and cannot be healed or truly understood. The sovereign God is capable of observing any person's heart and testing the mind of any evil one. God can and will judge each one and give each the right judgment *(Jeremiah 17:9-10)*. *Study Matthew 23:25; Psalm 116:11; Micah 6:12.*

> Micah 6:12   For the rich men thereof are full of violence, and the inhabitants thereof have spoken lies, and their tongue is deceitful in their mouth.

Failures in Institutional Management

There has been a breakdown in the reform of human institutions, from penal punishment centers to the institutions of higher learning. According to George Roche,[10] government funding is destroying higher education in many ways. Thousands of colleges students lack basic knowledge, such as when Columbus sailed to the New World, who wrote the Declaration of Independence, or why the Civil War was fought. College graduates lack academic skills in the language arts. Higher education in this nation is academically, morally, and financially going bankrupt.

On the surface, these institutions appear prosperous. The bigger the institution the greater the budget deficits. Defaults on student loans are due not only to the failure of students to repay them but to mismanagement, fraud and abuse. Taxpayers are placed under extreme financial burdens. The government has failed to withdraw grants and loans on educational schemes that have not proved worthy. It is no wonder the federal government is trillions of dollars in debt!

Higher education in America is in an academic crisis. Course offerings have been reduced. Large classes of up to a thousand students and televised courses that reach even more have been substituted. Graduate assistants teach lower division courses while professors teach less and less, on the grounds that they must do research and write in order to publish.

Some suggest that graduate education is the biggest consumer fraud in this country. However, the liason between higher education and the corporate world is well-known, and the United States is the economic leader of the world, because of this. Students who are able to secure training for that economic leadership are fortunate indeed.

Some say there is a moral crisis in American higher education. Indeed, in a society where student behavior and morals are of no concern to teachers in the colleges, we have simply the same free sex, homosexual activity, drug abuse, cheating, and sins and vices of all kinds in which the society as a whole engages. These are immoral destroyers of the leaders of tomorrow.

There has been a serious and collective effort to destroy the *in loco parentis* roles that colleges and universities assumed in the past. In most of them, in the name of freedom of choice, students have been given the right of adults to manage their own lives. Whether the role *in loco parentis* persists is dependent upon the influence of Christian principles and goals in the academic life of a particular institution.

However, it might be the responsibility of taxpayers, parents, and educators to alter the mismanagement of funds, academic and moral values, if they feel the mismanagement touches young people's lives. In the end, Roche fails to discuss the salvation of souls, but he suggests ways of recovery when restructuring education and the restoration of the values.

We need more than reform. We need the regeneration of souls that occurs when Christ takes over our lives. All things are possible with God as Biblical history has reported. When men with the ambition of their own energies and talents want to achieve without God in the center, they cannot fail to fall short *of pleasing God(Matthew 6:33).* Also study *Mark 10:17-27* and *Jeremiah 22:13-19.*

> *Matthew 6:33 But seek ye first the kingdom of God, and his righteousness; and all these things shall be added unto you.*

Man, in his blind sinful nature, has continued to fight for reform with all the energy of his flesh. He has throughout history sought to establish a utopian society that would correct the ills of human nature. Thomas More was such a man, who published a theory to solve political inequities in 1516.

All theory, all idealism seeking to create a more perfect world, however, has not had the desired result. The perfect society has not come about. Man of every generation becomes entangled by his own nature.

Robert W. Lundin,[11] a secular psychologist, interprets that a warfare goes on between the superego and the id. The id is completely unconscious. It is the source of psychic energy that emanates from instinctual needs and drives. The superego, which is another entity of the psyche, internalizes parental conscience and establishes rules. It also internalizes society's system of reward and punishment as expressed through guilt, conscience and moral attitude. The third entity, the ego, is the battlefield. Both the superego and the id involve the ego to their own advantage.

The apostle Paul urged Timothy to study earnestly and reconcile himself to God and to be a bondservant and an ambassador unashamed of rightly dividing the word of truth, for the soul of man never dies *(II Timothy 2:14-15)*.

The noble Bereans also received and searched daily the scriptures with a readiness of mind to verifying things *which had been preached to them (Acts 17:10-12)*. Even so, some will wrongly divide the word. Peter warns us of false teachers who make merchandise of the Scriptures. Cults, sects, and other assemblies have no shortage of Biblical "proof" in the form of selected texts to validate their apostate teachings. They make a private interpretation by distorting the Scriptures and adding to them—a problem centuries old.

Unsavory Foundations

Charity and Christian organizations have been trapped into investing large sums of money in unsavory foundations which have promised, convincingly, to double or triple the Lord's money in a short period of time. Many leaders of these groups have capitalized on the believer's desire to enlarge on the ministry of Jesus Christ by get-rich schemes which benefited themselves greatly and the church but little.

What is wrong with their approach? Apparently they want something for nothing. All of us are that way at times. There is no easy way to advance a ministry, however. Why should they gamble with our contributions? Is the motive to have the preeminence among others? No wonder Jim Bakker and Jimmy Swaggart have given Christians a bad name in the world by their life-styles and fraudulent practices.

Consider the bankruptcy of the Foundation of New Era Philanthropy which scandalously hoodwinked evangelical Christian organizations in investments. The Focus on the Family and Prison Fellowship was willing to invest the believer's money to become rich quickly rather than to await contributions. Their financial managers, in their desire to improve and increase the growth of a ministry, took the kind of risks that are inherent in the volatile financial world. They were lied to, told that there were anonymous donors who would put up matching funds, etc, but they were victims of a pyramid scheme. Contributors did not want their money to be put at risk in the stock market.

Ministries like the Radio Bible Class, Thru the Bible Radio, the Christian-Jew Foundation, In Touch Ministries and many others have no plans for gambling with contributions supporting the furtherance of the Gospel.

Christians must be aware how their contributions are being spent. The opposite is also true. When money is received for ministerial purposes, do churches account for funds received for God's glory? True Christianity can and will fail, as many religious groups do, if they exploit controlling funds for personal profit or false values in disobedience to God.

Corruption in Biblical Times

Study the minor prophet Jonah. Nineveh was a gentile city of wickedness and idolatry. God noticed the quality of life then as He does today. Jonah, God's agent, did everything he could to circumvent God's plan for Nineveh. God had to place stumbling blocks in Jonah's lessons of life. He had to remove the pride from his heart and change his attitude toward lost people. He was forced to obey God's loving call, and had to suffer himself to learn to pity the perishing. Jonah finally acknowledged that only the Lord God could change the indifference in his life. He finally perceived that *Salvation is of the Lord!*

For Jonah (and for us) it was a rewarding experience to face the truth and see victory rather than destruction. Jonah preached the Word to the Ninevites. The greatest revival ever recorded in history took place in Nineveh. Men cried out mightily to God and repented of their evil. In mercy and love, God relented, and He turned away His anger and destruction.

The conversion of Nineveh was another miracle from God, as was the parting of the Red Sea, and the story of Christ feeding the five thousand. We read in the book of Nahum that later on the Ninevites forgot their revival. They became depraved and God allowed Babylon to finally destroy this great city forever—the prophecy was painfully fulfilled.

It was a lesson Jesus taught promise keepers for all generations. Blessed are those that listen and understand the Word of God and keep it. As Jonah became a warning to the Ninevites, so shall Jesus Christ, the Son of God, be a sign to this generation—meaning all the generations in the church age of grace. Study *Matthew 12:39-42; Luke 11:28-32* carefully.

All around us we observe razzmatazz Christianity: light and sound, but no substance. It is imperative that we live as the Lord would have us to live. We must rediscover and embrace with endurance the fundamentals of the Christian faith. Today, we are to identify with the Godhead and be of one mind in Christ *(John 17:17-26)*. But how is that possible when Christians bicker about investments, doctrine, baptism, pre and post tribulation, etc? Everyone thinks he is right.

People become antisocial, isolated from one another, and the church becomes only a gathering place. *Isaiah 55:6-9* reminds all of us to seek the Lord while He may be found. To return to the Lord is the great invitation. Remember God's thoughts and ways are not our thoughts or ways. The invitation is that we should believe in the abundant life by way of God's truth and love and walk in it *(II John 1-6)*.

Therefore, focus on the ministry of Christ, for His grace and mercy is for each of us. Do not lose heart, but renounce the hidden things of shame and dishonesty. Spend not your lives in craftiness, nor in handling the Word of God deceitfully, but set forth to seek the truth, commending yourselves in good conscience in the sight of God. You will then overcome and pass difficult tests as the Lord refines you for everlasting life *(II Corinthians 4:1-2).*

In His Name

"GO YE!" the Lord commands of those
Who would his disciples be;
Tell all the world of Him who died
From sin to set us free.

Make known his love—for everyone
In His image He has made—
That has stood since the foundations
Of this old world were laid.

"Tis not the big things we must do
To please our Heavenly Father;
We cannot, friends, all preachers be,
But, we are taught that rather

The little things we all should do—
Tho we think they do not matter—
Jesus said, "Give in my name
If but a cup of water."

There are those around us everywhere
Who need that magic touch;
Sometimes a smile, a kindly word,
It doesn't cost us much

To scatter seeds of kindness
Around outside our door,
We may see blooming some bright flower
Where none e'er bloomed before.

So we need not go to foreign fields
To do a kindly deed,
We need not go to foreign fields
To find someone in need;

For, here is our America
For those who cannot roam;
And missionaries all may serve
In the "harvest fields" at home.

by Lillie Flanders Overholt

ENDNOTES

[1.] Wilson, Neil; editor. *The Handbook of Bible Application.* Wheaton, IL: Tyndale House Publishers, Inc.,1992, p. 532.

[2.] "Readers share views about death penalty." Salem, OR: *Statesmen Journal,* August 31, 1996, p.6A

[3] Lockyer, Herbert. *All the Doctrines of the Bible*; Grand Rapids, MI: Zondervan Publishing House, 1964, pp. 169-176, 186-190

[4.] Arvine, Kazlitt; *Cyclopedia of Moral & Religious Anecdotes*: New York: Funk & Wagnalls, 1890, p. 48.

[5.] Menninger, Karl. *Whatever Became of Sin?* New York: Hawthorne Books, Inc., 1973, pp. 18-37.

[6.] Colson, Charles. *Loving God.* New York: Harper Paperbacks, A Division of Harper Collins Publishers, 1987, chap. 9.

[7.] *Ibid.,* p. 113.

[8.] Kusumoto, Kay. "Remarks reveal hostility beneath Civil Society." Salem, OR: *Statesman Journal,* Dec. 9, 1993.

[9.] Griffin, John Howard. *Black Like Me.* Boston, MA: A Signet Book, Published by Haughton Mufflen, 1960.

[10.] Roche, George. *How government Funding is Destroying Americans Higher Education.* Hillsdale, MI: Imprimis— Hillsdale College, Oct. 1994, Vol. 23, No. 10, pp. 1-6.

[11.] Lundin, Robert W. *Personality - An Experimental Approach.* New York, NY: The MacMillan Company, 1961; p. 313.

CHAPTER TEN: Open Letter To Anyone Who Believes He is All Right

Place your name in the blank spaces as you read:

You must find the greatest joy in being involved in various trials. If you are deficient in wisdom which you seem to lack, let _____ ask of God, who gives generously and doesn't reproach one afterward, and he will give it to him. _____whose doubts are like the billowing sea, driven and blown about by the wind, is such a person who must not expect to get anything from the Lord.

You are on a collision course. You will disappear like a wild flower. Keep smoking, cussing, looking proud, being double-minded and manipulating people—that is the way the rich and poor will fade and die in the midst of their pursuits. When anyone is tempted, it is by his own desire that he is enticed and allured. The desire conceives and gives into the sin, and when sin is mature, it brings forth death. Please don't argue about heart attacks or some other disease.

Everyone, including _____ must be quick to hear, slow to speak, slow to anger, for men's anger does not produce the uprightness *God requires.* So strip yourself of everything that soils you. Judge yourself, not others.

Let the message open up blind eyes and deaf ears beyond the stench of your filthy, uncaring mind and in a humble spirit let this message (that has power beyond money, legality, and conventional wisdom), save your soul.

Obey the message, _____. Do not merely read it, and deceive yourself. For anyone who merely reads the message without obeying it is like one who looks in a mirror at the face God gave him and then goes off and immediately forgets what he looks like. He fails to recognize his condition, such as his temper, pride, deceit. etc. You name it! It's all sin that will be judged by God.

In your thinking you are all right. My, you have a short memory! You attend your own club or church, argue with your mother or wife, swap yarns for kicks, and you may be unfaithful to your wife. Daughters or sons don't have much to do with you anymore. Sure you pay your bills, look good on the outside, buy new things, but you are a sinner like all the rest of us. The only difference is you have not repented of your sins and asked Jesus to come into your heart and save you from your sins.

At age _____, you are on a collision course. Where will you spend eternity—in joy or torment? You talk about hell. What do you know about HELL? Your *will* is so strong to love this world that you have a disease called greed, selfishness, conceit, pride, self-righteousness, etc.

Judge yourself? Observe the law that makes man a slave to this world, and yet keeps him looking to be blessed by God in whatever he does. You may think you are high-minded or maybe even religious. Judge yourself? One who does not bridle his tongue deceives his high-minded self. Does your tongue outrun your brain? Are you partial—playing favorites?

If you really want to obey the supreme law where the Scripture says, "You must love your neighbor as you do yourself," you are doing right; but if you show partiality, you are committing a sin and stand convicted before the Law as a law breaker. Note in *Job 13:10; I Timothy 5:21,* and *James 2:3-8* that anyone who obeys all the law but makes one single slip is guilty of breaking all the law.

> *I Timothy 5:21 I charge thee before God, and the Lord Jesus Christ, and the elect angels, that thou observe these things without preferring one before another, doing nothing by partiality.*

What good is it to say you are a church member, Christian, or even to say you have faith (trust) when you do not show good works toward others. Therefore, faith without works is dead. It is nothing, my friend. You must learn to believe that faith and good deeds work together.

Multiply your age in years by 365 days. One computes about _____ days for a _____ year old person. Figure it out for yourself, the days of up-and-down living. With our tongues, blessing and cursing issues from the same heart. You war and fight against yourself and others. Daily, the media reviews the rage of savagery upon the earth. People look at it impassively and don't know what to make of it.

Is there one wise and intelligent person among you? If so, may that person demonstrate good will in what he does in the humility and wisdom of God. You cherish bitter feelings and wear your feelings on your sleeve. Jealousy and rivalry are in your heart. Do you pride yourself on it and thus misrepresent the truth? Friendship with the world means enmity with God. God opposes disobedient, haughty persons. Humbly submit yourself to God and resist the devil. He will flee from you.

Do not talk against your neighbor, business associate, or relative. God will judge in due time. So when a person knows what is right and refuses to do it, he is guilty of sin

(James 4:13-17). All are wholly under the power of sin. Without the sovereign power of God you are incapable of doing good, and you cannot honor and glorify God *(Romans 3:23-26).*

Only God is good. Judge yourself, not others. People are made right by the grace of God. Grace is a free gift from God. You are redeemed by the blood of Jesus Christ the Son of God. You were saved from your sins when Christ was crucified on the cross. He died for your sins and mine. By repenting and believing in Christ, all will receive His free gift of everlasting life.

Good works, education, even good looks will not give you eternity. Assurance of eternal life is provided for every individual with an unlimited guarantee by a sovereign God. You are given a permanent policy for your entire life. Here are the promises: study them from any Bible. Here are your benefits. The Holy Spirit is your God-given seal, a permanent promise for your entire life.

Maximum Future Benefits

1. Eternal Life - "For God so loved the world, that he gave his only begotten Son, that whosoever believeth in him should not perish, but have everlasting life *(John 3:16)*."

2. Eternal Home in Heaven - "Believe in God and His Son the Lord Jesus Christ. I go to prepare a place for you. This is a precious promise *(John 14:1-4)*." God wants to give you the gift of eternal life *(Romans 6:23)*.

> *Romans 6:23 For the wages of sin is death; but the gift of God is eternal life through Jesus Christ our Lord.*

3. An Incorruptible and Glorified Body - " We shall not all die but be raised and changed into what is immortal *(I Corinthians 15:51-54)*."

Certainly all of us want to go to heaven. Most assuredly

we want to take the proper route. What is the way?

God Tells the Truth About Man

"For there is not a just man upon earth, that does what is right and never sins *(Ecclesiastes 7:20)*."

"All we like sheep have gone astray; we have turned every one to his own way; and the Lord hath laid on him the iniquity of us all *(Isaiah 53:6)*." Christ is our kinsman and Redeemer, who has the power to buy us back to be glorified with Him *(Philippians 3:20-21)*.

"As it is written, 'There is none righteous, no not one' *(Romans 3:10)*."

"For all have sinned, and come short of the glory of God *(Romans 3:23)*."

"Your sins have made a separation between you and God *(Isaiah 59:2)*."

Maximum Immediate Benefits

1. Is the life of God in you? God provides a way to bridge the gap between Himself and you, and no one else can.

   a. By the Holy Spirit indwelling in you: *I Corinthians 12:13; John 3:36; Romans 8:9-11; I Corinthians 6:19*, your new nature is provided by God.

   b. In becoming a child of God: *John 1:11-12; Galatians 3:26*.

2. Victory over sin and the old nature. Jesus Christ, who had no sin, personally bore our sins in His body on the cross *(I Peter 2:24)*.

   a. Sin can't reign over you any more unless you let it *(Romans 6:12)*.

   b. All temptation will be limited to your personal capacity *(I Corinthians 10:13)*.

3. You receive God's gift of eternal life by believing in Christ as your Savior *(John 3:36)*.

4. You will have the gift of the Holy Spirit *(I Corinthians 12* [note *verse 7*]).

5. The fruit of the Spirit is yours: Love, Joy, Peace, Patience, Kindness, Goodness, Faithfulness, Gentleness, Self-Control *(Galatians 5:22-23)*.

6. A direct communication hot-line with God *(Matthew 6:33)*.

   a. For personal and a perennial care.

   b. Open at all times, 24 hours per day and 365 days a year—no holiday closures for sure *(John 14:13-14, I Thessalonians 5:17)*.

7. Private counseling services for spiritual guidance *(John 16:13; Romans 12:1,2)*.

8. Personal education program with the greatest Teacher of the universe *(John 14:26)*.

9. Supernatural power *(Ephesians 1:19-23)*.

10. Corporate body life, fellowship and care. Study *Ephesians 4:14-16*.

11. All the conditions provided in this policy are valid in accordance with the Bible as God's standard with unlimited guarantees during and after wars, peace, storms, earthquakes, terminal diseases, security *(Revelation 2:11)*, except death *(Romans 8:5, 6, 12, 13)*.

This is an eternal life decision. Your personal decision about Jesus Christ will determine whether you will spend eternity in joy and God's security *(Psalm 16:11)*.

God Tells His Remedy for Sin

(read carefully the Bible policy)

"Come now, and let us reason together, saith the Lord; though your sins be as scarlet, they shall be as white as snow; though they be red like crimson, they shall be as wool *(Isaiah 1:18)*."

"But God commendeth his love toward us, in that, while

we were yet sinners, Christ died for us *(Romans 5:8)*."

"Who his own self bare our sins in his own body on the tree, that we, being dead to sins, should live unto righteousness; by whose stripes you are healed' *(I Peter 2:24)*."

"But he was wounded for our transgressions, he was bruised for our iniquities; the chastisement of our peace was upon him; and with his stripes we are healed *(Isaiah 53:5)*."

"Not by works of righteousness which we have done, but according to his mercy he saved us, by the washing of regeneration, and renewing of the Holy Ghost *(Titus 3:5)*."

For Jesus, the God man, taught us that His blood was shed for the remission of sins. We were purchased with His own blood *(Matthew 26:28; Acts 20:28; Romans 5:9; Hebrews 9:12-14)*. Jesus *(Hebrews 8:6-8)* is an everlasting priest. He is the mediator of a superior perfect covenant. Therefore, we can tabernacle with Christ directly through prayer. The anointing Holy Spirit continually opens new understandings of His word to each of us. The Spirit intercedes and helps us grow spiritually and closer to Jesus Christ who reigns with the Father in Heaven.

This is difficult for some to believe that God and His Son are all truth and will not forsake you *(Joshua 1:5; Hebrews 13:5-9)*. Religious leaders are dead, but Christ is a living intercessor today. Christ died but He came physically alive, and ascended to Heaven to intercede on our behalf. If you really walk in this light of His presence, your relationship and fellowship with Him will continue until He calls you home to eternity to serve the living Messiah in glory. Suicide, religion, cults and devil worship will only end in eternal torment. These represent true bibulous realism. But God is never limited by humanity *(Colossians 2:8-10)*.

"For by grace are you saved through faith; and not of yourselves. It is the gift of God; it is not of works, lest any man should boast... we are the Creator's handiwork in Christ *(Ephesians 2:8-10)*."

God Wants to Save You

God wants to save you and will save you if you follow His instructions:

"He that believeth on the Son hath everlasting life; and he that believeth not the Son shall not see life; but the wrath of God abideth on him *(John 3:36)*."

"And they said, Believe on the Lord Jesus Christ, and you shall be saved, and your house *(Acts 16:31)*." Also *I John 1:9*.

"To him give all the prophets witness, that through his name whosoever believes in Him shall receive remission of sins *(Acts 10:43)*."

No Cost to the Believer

1. Repent (turn about) from your own ways *(Luke 13:3; Romans 3:23; 6:23; Acts 3:19)*.

2. Receive the free gift policy.

a. The price paid in full once-for-all by Jesus Christ with His death on the cross of Calvary *(Hebrews 9:12)*.

b. Accept Jesus Christ by faith *(John 1:11, 12; 3:16; Romans 10:9)* [Entrust Him with your life].

3. Jesus hears and loves you. He will not reject you *(John 6:37)*.

Maximum Limitations

This policy is as boundless as the Grace of God *(Ephesians 3:21, 22; II Corinthians 3:4,5)*.

"And God is able to make all grace abound to you, that always having all sufficiency in everything, you may have an abundance for every good deed *(II Corinthians 9:8)*."

"And many other signs truly did Jesus in the presence of his disciples, which are not written in this book; but these are written, that you might believe that Jesus is the Christ, the

Son of God; and that believing you might have life through his name *(John 21:24-25)."*

There is Only One Way to Be Saved

God does not save mankind by love, but through His unmerited favor for those who believe on Him in Christ.

"Jesus saith unto him, I am the way, the truth, and the life, no man cometh unto the Father, but by me *(John 14:6)."*

"Neither is there salvation in any other; for there is no other name under heaven given among men, whereby we must be saved *(Acts 4:12)."*

"For there is one God, and one mediator between God and men, the man Christ Jesus *(I Timothy 2:5)."*

Christ Extends a Personal Invitation

"He that comes unto me I will in no wise cast out *(John 6:37)."*

Now the message of the Bible to you is: "For if you shall confess with your mouth the Lord Jesus, and shall believe in your heart that God has raised Him from the dead, you shall be saved *(Romans 10:9)."*

"Wherefore He is able to save them to the uttermost that come unto God by Him, seeing He ever lives *(Hebrews 7:25)."* Because Jesus Christ lives in Heaven, those who trust Him for salvation have the assurance that they will live with Him also. "I am the resurrection and the life; he that believeth on Me, though he die, yet shall he live." Open your mind and heart and receive the Son of God as your Savior.

Bonus Riders

A. God's love is offered to you:

1. Provision: God's enabling for your daily work *and needs (Philippians 4:13).*

211

2. Cost: You must seek first the Kingdom of God and His righteousness *(Matthew 6:31-33)*.

B. Concern for life events about you.

1. Provision: all things will work together for good *(Romans 8:28)*.

2. Cost:

a. You must love God *(I John 4:14-19)*.

b. You must follow His call for your life *(I Peter 1:14-21)*.

c. Surrender your life-style *(Ephesians 5:18; Romans 12:1, 2)*.

C. Spirit-controlled life. The love of God is shed abroad in our hearts by the Holy Spirit.

1. Provision: He will empower you to do the right thing.

2. Cost: Surrender your Life style *(Ephesians 5:18; Romans 12:1, 2)*.

D. Future rewards:

1. Provision: God will lay up treasure in heaven for your arrival.

> *II Corinthians 5:10*
> *For we must all appear before the judgment seat of Christ; that every one may receive the things done in his body, according to that he hath done, whether it be good or bad.*

2. Cost: Service to Him now *(Matthew 6:19-20; 13:44-53; 19:21; I Corinthians 3:11-18; II Corinthians 5:10)*.

E. Position of authority in the future.

1. Provision: you will be given the right to reign with Christ in His Kingdom.

2. Cost: You must utilize well whatever Christ has given you on earth for His profit or gain *(Matthew 25:14-30; Luke 19:12-26)*.

This policy demonstrates the way we view ourselves as sinners and will determine how we live our lives, how we will relate to others, and how we fulfill our responsibilities.

All bitterness, guilt, sin, etc. is taken away through the shed blood of Jesus Christ who died for the sins of the world. What are you going to do about it?

In summary, this policy is discovered in the Bible. The Old Testament and the New Testament present all the information God knows we need. The salvation policy gift is offered as a free trust to anyone. There is no probate in a living loving trust with Jesus Christ, the Savior of this world. Make the decision today. This is the only Eternal Life Assurance Company in the world.

This witnessing tool is used with your Bible on a one-to-one basis. Sharing your faith without an argument is usually carried out well with the assistance of the Bible for the Glory of God. Manfred George Gutzke[1] addresses unbelief. His book, *Help My Unbelief*, raises some interesting questions.

You put your total trust in a stranger. He is knowledgeable and well-trained. He has performed over two thousand heart surgeries in three years. Only three percent have failed, and that is an excellent record.

You are rolled into the operating room. He is going to perform a quadruple bypass on you. You are completely helpless by the use of anesthetics. You trust the doctor (stranger). The doctor has your rib-cage open. He discovers a decision change must be made. The surgeon performs a five-bypass to satisfy the medical condition of the patient.

Today you are running around in a reasonably normal fashion. By God's grace and the surgeon's skill, your life is extended longer.

Another example: The pilot (another stranger) flies you from Portland to New York. You have an inner trust in the surgeon and the pilot. You have a trust in people. You even trust your banker or financial advisor to oversee your money and investment. You have trust in physical things and affairs. You really depend on people and conditions of value. You

213

trust according to human worth and reasoning. You trust in the physical aspects of life even though everything cannot be seen at the moment.

Some people are placed in a position where they must blindly trust incompetent persons. Critics and victims report various torts and criminal or erroneous acts, such as surgically removing the wrong leg or breast from a patient, a pilot not completing a plan prior to flight or a guide not adequately preparing for a mountain climbing trek.

Anyone can make a mistake. But when a professional worker and his staff have the responsibility to complete a task that involves one's life and the lives and welfare of others, then legislators, licensing agencies and citizens must demand rigid requirements. Self evaluation is not sufficient. Continual monitoring by teams much like space-travel teams is mandatory. Churches could follow this example but rarely do.

When putting your trust and your very life in the hands of someone else, all elements of burnout, disharmony, maladjustment, fatigue, and indifference must be avoided. Backup people need to be available to avoid problematic errors in executing a significant act. You expect to live beyond your operation, and your investment, too.

You put your trust in this temporary situation as if your whole life depended upon it, which it does. But in whom do we trust for that final outcome?

Yes, the final outcome is physical death. We all die with no exception. Even good, moral, trusting, loving, law-abiding people face an appointed time of death. You run out of time and space to express yourself. You qualify for death from the day you are born. You reach a peak, then pine away. So where do you put your trust now?

Now review the section of the chapter on the spiritual worth of man. God is offering you eternal life and a legacy of benefits while living on His earth.

Your Sinful Condition

Only when a person becomes aware of his sinful condition can a new consciousness be established with the assistance of the Spirit. This is called a true conversion, or born-again experience given by the grace of God *(Ephesians 2:8-9)*. Only the Spirit is capable of saving a sinner and placing him in a position of being a child of God. No mortal is capable of doing this. The Holy Spirit takes a body, a spiritually hungry, blind person living in the dregs of this dark world and turns him around into a life of God's love and light. He inherits a new nature. A new creation in Jesus Christ is born from above.

Then you discover that the free gift of salvation has been paid. You realize that Jesus Christ died on the cross for you. His blood was shed for all sinners. He was sinless, but He took on all the sins of every age and blessed us with His *free gift (Ephesians 2:8; Ephesians 1:7)* of eternal salvation.

> *Ephesians 1:7 In whom we have redemption through his blood, the forgiveness of sins, according to the riches of his grace...*

Until the spiritually blind person can see this under the authority of the Spirit, that person will remain in unbelief. But if he believes, he may still be physically hungry but never spiritually hungry. After Christ arose from the dead and ascended to be with the Father in heaven He sent the Holy Spirit as a comforter to minister to the true believer and to live and work within each of the saved.

After the conversion, the Spirit, coequal with God and the Son, continues to minister to all regenerated children of God. They are called Christians and are continually being Spirit-nurtured as they study the Word of God. Read *Galatians 6:8-9; 5:16-18*. Christians still have the old nature until physical death. The physical body hungers and is subordinate to the Spirit-controlled new nature that only true Christians possess. God will test your faith and Satan will tempt you.

God will not forsake you. God will discipline and nurture you, for He loves His children in truth *(Psalm 89:33-37)*. The believer who exercises saving faith in Christ possesses eternal life and is eternally secure *(John 10:28-29; John 5:24)*. Works are the outgrowth of our salvation *(Ephesians 2:10)*.

The works are spiritual works for the glory of God. Grace teaches good works *(Titus 2:11-15)*. All believers will be judged according to their works *(II Corinthians 5:10)* over and above the free gift of salvation. Believers will receive rewards, for all works that shall abide *(I Corinthians 3:12-15)*. Our job is to share our faith in Jesus Christ with the poor and disabled in the world *(Acts 1:8; Matthew 28:18-20)*. The Christian community is not doing this very well as observed in most local churches.

> *Acts 1:8 But ye shall receive power, after that the Holy Ghost is come upon you: and ye shall be witnesses unto me both in Jersalem, and in all Judea, and in Samaria, and unto the uttermost part of the earth.*

Radio and television ministers reach far more people in national and international networks, but the cost is very high in broadcasting the gospel[2]. Prime time during weekdays is impossible to purchase, and many secular networks refuse to sell time to ministries. The local churches assume that the time and money spent on national and international broadcasting is sufficient for Christian ministry.

Of course it is not. Sharing our faith in Jesus Christ to the lost can be done more efficiently if all people in the local Church would bear the burden of witnessing for Christ, too. Christians are reluctant to witness, without an argument, to the lost world. The act of witnessing embarrasses them and puts them on the spot.

Therefore, they cannot be fully aware of what Christ did for them. They have never tried to share Christ with a pagan. Or perhaps they fear they will be persecuted or ridiculed as Christ was.

Yet, during the 20th Century thousands of Christians have been martyred. The Great Commission is to make believers of all nations *(Matthew 28:19)*. That is the ideal for which we should strive.

> *Matthew 28:19 Go ye therefore, and teach all nations, baptizing them in the name of the Father, and of the Son, and of the Holy Ghost...*

When was the last time someone witnessed to you? Perhaps it has been a long time, or perhaps never. Ask a Christian, "How do you become a Christian?" A positive response is seldom supplied. Maybe such a question surprises the person or he really does not know the plan of salvation. Scripture tells us to be ready to give an answer to anyone who asks the reason we have for assurance that we will live forever.

ENDNOTES

[1] Gutzke, Manfred George. *Help Thou My Unbelief.* Nashville, TN: Thomas Nelson, 1974, pp. 43-49.

[2] McGee, J. Vernon. *Joel.* Pasadena, CA: Thru the Bible Radio, 1978.

SUMMARY OF MAN'S SEPARATION FROM GOD
Isaiah 59:1-3; John 17:14-17; Romans 6:1-11; II Corinthians 6:14-18; Galatians 6:14; Matthew 13:47-49

BASICALLY GOOD
Romans 3:12 They are all gone out of the way, they are together become unprofitable; there is none that doeth good, no, not one. (KJV)

DESTRUCTIVE
Romans 3:16 Destruction and misery are in their ways; (KJV)

NOT GOOD
Romans 3:12 They are all gone out of the way, they are together become unprofitable; there is none that doeth good, no, not one. (KJV)

RIGHTEOUS
Isa 64:6 But we are all as an unclean thing, and all our righteousnesses are as filthy rags; and we all do fade as a leaf; and our iniquities, like the wind, have taken us away. (KJV)

UNFAITHFUL
Psalms 5:9 For there is no faithfulness in their mouth; their inward part is very wickedness; their throat is an open sepulchre; they flatter with their tongue. (KJV)

DISOBEDIENT
Isa. 53:6 All we like sheep have gone astray; we have turned every one to his own way; and the LORD hath laid on him the iniquity of us all. (KJV)

KIND
Romans 1:29 Being filled with all unrighteousness, fornication, wickedness, covetousness, maliciousness; full of envy, murder, debate, deceith, malignity; whisperers. (KJV)

PROUD
Romans 1:30 Backbiters, haters of God, despiteful, proud, boasters, inventors of evil things, disobedient to parents. (KJV)

UNHOLY
2 Tim 3:2 For men shall be lovers of their own selves, covetous, boasters, proud, blasphemers, disobedient to parents, unthankful, unholy. (KJV)

GIVING
Rom 1:29 Being filled with all unrightousness, fornication, wickedness, covetousness, maliciousness; full of envy, murder, debate, deceit, malignity; whisperers. (KJV)

GREEDY
Romans1:29 Being filled with all unrighteousness, fornication, wickedness, covetousness, maliciousness; full of envy, murder, debate, deceit, malignity; whisperers. (KJV)

DISHONEST
Jer 17:9 The heart is deceitful above all things, and desdesperately wicked: who can know it? (KJV)

LOVING
2 Tim 3:2 For men shall be lovers of their own selves, covetous, boasters, proud, blasphemers, disobedient to parents, unthankful, unholy. (KJV)

SELFISH
Phil 2:21 For all seek their own, not the things which are Jesus Christ's (KJV)

		MAN IS NOT GOOD
Man is not basically good	Man is naturally destructive	MAN IS DISOBEDIENT
Man is not basically righteous	Man is naturally unfaithful	MAN IS UNHOLY
Man is not basically kind	Man is naturally proud	MAN IS DISHONEST
Man is not basically giving	Man is naturally greedy	MAN MUST CHANGE IN
Man is not basically loving	Man is naturally selfish	ORDER TO LIVE WITH GOD

218

CHAPTER ELEVEN: Confused Members of the Church

Our Church and Its Ministry

The Stranger in our Midst

Another problem in our churches is the sin of selfishness. Church members want to promote their own activities. When strangers join the church, new ideas are not appreciated. Members then feel an attack is made on their way of doing things.

Do we listen, understand, reflect, share and accept a better way of teaching a Bible class, of presenting a sermon, of offering activities for the youth that will be constructive to all members of the group? Perhaps too much of the "ego" gets in the way.

Jesus taught us to love, not to ignore and reject the stranger. Take the stranger in and accept him as your own *(Exodus 22:21)*. Neither vex him nor oppress him. Remember, you were a stranger once.

The future for every child of God is in the gospel of Jesus Christ. People would rather fight, argue, struggle to be

> *Exodus 22:21 Thou shalt neither vex a stranger, nor oppress him: for ye were strangers in the land of Egypt.*

heard, to be recognized for their own supremacy, and they refuse to accept criticism *(Proverbs 13:18)*.

We should be concerned about caring for sick and terminally ill persons. Teach us, Lord, to love in Word, but also to love in action, work, etc. Do it in truth *(I John 3:18-22)*. The problem is pride in one's life, finally admitting it, and doing something about it *(Proverbs 23:12, 25:12)*.

In his ministry, Paul quoted from the psalmist of *Psalm 44:22* who said, "Yea, for your sake we are killed all the day long; we are accounted as sheep for the slaughter." Therefore, in all things we can be much more than conquerors through Christ Who loved us. We are servants to minister to others even though we may be persecuted, harassed and ignored, all for the glory of God. The reward is to be an eternal winner at the Day of Judgment.

Leadership in the Church

Many church bodies, as well as secular groups, want our time and money. Then, some enamored and obsessed idle talkers wants to lead the body. Their tongues outrun their minds. The cry is for volunteers and participation as a life service.

Sometimes people manipulate others for their own purposes and goals. The election of leaders is fine if fairness governs generally, but popularity enters the selection process. Usually if a person has money, or is young, or is recognized in the community (such as a doctor, lawyer, business man, organist or retired officer from the Armed Forces), he is given priority over others who do not have recognizable status.

What biases and partialities are experienced among the

members of the Church! The social climber is the carnal Christian immersed in church doctrine but brainwashed with self righteousness. He is tainted and contaminated with unbelief and blind to the outcome for the less fortunate. Others may either rebel or leave the church group. The status climber will not listen to or understand the call of Christ to serve mankind and to glorify God.

There are always psychological mechanisms that can be used to protect one's boundary of security[1]. Support in the form of contributions for church revitalization and for war-torn countries is a necessity. This is fine when results can be seen and appreciated, and when most of the money, food and materials, Bibles, etc. are sent directly to the needed area with purpose.

When administrations swallow most of the money just to put it where they were told it would do the greatest good, usually little is accomplished. The job is to put people in a spiritual setting that allows them to offer their gifts and talents where they will do the most good both in their own eyes and in the sight of the Lord. The way to go about this—for the local church, mission, youth groups, older Christians, etc.—is to:

1) Give all the believers responsibilities. The attitude is to get the Lord's job done together. It is a sin to put people down and not allow them to work for the Lord in this world. Let them know realistically that when they accomplish something, they share the glory of the Lord.

2) Be sure the leader cares about the participation of others. The involvement must be both spiritual and social. The followers are then led to obedience and loyalty in the ministry of Jesus Christ. Examples of ministry would be to:

   a. Feed the poor physically and spiritually.

   b. Discover and create jobs for the poor who are willing to work.

   c. Help the elderly, the bereaved, the grieving, those with

terminal diseases, etc.

    d. Offer assistance for those who are willing to grow spiritually.

3) Offer people in any church or group encouragement and direct them to make sound decisions, under the guidance of the Spirit of God.

    Study some of the great challenges as they apply in your personal life. God's grace transformed Peter's timetable from a late bloomer to a powerful leader able to endure submission and suffering as a lesson for all of us. In *I Peter, chapters 1 through 5:10* numerous lessons of trials are taught for your spiritual growth. Jesus, the Master Teacher, transformed Peter from a weed to a solid rock for the purpose of living *(I Peter 1:3-9)* in preparation for everlasting life. He was an encourager to the apostles and others in the Church. Peter in his epistles and in the *Acts of the Apostles* grew with endurance as a fearless witness before a sovereign God. Nowhere do we see any prerequisites for approval in the Church other than being an obedient child of God.

Witnessing

    The evangelist Philip, not an apostle, in a very practical way preached for Christ only and mightily increased the faith of the masses. Study *Acts 6:1-5; 8:1-40.* How are we witnessing to the lost world today? He who has total faith in Christ dares to witness. He who will endure trial to the end shall be saved though the world despises him *(Mark 13:10-13).*

    There is a witness outreach everywhere. Sharing our faith without an argument has been the great failure among the Christian majority. It is only a small minority of Christians that are the fruit-bearers for Christ. The rest are bottled and sealed for their nonproductive complacency. In America, where numerous opportunities for daily witness are available without persecution, few there are who gladly accept the injunction to proclaim for Christ. He loves us beyond words to express.

In Muslim and Buddhist territories today, Christians are being martyred for their love of sharing Christ. Christians worldwide must recognize that those who endure such persecution bear a much lighter cross at the end. They will then possess loving insight, forgiveness and belief. Gentle Stephen, an example of martyrdom, was a powerful Spirit-driven speaker *(Acts 7:1-8:3)*. He was filled with faith, courage, wisdom and grace that only God could bestow upon him.

Stephen did not have to wait and be trusted before gaining acceptance, church membership, accountability, etc. He was given power to perform acts of God far beyond the requirements Christians demand of the believing stranger today. There are many challenges missed by ministers and Christian workers who confess, preach, teach and live in the full counsel of God.

Some Christians are fearful and therefore lack faith in trusting other Christians. Ministers have to study and analyze how they can use the Christian stranger in the Church. He may feel his authority is threatened. God help the ministers and workers who are afraid to permit the Christian stranger to express his calling early in the ministry. *For the love of Christ, why don't Christians accept each other more freely without suspicion?*

A genuine Christian is like a lighted candle. You never see his true values until he suffers pain or stress. He should never be ashamed, for he is delighted to glorify God under all circumstances. Among visible members of the Church, we may observe great participation. Programs, workshops, conference speakers, dinners and musical praise are seen in many churches of today.

But numerous Christians are contentious with each other. They differ in church organization, doctrine, and witness. They ignore the Great Commission Jesus taught *(John 8:16-20; Isaiah 43:8-12; Acts 22:14-15; Mark 16:14-16).* The Holy Spirit must be grieved because of our self-righteousness. Some brethren are hypercritical of how others witness. Remember, witnessing must be done cautiously in the spirit of love. High-pressure tactics are nonproductive in leading another to a genuine lasting conversion by the Holy Spirit.

People everywhere are looking for a warm and accepting place, full of life and purpose, where there is a sense of participation for all members of the family. This is the place to make new friendships and find practical advice for every-day living.

Time and Gifts

If you have money or are a college professor or medical doctor, you are readily accepted and quickly used in the ranks of the ministry. Therefore use your time wisely by investing the life God has given you in His will *(Matthew 6:33; Ephesians 5:15-17).* You have an opportunity each day, as God gives you time to use for His purposes. Times are evil. It is essential that you pray and study to obtain spiritual knowledge and wisdom so that you can be effective.

> *Matthew 6:33 But seek ye first the kingdom of God, and his righteousness; and all these things shall be added unto you.*

The world and many pseudo-Christians live only for self. Preoccupation with self, and time when mismanaged are both sins. Do you recall that God overlooked our sin and ignorance and commanded us to repent? God has set a day in which He will judge the world fairly *(Act 17:30-31).*

You may think you have no time for God. Who gave you life, time, talent and treasure? Of course, it was God.

224

Time is where you place your efforts and manage your values in this life.

Jesus taught us to pray to our heavenly Father. When you pray as Jesus prayed *(Mark 1:35; Matthew 14:23; Luke 6:12-13; Luke 5:15-16),* you will discover how recovery takes place. You will never be forsaken. God will turn your fear into faith. He will answer your prayers and you will be His faithful vessel. He will use and bless you in His time.

The responsibilities of the Church will be carried out the way God established it. The Church will thrive even under persecution when responsibilities are carried out in faith and in love. His plan of redemption will constantly unfold.

Sound Doctrine

Of course there is a difference in the belief of liberals, cults, and evangelical fundamental assemblies. Sound doctrine makes all the difference *(Titus 1:9).* Religious and cult doctrines must be distinguished from Bible doctrine. When church politics and apostasy enter an assembly, Satan is not troubled for he is in control.

> *Titus 1:9 Holding fast the faithful word as he hath been taught, that he may be able by sound doctrine both to exhort and to convince the gainsayers.*

It is the evangelical fundamental church that teaches the unadulterated Word of God. Satan is constantly lashing out to hinder the fundamental teachings of Christ to the church. Yes, Satan is divisive and influential in splitting churches and creating contentions among true believers. Unity is only achieved through Christ.

Let us encourage one another in our faith and love for Christ. Put aside every hinderance in your life. The Spirit constantly refines each of us to teach us the value of prayer, and He reveals spiritual knowledge and wisdom from the

Bible. Christ directs our path toward the heavens. So fix your mind in Christ, the perfecter of your faith *(Hebrews 10:19-36, 12:1-11)*. Furthermore, retain your confidence and endurance in the Savior. What a divine promise! You will never experience a more serious and joyous decision than at this time and thereafter!

> *Matthew 5:10 Blessed are they which are persecuted for righteousness' sake: for their's is the kingdom of heaven.*

Jesus Christ will affect every corner of your life here and into eternity *(II Peter 3:1-9, 18)*. The true believer in this cosmetic world may be martyred for the cause of Christ or die for the brethren, kicking and screaming as he is dragged down, for his call in Christ *(Matthew 5:10)*.

Problems that Hamper God's Legacy

Exploitation

Sin-blight in many thousands of settings is observed and experienced in our world: the storage of radiation substances, fuel spills, landfills full of garbage, and toxic dumps left by various agencies. Man exploits the land. Man also exploits his finite resources such as lumber and oil through conspicuous consumption. Man exploits himself, through overindulgence in food, medicine, drugs and alcohol. And man exploits womanhood; women exploit manhood.

Why doesn't humanity address the problem of sin *(Romans 3:23)*? Society does not know how to manage the sins of exploitation. True acknowledgment of our sins, repentance of our sins, and believing in Christ who died for our sins is the only agent to help us manage our sins. The seven deadly sins of man, including greed, also apply to our nation and the world.

Wars and Weaponry

Many wonder whether Japan would have used the atomic bomb to conquer our nation if they had the time, funds, and materials. America trained many of Japan's scientists prior to World War II. Because of their depraved sinfulness, Japan admitted they would have used the bomb on America.

America's decision to use the bomb in Japan was the last option. All other options to end the war were stalemated. America never turned to God in unison in prayer to end the war. The tragedy of war is the outpouring of sin that the world has not acknowledged and has been unable to manage. Man needs to be regulated. He is the most vicious creature on earth.

No wonder there is a rising risk in cardiovascular and circulatory diseases. We are given the stress test. But we are missing the *sin* test. We talk until the death-rattle arrives, but the depraved man sees no sin in his caustic, insensitive living as he relates to the world and other people.

Avoidance Mechanisms

If you really can relate to God through Jesus Christ— and not through religion, philosophy, psychiatry, etc.—then there is great hope that you may relate to your fellowmen. Until then it is difficult to do. You relate to what is easy. You create a barrier of psychological mechanisms, e.g., rationalization, to preserve or protect your ego. But you can relate to your fellowman through love. That would be the starting point.

There are numerous fleshly mechanisms that the old human behavior expresses to avoid love, such as worry, back-biting, apple-polishing, and ear-banging. Or you can be a killjoy, a slave-driver , a bully, a whiner, a redneck or a hothead. You can also be, collectively, invaders of privacy, milquetoast wimps, instigators, imposers and perfectionists, etc.[2] Rela-

227

tionships are difficult to build with people with different motives. Submitting to the pulses of the irritable, human nature is contrary to God's will, but it is the path of least resistance. Yet Scripture warns us to resist the devil.

Financial Planning

Robert Fulghum was well known for his writings on the question of life and death. People study his philosophical views with intense interest. They become motivated to prepare a will or an estate plan program. But he can point out to them some drawbacks.

Why leave a legacy of property and possessions behind when you die? It is fine to make preparation for your death after years of earned cumulative assets. Anyone with good earnings can readily comprehend advantages and disadvantages. Retirement groups encourage you to avoid taxation by protecting your assets in a trust.

There are numerous financial encumbrances, such as the marriage penalty, for persons endeavoring to uphold those family values gleaned from Biblical teachings. Pensions, tax changes and probate laws also penalize persons remarrying. Because benefits would be lost, couples live together unmarried. Especially for the divorced or those with death benefits, remarriage can alter or may do away with former benefits. Therefore people often live together without disturbing pensions and other fringe benefits.

The world does not see how freedoms are gradually being removed. People are manipulated into sin, foregoing legal marriage in violation of conscience for the sake of financial survival. Some still long for a family, although not one with a man in it. Some adopt, but others use devious means to become pregnant. Both men and women avoid attempting to resolve what they deem to be irreconcilable differences.

The Reprobate Mind

At the other end of the spectrum wealthy career women, and also lesbians, avoid marriage, but selfishly desire a family by way of artificial insemination. Men and women desire not to solve irreconcilable differences in their lives. Therefore they become controlled by them or managed by others. Study *II Timothy 2:15-3:7.* Laden with sins, they are never able to come to the knowledge of the truth.

God is totally left out of their plans. The sting of death will come quickly, but the plan of everlasting life is entirely snuffed out of existence. The loving God is totally given up to a refined reprobate mind. Search the Scriptures and believe it!

Torment and unimaginable suffering are scheduled for those with unbelief. Even a good moral person will be caught in the entrapments and cares of this life, and neglect to manage life in the presence of an awesome God *(I Corinthians 15:26,54-58; II Corinthians 4:10-14; Philippians 2:5-11; Isaiah 25:8).*

A large segment of our society disobeys God. They choose to do something wrong and then want to blame someone else rather than take responsibility for their actions. They blame the parents, the teachers, or the police! A positive injunction would be that everyone is indeed responsible, and it is the responsibility of every adult in some way to direct and teach children the way that they should live so that they seldom will depart from such training.

Is it a thrill to speed in a stolen car to your death in the wee hours of the morning, or to perform illicit sexual acts, or to become incoherent in gang activity? Should state lottery dollars be used to finance public education? Why should monies from an addiction support our youth? The money from the gambling act is denying many the good food, clothing, and warm homes they ought to have. Picture yourself in such

229

a quagmire of circumstances.

Death swallows up young people every 15 minutes in the United States through addictions. It is as tragic as a full-blown war among nations. All the media reviews and medical reports cooperate with television to teach the young every conceivable way to kill, commit suicide and take uncontrolled ego trips for fun and thrills. They play irresponsibly with souls. Too many people are morally confused, spiritually blind, ill-informed, and adrift. Do they really want to know the difference between right and wrong?

Death goes far beyond the burial lot. Biblically, physical death is a separation of the soul and spirit from the body. When values become degenerative, the pagan could care less, the carnal Christian looks to establish civil and social reform, and the real believer may step into the ways of the pagan. Therefore true believers must be of one mind in Christ.

Therefore do not become contaminated or complacent in this world *(Romans 12:1-6; I Corinthians 2:11-16; Isaiah 64:4)*. Your thoughts are to be in truth, a purity that weaves the web that shares your deeds and serves others unto the Lord. You will not then desire the *(Micah 4:12)* trash offered by the world. The brain is the center of our thoughts. Thoughts affect how we will behave *(Colossians 3:12-17)*.

> *I Corinthians 2:16 For who hath known the mind of the Lord, that he may instruct him? But we have the mind of Christ.*

The True Believer

To be holy, let the Word of Christ reside in you richly with the wisdom and glory of an awesome God. Continue thanking God for His direction in your life. Walk in the Spirit; Talk in the Spirit; Pray in the Spirit and you will Think in the Spirit. Then you will think the way God wants you to think, live, and serve. *(I Corinthians 2:16; Isaiah 55:6-11).*

Review the following portions of Scripture concerning the power of God's Word on your thinking: It is written that the living Word of God is powerful and sharper than any two-edged sword, penetrating even to the severance of soul from spirit and of the joints and mar-row, and it is a distinct discerner of the very thoughts and motives of the heart *(Hebrews 4:12).*

God's thoughts are precious unto each of us. Great is the sum of them *(Psalms 139:17).* Our sovereign God knows the thoughts of vanity in man *(Psalms 94:11).* For someday man's works and thoughts shall experience God's glory *(Isaiah 55 :6-11).* Henceforth, may the wicked and unrighteous man relinquish his thoughts and let him become

> *Hebrews 4:12 For the word of God is quick, and powerful, and sharper than any twoedged sword, piercing even to the dividing asunder of soul and spirit, and of the joints and marrow, and is a discerner of the thoughts and intents of the heart.*

bonded to the Lord. Being made aware by the Great Entrapment is useless unless God will have mercy on his soul when true repentance takes place. For God's ways and thoughts are not your ways *(Isaiah 55:7-9).* Seek the Lord. The mission of every Christian is to allow the Spirit to make its point in Scriptural study, and thus enable us to walk circumspectly with Christ *(Exodus 23:13; Ephesians 5:13-16; Psalm 24:3-6).*

Awareness of *The Great Entrapment* is useless unless you study the context of the inspired Word of God. The purpose of study is to prime a person to become literate in spiritual Bible knowledge and wisdom. Listen to Peter. As *true believers* we will have numerous trials even though we will not spend our lives as we did before. We run the race with our Savior, for He is helping us endure all things that come into our lives.

God knows you will suffer with Him, but He will enable you to rejoice in the tests, trials and tribulations, for Christ will take us from suffering to total joy and love where we will be with Him. Our suffering will increase our faith, hope, and service to Him as we experience His deliverance in trials. Our suffering will produce patience, strength, and humility as He constantly refines each of us daily.

Therefore, as a bond servant, you have inherited precious promises through the righteousness of God. As you grow spiritually, God generously gives each of us grace and power as we receive the knowledge and wisdom of God through Christ, our Savior and Priest, who intercedes for us in our daily prayers. Sins will diminish as you run the race with Christ. When you fall, He loves you and will pick you up so you can continue to walk with Him toward eternity.

Whether you are rich or poor, your sacred life is changed forever. You have received His free gift of salvation and eternity. The purpose of living from this moment on is to be used by God while you are physically present. Death only ends the physical presence here, but the soul is the immortal spirit of the person that possesses no material reality. The soul shall return to God who gave it *(Ecclesiastes 12:7; Genesis 2:7; Psalms 119:175; Jeremiah 38:16)*. Refer to a concordance for further inquiry.

The Lost

The physical body houses the soul. The spirit serves the soul (inner man) and provides the consciousness of God. In *Matthew 10:28* Jesus comforts one not to be afraid, for the Father has told us that the soul is immortal.

Yes, the physical body can be killed. So what does it mean to fear God who can destroy both soul and body in hell? It means that God has the power and ability to destroy.

Then you will discover the unremitting consequences of sin without God as your Savior: punishment, weeping, rejection, anger, and darkness *(Matthew 8:12; 13:42,50; 22:13; 24:51; 25:30).*

> *Matthew 8:12 But the children of the kingdom shall be cast out into outer darkness: there shall be weeping and gnashing of teeth.*

Then you could know the despair that you had rejected faith, hope and the love graciously given by God *(Matthew 25:41-46; I Corinthians 13:1-13).*

It is prudent to review what Jesus has told us concerning Eternal Life and the judgment (John 5:24-29; John 14:6).

-The judgment of the believer's self is revealed. See the significance of the Lord's supper *(I Corinthians 11:31-33).*

-The judgment of the believer's works is revealed *(I Corinthians 5:9-13; Deuteronomy 22:24).*

-The judgment of the nations is revealed in all its finality *(Matthew 25:31-46).*

-The judgment of the wicked is revealed *(Revelation 20:11-15).*

Promise breakers abound, and as a consequence we live in a disjointed society. People exist in squalor. There may be splinter groups in the same setting that manage to keep things organized and clean, but they allow controlled substances, alcohol, even coffee to rule their lives. Then there is temper and tongue that cannot be controlled *(Matthew 12:34-37 and James 3).* Hunger, thirst and sex are difficult to manage *(Romans 13:14; I Corinthians 9:25-27; Philippians 4:5; I Thessalonians 5:6-8; Titus 2:2, 3, 12).* There is a constant void expressing itself in temporary satisfactions.

Peter *(II Peter 1:5-6)* describes all the attributes that go into temperance. Remember, you may have faith, virtue, knowledge, etc, but is there a false balance in your life? Is temperance under control, or are you an abomination to the Lord *(Proverbs 11:1)?*

Whether you are strong or weak in will, the energy of the flesh wins. God understands your failures and weaknesses. Sin is the common denominator. When you become converted, Jesus gives you a free gift of eternal life. But upon your *true conversion*, beyond self-control, will, logic, philosophy and reasonable expectations, God and Christ places the Holy Spirit inside you and sets you apart from your old uncontrollable nature, for you have been adopted and bought with a price *(I Corinthians 6:20)*.

> *I Corinthians 6:20 For ye are bought with a price: therefore glorify God in your body, and in your spirit, which are God's.*

The Temptations

With that, the new born-again nature grows as the Holy Spirit spurs you on to eternity. You can still fall into sin.

The demonic powers of the New Age Movement and many cults can cunningly brainwash a person. Their agents, with powerful, persuasive language can promote themselves and their platforms among the gullible recruits. The ensnared cult members then give over their worldly goods and their wills to satanically-contrived practices for entrance to a pseudo-heaven. In this way many members of humanity have gone out like fools into a lost eternity.

When you follow the leading of the Holy Spirit you will have a set-apart, sanctified life. You will never do it under your own will so as to please God. Are you mocking Almighty God? Are you building any purpose in your life? Where do you invest your life?

Love, hope and faith is in the living Christ *(I Peter 1:3)*, not in self or another person. Most people believe in God like they believe in the devil. Surveys report that people believe in angels, miracles and shortcuts to heaven. Seldom do they report belief in Jesus Christ and acknowledge the problem of sin.

Religious researchers report about belief in hell and the devil as well, but they rarely report people believing in the plan of Salvation in Christ. Many people are blind, indifferent and smothered with adversity, and they shunt the spiritual will and wisdom of God. Until they turn from their limited humanity to the unlimited benefits of the grace only God can offer, they will not discover that God is with us *(Ephesians 4:7; Romans 12:3)*.

The Promised Land

Centuries ago, Moses trusted God to lead the children of Israel out of Egypt *(Exodus 3:10-12)*. God's promise to Moses was: "I will be with you." When Moses did not think he was worthy and expressed a negative reluctance to be used by God, God was angered by his reaction. Still God used Moses and his brother Aaron mightily as His agents.

God is always right and He always has His way. Again, God chose Joshua for a minister *(Joshua 1:2,9)*. With His chosen leader He led the people into the promised land. God provides His way to all truth. Within the truth, He is all-knowing, all-powerful and ever-present. We must abandon contrivances. We have surety in the promises of God *(Isaiah 41:8-10)*.

Some Old Testament characters refused to acknowledge by faith the love of God for them. God communicated to them through angels, visions, dreams, signs, etc. *(Exodus 23:20-23; Numbers 20:16; Psalm 91:11-12; Joshua 5:13-15; Revelation 1:10-20; Genesis 40:8-23; Daniel 7; Matthew 1:20-21; Genesis 15:8-17; Matthew 16:3-4; 24:3-14)*. The people had to have total faith in God's leading them. Some believed fully while others were smothered in unbelief.

During the wilderness march, God gave the Israelites

food from heaven. Also, their clothing would not wear out. The discontented Israelites desired to return to Egypt for the earthly food. Their human appetites made them incapable of appreciating all God's miracles on their behalf. Instead of responding with faith, love, and gratitude, they continued in the blindness of the heathen from whom God wanted them to separate.

The Entrapment of Sin

The great entrapment of sin is revealed in all periods of time. People are attracted to false doctrines in every aspect of life. Man's attempt to explain the world around him has created theories and belief systems such as evolution, socialization, secular humanism, behaviorism, and even the New Age Movement, all in a vain effort to avoid the truth.

Beware of philosophies, for the world is unable to deliver anything better. We see God left out of the chain of events repeatedly. God's revealed will is not considered by the governing bodies in their decision-making.

By Faith Alone

Study *Hebrews chapters 10-12* and make them the bone of your soul. We are thrilled as we read of the heroes of faith who were strengthened by their sure hope of heaven, of how they endured all manner of affliction, and of how they were preserved from the enticements of a depraved world and triumphed over sin as by total faith. They laid aside every entrapment and took Jesus as Lord and Savior.

In a like manner your spiritual life is constantly being renewed as the Holy Spirit lives in you and governs you in total faith. There is no leaning on your own understanding, no murmuring, no idols, but the unlimited faith in your heart and mind are open to please God and accept all His promises.

You are a servant of Jesus Christ Who bathes you constantly in the Holy Spirit and Who enlightens you in prayer and the Word. God feeds you with all grace, and you have salvation from iniquity, guidance, care, and strength to manage sufferings. Physically you are dying by degrees, but spiritually you are growing by His grace *(Romans 3:22-24; 1 Corinthians 1:4-8; Colossians 1:10-11; 1 Peter 2:1-3; 3:14-18)*. Please note: *1 Timothy 4:3-16; II Timothy 2:1-25; Titus 2 and 3*. After Paul's conversion, God established in his life a pattern for believers today *(1 Timothy 1:12-16; Daniel 4:2-3)*.

The divine preeminence of Christ is declared by Scripture which tells us that all things were created by Him and for Him *(Colossians 1:16, 20-29)*. You see, God, Christ and the Holy Spirit are one. The triune God exists in three persons: God, Son, and Holy Spirit, yet the three are united as one God. The Holy Spirit lives in every true, converted Christian. Christ baptizes you with the Holy Spirit after you repent of your sins. Herbert Lockyer[3] has stressed that believers need to understand the truth of the Holy Spirit. Why?

1. It is a neglected doctrine.

2. It is a misunderstood doctrine.

3. It is a sacred doctrine which some have sought to pervert.

4. It is a Scriptural doctrine to be taught.

5. It is a practical doctrine.

Preconceived understanding and theories must be reexamined carefully and thoroughly and made to bend to the will of God. Only when they are reviewed and approved by the Holy Spirit are they to be used in the believer's walk of victory on this planet.

The Holy Spirit... "is referred to some 90 times in the Old Testament with 18 different designations applied to Him; and around 260 times in the New Testament with 39 different names and titles. We realize His conspicuous place in this age of grace, which is the dispensation of 'the ministration of the Spirit' *(II Corinthians 4:8)*: and that it is spiritually disastrous to neglect what the Bible reveals of His activities. Pre-eminence is given to 'church work' - 'social work' - 'Mission work,' but the apostles knew only one kind of work, namely the Spirit's work. This is why The Acts is saturated with His presence and presidency, and should be renamed 'The Acts of the Holy Spirit through the Apostles.' "[4]

> *Isaiah 61:1 The spirit of the Lord God is upon me; because the Lord hath anointed me to preach good tidings unto the meek; he hath sent me to bind up the broken hearted, to proclaim liberty to the captives, and the opening of the prison to them that are bound...*

The Holy Spirit indwells in the believer *(Joel 2:28-32; Zechariah 12:10 (Isaiah 61:1)* and is a constraining presence, casting off the great entrapment rampant in the unbridled church.

Divine Assurances

There are great promises inherent to a life in Christ. Believers through the Spirit of God are regenerated and sanctified with a divine nature to serve and glorify the Father. With that divine nature God gives these assurances:

1. The Spirit will baptize you with His Spirit and fire *(John 1:33; Acts 11:16; Acts 1:5)*.
2. The Spirit of God will speak in you *(Mark 13:11; Matthew 10:20)*.
3. The Spirit shall teach you *(Luke 12:12)*.

4. The Spirit is another Comforter who abides with you for-ever, teaching and directing you in truth *(John 14:16-17, 26)*.
5. The Spirit is truth, righteousness, and judgment *(John 15:26; John 16:7-14)*.
6. The Spirit is a guide and has power *(Acts 1:8-16)*.
7. The Spirit is a gift *(Acts 2:38; Acts 10:45)*.
8. The Spirit endows you with boldness *(Acts 4:31)*.
9. The Spirit allowed some to speak in tongues and prophesy *(Acts 19:6)*.
10. The Spirit makes overseers of some believers *(Acts 20:28)*.
11. The love of God is spread in our heart by the Spirit which is bestowed upon each grace believer *(Romans 5:3-5)*.
12. When you walk in the Spirit there is no condemnation *(Romans 8:1)*.
13. The law of the Spirit of life in Christ has freed us from the law of sin and death *(Romans 8:2)*.
14. The Holy Spirit who raised up Christ Jesus from the dead lives in you; He will make your dying body live again after you die by His indwelling Holy Spirit within you *(Romans 8:11)*.
15. The Spirit Himself bears witness with your spirit that you are a child of God; you are a joint heir with Christ; but to share His glory, you must now share His sufferings. *(Romans 8:16-17)*.
16. The Spirit helps your infirmities and the Spirit intercedes for you *(Romans 8:1-27)*.
17. The power of the Spirit sets us apart from the world and gives you abounding joy and peace in faith believing *(Romans 15:13-30)*.
18. For the love of the Spirit, you strive with others in your prayers to God *(Romans 15:30)*.
19. Your speech, teaching and preaching may be Spirit pow-ered *(I Corinthians 2:4,10-14)*.
20. The Spirit teaches you spiritual things from God only *(John 14:26; Luke 12:12)*.

21. Your body is the temple of the Holy Spirit, and you are not your own any longer *(I Corinthians 6:19)*.

22. Only the Holy Spirit can make you say Christ is Lord *(I Corinthians 12:3)*.

23. The Spirit gives to you a gift or talent to profit and use *(I Corinthians 12:3-11)*.

24. God has set His seal upon you, and given you the pledge of His Spirit in your heart *(II Corinthians 1:22)*.

25. You are a minister of God by the Holy Spirit *(II Corinthians 6:4-6)*.

26. You receive the promise of the Spirit through faith *(Galatians 3:14)*.

27. If you walk in the Spirit you will not perform or satisfy the lust of the flesh *(Galatians 5:5, 16-26)*, since you are not under the law. You are given the fruit of the Spirit: love, joy, peace, long-suffering, gentleness, goodness, faith, meekness, and temperance, against which there is no law. Therefore keep in step with the Spirit.

28. You have access by one Spirit into the Father's presence *(Ephesians 2:18)*.

29. The Spirit strengthens your inner self *(Ephesians 3:16)*.

30. You will love to keep the unity of the Spirit by not grieving the Spirit. You are sealed by the Spirit unto the day of redemption *(Ephesians 4:3-30)*.

31. You will pray unceasingly in every battle for you will need faith (your shield) to stop Satan's fiery darts. He is out to get you! Wear the belt of truth, the breastplate of righteousness, and have your feet prepared to present the Gospel of peace *(Isaiah 52:7)*. Take the helmet of salvation, and the sword of the Spirit, which is the Word of God *(Ephesians 6:13-20)*.

32. You have companionship and fellowship with the Spirit *(Philippians 2:1)*.

33. Your love springs from the Holy Spirit within *(Colossians 1:8)*.

34. You do not suppress the Spirit *(I Thessalonians 5:19)*.

35. You are sanctified by the Holy Spirit. The Spirit says, if you hear God's voice today, continue not to harden your hearts, or wander in your ways, or wander in your heart. Continue to learn the ways of God so you will enter into the rest and joy of the Lord *(Psalm 95:71; Hebrews 3:7-11)*.

36. The Spirit is a witness to us *(Hebrews 10:15)*.

37. You obey the truth through the Spirit unto unfailing love out of a pure heart for the Saints (I Peter 1:22).

38. You know the Spirit of God. How? Every Spirit-born person agrees that Jesus Christ, God's Son, really appears as God-man with a human body. You know you live in Him, and He (Christ) is in you, because He has given you His Spirit *(I John 4:2)*.

39. You believe the Spirit is a witness and is all truth.

There are three that bear record in heaven, the Father, the Word (Christ) and the Holy Spirit, and these three are one. There are three that coincide and bear witness in earth, the spirit, the water and the blood. Therefore the Spirit witnesses and acknowledges the Messiahship of Christ and to the nature of His work as Messiah *(I John 5:6-12; John 16:14; Romans 8:16,17)*.

We can see that the Holy Spirit indwells, controls and seals every spiritual Christian who glorifies Christ. This is the ingredient that is totally missing in the society today. The seed of unbelief leaves a famine within each of us. We are caught up with the glamour and glory of worldly activities, money, idols, and preoccupation outside God's will. The devil and his advocates subtly entrap men and women who try to be good church members, to be morally correct, and even those with a definite commitment and daily walk with Christ *(Titus 1:16; Matthew 7:20-23)*.

We acknowledge from Scripture that our mortal bodies will return to dust, but the soul of man will live on in an eternity of torment or joy. Therefore, a positive eternal decision must be made. World television audiences rejoice in the pleasures of this world! The selfish view demonstrates man's indifference to relating intimately with Christ. It is self-centered for anyone to attend church because of duty or for any other reasons outside the Spirit of Christ. After an hour of worship and conversation, you are ready to depart with the blessing of God.

Even nations possess a famine of faith *(I Corinthians 11:30-32)*. This is why many among us are feeble, sickly and indifferent. Some seek a role in postwar dialogue of peace. Even Nobel prize leaders strive for peace. All fear impending annihilation.

Europe quietly and slowly presses for diplomatic solutions to the Middle East problem that is centuries old. No one has been capable of finding solutions to the economic warfare. Another Arab state which takes a position of making peace, will ultimately oppose Israel like other nations. Not everyone desires to work for security, peace, rightful land ownership and strive for economic cooperation.

What we have is a diplomatic test! European and Western nations participate in the Middle East settlement. Small countries strive for freedom, self-determination and final independence. All fight, bicker, argue, and push for their rights. Nations want their way like children, lining up for a merry-go-round ride.

Who is right? Everyone thinks he is right, from the infidel to the theologian! Sorry, the sovereign God is the only right one. He is the only One who has the capacity to judge and determine righteousness. Christ is the ingredient that is missing in the lives of people.

The day will arrive when the Antichrist will rise up with a manipulative plan. The majority of the world will be entrapped with his clone stratagem. When you study *Daniel, Revelation* and other portions of Scripture, you will discover the entanglements he will order for those who are hard of heart.

They will experience a living Hell-on-earth called the tribulation. The unrighteous shall perish, with all the perversity and deception that is in them, because they refuse to recognize and receive the truth. God sends a strong message that the unbelieving sinner would accept a lie rather than the truth about God *(II Thessalonians 2:11-12; Hebrews 3:12-14).*

Your Spiritual Checklist

Now is the time to make a personal inventory on the outreach of your life. A spiritual checklist would be fitting.

Please read the self-evaluative scale of instruction very carefully. Indicate on a scale from 1 to 5 how you view yourself. Write any comments which might help clarify your evaluation. Though you may fall short of your goals, indicate how well these precepts guide your life. (*Proceed prayerfully.*)

Weak........ Strong

1 2 3 4 5   a) You strive to be blameless, above reproach and of unimpeachable character.

1 2 3 4 5   b) You enjoy a good reputation among those outside the church.

1 2 3 4 5   c) You are faithful to the one woman who is your wife.

1 2 3 4 5   d) You are able to manage your own family and personal affairs well, and to have your children under control.

1 2 3 4 5   e) Your children are not be under suspicion of loose living, rebellion, unruliness or insubordination.

1 2 3 4 5   f) You strive not to be self-willed and/or arrogant.

1 2 3 4 5   g) You strive not to get angry quickly, brawl, fight, or be abusive.

1 2 3 4 5   h) You are mostly patient, courteous, and not argumentative.

1 2 3 4 5   i) You are not addicted to tobacco, drugs or alcohol, nor do you feed upon vanity and emptiness.

1 2 3 4 5   j) You are disciplined, temperate, and a sober individual in control of yourself and your life.

1 2 3 4 5   k) You are not greedy, a lover of money nor eager for money made in underhanded or evil ways.

1 2 3 4 5   l) You genuinely love righteousness, truth and all that is good.

1 2 3 4 5   m) You are a fair, just, and equitable person.

1 2 3 4 5   n) You are a sensible, discreet, and prudent (wise) person.

1 2 3 4 5   o) You enjoy being hospitable and kind to strangers.

1 2 3 4 5   p) You are not a recent convert, nor immature in the faith so as to be vulnerable to pride.

1 2 3 4 5   q) You are a genuine faithful Christian firmly devoted to the Lord.

1 2 3 4 5   r) You adhere to sound doctrine found only in the Scriptures.

1 2 3 4 5   s) You are able to teach the Word of God and encourage believers in principle and by example or verbal witness to others.

1 2 3 4 5   t) You are able to refute, contradict, and expose unbelief and defend the faith.

Additional Queries

Do you overextend yourself in the Christian life? Is your time so taken up with activities and projects that you are counterproductive to yourself and others? How can you glorify God with this kind of life-style? Who do you edify?

People have problems with the heart. They are more concerned with the physical heart than the spiritual heart—i. e., low fat-diets, exercise, less stress, change in one's life-style, non-smoking and non-drinking, walking so many miles a day, etc. Yes, all of these concerns and clichés allude to your heart.

What about your spiritual heart? This is a problem unknown to the natural man, underestimated by him. Nobody notices the unknowns. Where are you going to spend eternity? Is it too late when the death rattle appears? Yes. It is just around the corner.

What does the future hold? Will the church go through the tribulation? Will we be destroyed in a nuclear war? In desperation, people worry, ponder, philosophize over such questions; they are fearful or apathetic about life after death. People are more concerned about earning an education, studying cultural and societal trends. Physicians inform us of the lethal affect tobacco has on the human body, but what does sin do to the human body?

When working with people, we must recognize, love and accept people as they are. Are circumstances truthful? This can be expressed as a spiritual veridical perception that only the child of God possesses. Spiritual veridical perception is activated when the Spirit of God informs the believer and directs, comforts, and teaches him God's genuine truth released from the Holy Scriptures. We will discover when reading the Bible that God's promises mean just what they say.

Feelings cannot overrule a person's perception of spiritual truth. Two essential things surface repeatedly, sin and pride. Each person is tempted by his pride which entices him. Pride conceives and gives birth to sin; and sin, when it is mature as a master of consequences, brings forth death *(James 1:14-15)*.

245

Truth, Before Feelings

Christians engage best when offered some latitude in studying Scriptures. All the answers of life are discovered as the feeding Spirit reveals new truths daily. With prayer and the application of Scripture to life's problems, the believer will sustain interest and grow as the Lord does the leading. This is a long-life struggle, for the old nature can and does get in the way while the new nature is directed by the Spirit *(Galatians 5:16-17; Peter 2:11)*.

Loving parents also must continuously endeavor to work with and encourage their children continuously to love and obey the Lord *(Proverbs 22:6; I Timothy 4:6-8)*. You cannot buy them truthfulness, love, honesty, etc *(Matthew 5:8)*. Only God can bestow it as you pray and lead them in the study of God's inspired Word.

Proverbs 22:6 Train up a child in the way he should go: and when he is old, he will not depart from it

Comparative Religions

The following approach to comparative politics is given by Edward Feit in *Governments and Leaders*:

"China's three major religious traditions have been Confucianism, Taoism, and Buddhism. Confucian humanism has always been the mainstay of the Mandarin elite, while Taoism and Buddhism have found greater support among the masses. China's peasant masses, with 20% of the world's population, have not been particularly sectarian about religious dogmas and, in fact, quite freely intermixed the rituals of all three on an eclectic, pragmatic basis.

"Certain religious tenets became almost universally accepted: filial piety within the family, which entailed respect for the old and care for the young; political relationships based on strict hierarchy, with mutual obligations binding superior and inferior; loyalty among peers; and a situation ethics that prescribed rules of propriety for various different contexts."[5]

"Religious affiliations of a country's population often have an impact on its historical and political development. From 1871 to 1945 German Protestants outnumbered Catholics by a two-to-one ratio, although Catholics formed a majority in several regions, such as Bavaria, Selisia, and the Rhineland. Thus Protestants had a greater impact on national policy than Catholics, while educational and cultural policies of the constituent states varied depending on which religious group had a majority."[6]

"In the post-World War II period, the situation has changed dramatically. In East Germany the preponderance of Protestants is striking; only 11% of the population is Catholic. In West Germany the religious affiliation is more nearly balanced with 45% Catholic, 40% Protestant, and 6% other or no denomination. Only 0.1 % is Jewish."[7] Religious beliefs have had a strong influence upon political parties and on public issues."[8]

"During the 19th century, Latin American landowners and the Roman Catholic Church have been strong politically. Cuba has been different. Foreign-controlled interest in acreage and the sugar market were less influenced than in sister nations. The Catholic Church was less powerful in that country. Usually Latin American countries have been more powerful where land, wealth, and obedient followers of the church exist."[9]

"Under Fidel Castro's rule the educational system was nationalized in 1961 and the Catholic Church authority was decreased and Catholic schools closed. The Catholic Church suffered under his regime. The Roman Catholic Church was never as strong as observed and studied in other Latin American countries. Cuba, like most Latin American countries had a great deal of immorality and promiscuity beneath the Roman Catholic Church dogma.

"There were registered and illegal houses of ill repute. Sex was practiced openly in most of these countries. Did the church have any control or influence of the sex practices of the people of the land?"[10]

The Castro regime has consistently persecuted the Christian church and incarcerated its leaders. Media sources inside and outside of Cuba observe after forty years of Christian oppression that some freedoms have been given, while evangelical groups have still been incarcerated for their worship, fellowship and witnessing. God wants the Cuban dictator to turn his life around and become a real Christian. What is the destiny of this leader?

God has called believers all over the world to new levels of spiritual thought *(Isaiah 55:8-9; John 12:24-28)*. The American Church has not really been persecuted yet, but segments of government, industrial and social institutions have endeavored to remove the free speech of prayer and Bible study from our multi-cultural society. Also, the godlessness of the A.C.L.U. has repeatedly suppressed the freedom of this nation with legalism that violates constitutional rights.

We have people and leaders that have refused, because of their unbelief, to carry on the Christian heritage that laid the foundation of this country. Have not the regimes of Stalin, Mussolini, Franco, Hitler, Castro and others plainly exhibited horrible turmoil, suffering, pain for our generational children?

True Christianity, not religion, ought to guide us, from our top leaders to people at poverty levels, into love and genuine acts of charity toward those who need them. Our leaders need the total Word of God in their lives and to participate in assisting each other without political or monetary gain.

Biblical history clearly records that the Old Testament prophets like Amos, Daniel, Isaiah, Jeremiah and others, forewarned the people that God's plan will not be disturbed. God would not allow His people, whom He loves, to disobey and rebel against His ways.

Today we are experiencing the same turmoil and behavioral patterns against which the prophets warned. People refuse to acknowledge God's way, and few Christians possess the grace only God can give them to witness to a lost world. God can see that people have no love for Him and little love for each other. Therefore God will harden their hearts and will no longer sustain a loving mercy upon the world *(Hebrews 3:7-19; Ephesians 4:17-24; Romans 9:14-32)*. They are skeptical, and not easily persuaded, due to so much anxiety and unhappiness in the world.

Before we can achieve eternal assurance and security, Jesus tells us to follow Him, renounce self, and take up His personal cross. If you gain the whole world in fame and temporal goods and lose you soul, what shall it profit you? You cannot give anything in exchange for your life *(Proverbs 8:32-36; Mark 8:35-36)*.

With a true conversion, the saint will follow Christ daily until taken to heaven *(Romans 6:11-14)*.

It is depressing to acknowledge there is conflict within ourselves. Paul recalls the inward struggle with sinful desires in Romans, Chapter Seven. Other relations to note are: Samuel with Saul; Saul with David; David with Absalom; Peter with Christ.

> *Mark 8: 35-36   For whosoever will save his life shall lose it; but whosoever shall lose his life for my sake and the gospel's the same shall save it. For what shall it profit a man, if he shall gain the whole world, and lose his own soul?*

Martha with Mary is also a lesson to learn and apply in our own personal lives. The struggle is with sin as expressed by inborn selfishness *(Ruth 1:14)*; desire *(John 7:37)*; depression *(I Kings 19:3-4)*; pride *(Matthew 26:69-72)*; and spiritual immaturity *(I Corinthians 13:11)*.

> *Luke 13:24 Strive to enter in at the strait gate: for many, I say unto you, will seek to enter in, and shall not be able.*

Each wants to go to heaven in his own way. Nevertheless, the Lord Jesus Christ has acknowledged that to enter the narrow gate is difficult *(Matthew 7:13-14; Luke 13:24)*. Jesus is the way, the truth, and the everlasting life. No man or woman ever comes to the Father but by Him *(John 14:6-7)*. Some are chosen by God; others come by free will; but few are saved. It is sad, but we are told these things clearly *(Luke 13:23-30)*.

The Lord will not acknowledge evildoers. Yes, there will be weeping and gnashing of teeth when they will actually see the faithful patriarch and all the prophets in the kingdom of God, and will find themselves cast out because of their spiritual blindness and unbelief.

It is easy to go to hell! Before you arrive there you must avoid the Church, the teaching and applying of Scripture to your life, and the praying for the help of the Holy Spirit and all the providence God offers you. Finally, you must reject Calvary and trample upon the loving Christ who died for your sins so that you could have eternal life. What a tragedy!

It has been reported that in the United States, as well as in the entire world population, 5% of all individuals have changed their sex code. Multitudes talk about it, and these many engage in it, blinding themselves to God's teaching and their own conscience. Government, business and church leaders have done little to discourage such practices. God tells us sex is to be confined within the sanctity of marriage.

America has lost its grip on its relationship with God. Authority is defied and people live lives of regret. As examples there are the AIDS victims. When facing such tragedies, a thousand words could not have deterred them from destruction. Yes, our country is on a collision course.

Have we truly achieved sustainability? We must recognize the existence of conflict in global economies, where the financial markets are a god to powerful people. The global ecology is torn apart by man, partially rebuilt, and again destroyed by man.

People follow many gods that make no demand on them. They lack a confession of sin to an Almighty God who loves and demands obedience. No wonder society continually opposes or ignores God's divine standards. Prosperity is their god. Their value judgments are distorted by sin.

Daily we experience political anarchy and spiritual and moral poverty. Politics too often are corrupt, and godless men who are blind to the truth lead us in spiritual poverty *(I Corinthians 2:14-16)*. Society does not exercise self-control, establish a work ethic *(II Thessalonians 3:10)*, remain married *(Genesis 2:1-25; I Corinthians 7:1-2)*, gain honesty *(Micah 7:1-20)*, kindness *(Luke 6:27-36)*, humility *(Joshua 7:1-26)*, or establish a life-style in harmony with God *(I Thessalonians 5:15-24)*.

We learn from Scripture that the value of working or creating work reduces poverty *(II Thessalonians 3:8-16)*. Yet today we have all kinds of poverty programs and multigenerational welfare. People learn not to work if they can receive free handouts, but they doom their children to living poor.

A lesson in *Nehemiah 5:1-19* urges the return of the people to their fields so they could work, regardless of usury. The godless rich then were told to keep the poor employed, but they were implored to return the lands to the people. Families and church bodies today are urged to care for those who are physically and psychologically unable to support themselves. Greed and affluent living have made too many of us insensitive to the care of others, just as greed and affluent living had led to oppression and insensitivity in Nehemiah's time *(I Timothy 5:1-25; Amos 18:24-27; Acts 4:34-35)*.

Bible Ministry

Can you respond to the urgent call to help others who are starving, depressed and in religions which offer no genuine hope? There is an exciting ministry in assisting countries awaiting you This ministry includes the unique challenge of introducing Bibles and medical and industrial assistance into countries of the world, distribution of evangelistic literature and hymnals, and the groundbreaking of new churches for people who have not had freedoms in their lives for years.

Still crime, inflation, censorship and governmental corruption prevail in countries that do not yet have real freedoms. True Christianity is struggling to reach people who are just beginning to worship and study the Bible freely. It will take years for the Church to learn to aid these people who desire to search God's truth along with prayer, Bible Study, and fellowship.

People in poor countries need physical sustenance, encouragement, love and some guidance in adjusting to their new freedoms—to vote, express themselves, and travel if they have money, to new locations inside and outside of their country. World and church organizations have gone into troubled areas of the world, but have consistently attempted to take care of physical rather than spiritual needs. Both are required.

The people in countries which have undergone great political and economic upheaval are victims. Crime has come to the forefront in depressed, civilian life. Place yourself in their position. When daily food, shelter, clothing and jobs come but slowly in their economic recovery, they take on the first help coming in their direction.

Depressed and despairing people are slow to respond to offers given to them. They are ignorant and lack knowledge when new treatment is offered in the reorganization of a country. Our Christian purpose is not only to help in matters of health and food but to witness for Christ.

In and around Sofia, Bulgaria, Richard Jordan[11] observed and experienced a depth to the culture that is not apparent on the surface. He saw the aftermath of fallen communism and a present political system that has not yet achieved economic recovery in that poverty-stricken country. Services such as electric power, water resources and other public works are neglected. The government alienates the people. Godless communism has taken its toll. It will take years to rehabilitate a country that inevitably failed, but slowly it will rise if given the opportunity.

Indeed, people are receptive to the gospel—meaning the harvest is white. People in countries where new freedoms have come about have fewer amusements, such as going on tours, vacations and entertainment. In contrast, America is "gospel hardened" due to unbelief, sin and an abundance of material goods, affluent living, and technological automation.

We are a nation on a collision course. We indulge excessively in our wants, needs and freedoms. In Sofia, people have imprisonment, poverty, unemployment, and so forth, but eagerly desire to hear and study God's Word as they build their lives.

Richard Jordan's travels were to exalt the Lord Jesus Christ. Hungry hearts were open to the plan of salvation and eternity. The people there seek stability in Christ for their families and for their daily living. However, reformation and education by man's efforts alone have never been successful unless God is at the center of life.

Elsewhere, the world over, hungry hearts are being sucked in by every conceivable "ism and schism." Open persecution and martyrdom are mounting as extreme nationalists, skinheads, Orthodox extremists, and communists have mounted joint opposition against evangelical Christians. In January 1997, David B. Barrett[12] reported that an estimated 160,000 Christians have been martyred for the cause of Christ.

Tom White,[13] director of The Voice of Martyrs, reports

that the Iranian government does not want ministers to preach in the national language (Farsi). Mission workers who use Farsi to evangelize among the Muslims are threatened, beaten and killed. Great risk is taken by Muslim converts themselves. They are rejected and persecuted when they reach out to introduce Christ to the people of Egypt, Iran, Malaysia and other unreached areas.

In order to support the cause of Christ, fund-raisers are struggling to forward Bibles and soul-winning programs throughout the world. The problem is that frequently what is being taught is not biblically or interpretatively correct. The first big thrust is selling Bibles. The second thrust is teaching Church doctrine.

Who would know the difference if the doctrines taught are correct? People seldom search out the true doctrinal teachings of the Scriptures. They lean instead on their own understanding and opinions. Bible illiteracy is worldwide. Sound Bible doctrine is neglected *(Proverbs 4:1-2; Titus 2:1; John 7:17).*

> *Titus 2:1 But speak thou the things which become sound doctrine.*

These things are forwarded in order to caution any of those who would spread the Word of the Lord. If any should preach God's Word, it must be with an understanding of the true doctrinal teachings of the Scriptures.

> *John 7:17 If any man will do his will, he shall know of the doctrine, whether it be of God, or whether I speak of myself.*

Euthanasia

Is America blazing another trail of unbelief among permissive pagans? Michigan has been testing in- and out-of-court physician-assisted suicide for the terminally ill. Oregon has grappled with and finally affirmed a new suicide law which would allow people to take God's prerogative into their own hands. Governmental and social institutions are playing God by stamping out sacred, human life.

Who is to decide if a poor quality of life should then cease or be prolonged? By whom, indeed, should be the decision be made?

1. By the terminal patient?

2. By his family?

3. By the physician passing judgment that such a life does not merit saving?

4. By the physician who values life according to his oath and will sustain life, but with medications to minimize the suffering of the patient?

5. By the patient experiencing through tribulation that God destines his end.

The answer must take into consideration this overwhelming conviction:

1. That the medical doctor is subordinate to God.

2. His role is to sustain life while administering pain medication to reduce suffering.

3. Life must be allowed to terminate according to the body's own, and God's schedule.

Check an expanded search computer magazine index in the library. You will discover the numerous articles on the "right to die". Most of the articles neglect to include God into the subject *(I Corinthians 3:16-17, 6:19-29)*. We predict that termination clinics will be as common as abortion clinics predicted by the turn of the century.

God gives us the strength we need to bear all things. When someone is in pain and feels himself to be a burden, we should share that burden. We can choose to love him more, in order that he might bear his suffering. Christ died for our sins. If we choose to love Him and obey His plan for our lives, we can defeat that Satan. We can bear all things. We can conquer all things by our faith and love in Christ.

Harassment

It may take long periods of time to legislate reform acts and remedies to alter attitude and behavior. Let us examine other types of sin, persecution because of deformity, race, religion, accent, age, sex, etc.

Sexual harassment[14] has been an age-old behavior of all human beings in most cultures, societies, organizations, etc. The problem has plagued humans with the same sex or with the opposite sex. Harassment goes beyond teasing. It is bullying, annoying, disturbing, and tormenting another person beyond his or her consent. Sexual harassment is similarly motivated behavior with sex-oriented goals.

Is harassment considered sinful according to Judeo-Christian law? Study *Genesis 39:6-23* in which the harasser is a woman. The lead-on, temptation and fleeing of Joseph against the accuser is classic to contemporary behavior. Harassment is unmistakable.

Currently, we have other kinds of intentional harassment:
- A medical doctor is unnecessarily invasive or insensitive during a physical examination.
-The silent harassment of, ignoring, and maybe resenting a person's value judgments, political and even Christian teaching.

There is little doubt that the driving force behind sin of all kinds is the depraved condition of all humankind. The reign of the Prince of the Power means that man will continually struggle against his old nature. Why a sovereign God allowed man, as the image and likeness of God *(Genesis 1:27-28)*, to fall into disobedience and sin is yet to be answered. God will answer that in Eternity.

Prayer in the Schools

Jay Sekulow litigates with high courts over prayer and Bible study in schools.[15] The Supreme Court has acknowledged that prayer is a private protected right of free speech established under the First Amendment. Sekulow and associates consistently challenge school districts in regard to the Free Speech and Free Exercise Clauses of the Constitution. The impact of their litigation can be observed throughout the country. Churches and local community groups need to continue their support of the Sekulow Christian Mission.

Their efforts may also challenge the intrusion of other truly unwarranted topics in the school environment, i. e., extreme liberalism in matters of homosexuality, drug addiction, abortion, the use of contraceptives by juveniles, and other aberrant and unrighteous human behaviors. What right has society to inflict immoral positions on young minds while denying them access, through prayer, to a living, loving God?

Only God knowingly retains the thread of life. Of all creatures, only Almighty God has the omnipotence to create, protect and preserve the minds of our young. Only God is the Great Shepherd (Hebrews 13:20-21) of life that unites all natural things.

We must allow God to become an active influence in our lives and in the lives of young people. Can you imagine what might happen if a significant number of our leaders began each day in prayer before the Lord?

ENDNOTES

[1]. Enroth, Ronald M. *Churches That Abuse*. Grand Rapids, MI: Zondervan Publishing House, 1992, pp. 75-90.

[2]. Solomon, Muriel. *Working With Difficult People*. New York, NY: Prentice Hall; NY., 1990.

[3]. Lockyer, Herbert. *All The Doctrines of The Bible*. Grand Rapids, MI: Lamplighter Books, Zondervan Publishing House, 1964, pp. 60-64.

[4]. *Ibid.*, pp. 60, 121.

[5]. Feit, Edward; Contributing Editor. *Governments And Leaders - An Approach to Comparative Politics*. Boston, MA: Houghton Mifflen, Co., 1978, pp. 442-443.

[6]. *Ibid.*, p. 187.

[7]. *Ibid.*, p. 374.

[8]. *Ibid.*

[9]. *Ibid.*, p. 398.

[10]. *Ibid.*, p. 420.

[11]. Jordan, Richard. *Macedonian Trip Report: The Grace Journal*; Volume 7, Number 3. Bloomingdale, IL, December, 1994.

[12]. Barrett, David B. "Annual Statistical Table on Global Mission, 1997." *International Bulletin of Missionary Research*, January 1997, p. 25.

[13]. White, Tom. *The Voice of the Martyrs*. Bartlesville, OK: April 1997, p. 11.

[14]. Cater, Ralph. "Sexual Harassment Is A Centuries Old Problem," *Statesman-Journal*, Letter to the Editor, Section A, October, 1991.

[15] Sekulow, Jay. *Casenote* . Atlanta, GA: The American Center For The Law And Justice, June, 1994.

CHAPTER TWELVE: Caught in the Entrapment

Spiritual Poverty in Worship

Many churches have changed their worship service to a celebration. Announcing the celebration is a gossipy newsletter, with cartoons belittling people or situations or questioning why anyone would want to be a mother, father or a parent. These may be amusing to some people; but they are bewildering to many others, who don't have to be enticed to come to worship with gimmicks resembling movie previews.

At the celebration, music and announcements swallow up most of the hour. Then there are numerous choruses of pop/jazz music, and young ministers who speak rapidly and are poor communicators. There is a great deal of clapping and laughter, and amusing yarns for itching ears.

A well-developed sermon with sound biblical teachings would be appreciated, but the Word of God is not being taught in the strictest sense. Money, sports and social events take priority over the message. The assembly needs to be fed the Word of God, not secular humanism. Indeed, the church is ill-informed and adrift.

According to a 1978 research study among numerous ecumenical church bodies, but not including evangelical fundamental churches, churches are spiritually dry.[1] This must mean they are spiritually deprived.

Therefore, church bodies are not effective in helping people to cope with their problems. As we approach the twenty-first century, people in general are totally apathetic toward Bible teaching.

Not having been taught the necessity of pleasing God, the younger generation accepts marijuana usage and sexual freedom. Why the change of attitude? There is a persistent breakdown in the spiritual values in the home, schools and churches. Schools have prayer and Bible study, but of what caliber? Secular humanism has invaded our social institutions.

The research stated that in the last half of the twentieth century, Americans as a rule believed that Jesus Christ is God or the Son of God. However, only 70% believed in life after death. The study further elaborated that people believe in:[2]

1. a resurrection of Jesus Christ; 2. a born-again experience

It is interesting to note that the Church is about equally divided between those who believe the Bible to be:

1. the actual Word of God, or 2. the inspired Word of God

These are the reasons, in the study, that people join a church:

1. Raised in the congregation; 2. Friends; 3. Good programs (must be defined); 4. Self needs; 5. Children need Biblical training

Some of the reasons given for not attending a church:
1. Not raised in a specific church; 2. Sports, hunting, fishing, travel, etc.; 3. Social activities with friends; 4. More time for self and family

A significant finding was that 20 percent of the people

wanted a deeper meaning than the church could offer. So their reasons for leaving and returning to a church deal with human factors. Even some ministers commit sinful acts against the members of the church.

Since these studies were of ecumenical, but not evangelical populations, it is evident that the spiritual poverty we see in many churches is due to their attempts to deal with social and human needs in order to win back those who normally do not attend.

In the second half of the century, studies indicate a gradual shift from a fundamentalist interpretation of traditional Christian doctrine to symbolic-liberal interpretations. Church groups dealing with a hedonistic society feel they need to entertain people to hold them in church as a captured audience. Many allow the carnality of the world to creep in and alienate the life of the church.

People feel unable to come to the altar of the church or to confess their sin. They run with the world, and they want the church to accept an unbridled condition and to operate with the world. Because of these factors we see significant changes coming about which are beginning to affect also the evangelical and fundamentalist churches.

People are trend watchers smashing down upon customs and traditions. Church officials avoid Bible doctrine, but stress unity without sound doctrine.

A 1988 extended survey of 2,536 persons,[3] which was a follow-up to the previously cited study, sifted out the following findings and showed the following changes:

1. Do you believe Jesus Christ was God or another religious leader?

	1988	1978
God or Son of God	84%	78%
Another Leader	9%	13%

2. Do you believe the Bible: as the actual literal word (31%); as the inspired word of God with no errors (24%); as inspired but contains some errors (22%)?

3. Do you believe a person can be a good Christian or Jew if he does not attend church or synagogue?

	1988	1978
Yes	76%	78%
No	20%	17%

4. Genre of religious training as a child?

Sunday School	81%	76%
Religious School	22%	22%
Home Instruction	28%	41%

5. Have you made a commitment to Jesus Christ , or not?

Yes	66%	60%
No	27%	37%
No Opinion	6%	7%

6. The percentage of persons who believed in life after death decreased, in general, from 1944 to 1988:

1944	1948	1957	1966	1978	1988
76%	66%	74%	73%	71%	71%

Likewise, over the centuries, differences in belief have arisen over sound Bible doctrine. As a result, these differences have split assemblies and caused disunity in the body of Christ. One thing we must remember, Bible doctrine does not cause disunity—people do.[4]

Specifically, the truth of the power of God's Word versus the traditions and reasoning which men have imposed upon it has always been the struggle. Moreover, when traditions of men are introduced, then we have the entrapment of religious systems and vain philosophies of men creeping in and corrupting the church.

Chapters one and two of this book discuss the depraved reasoning of men. Men's egos swell in religions, traditions, and entrapments of the world. This book alludes to the legacies of the Bible alone.

There are many sects, denominations, and writers[5] who do admit that the Bible should be acknowledged as serious reading for intellectual growth, as are the works of Homer, Dante and Milton. And there are those who judge the works of Marx and of Mao Tse Tung equal to the Bible as a guide to mankind. Others place the Koran, considered the sacred book of God's revelations to the Moslems, as equal to the Bible.

Although those works may possess moral or canonical character and be considered sacred literature in some parts of the world, only the Bible is divinely inspired by God's intervention upon the minds of its authors. This cannot be said truthfully of the works of Marx, Mao Tse Tung, Homer, Dante, Milton and even of the Koran.

The Bible may be read as literature per se, but for spiritual growth it must be read and received as the Word of God. This study is designed to urge the reader toward an arduous study of the Bible with that in mind. The study-management technique described in chapter eight may be used to great advantage in gleaning an abundance of inspired new truths, as the Spirit opens your mind and heart.

That inspiration may be summed up thus: *All Bible references resolutely point to a risen Christ who abides with God in the Heavens. No other book or teaching can claim that its inspired leader is living and reigning with God, for Christ is God.*

The Bible—The Inspired Legacy

The Bible contains the mind of God, the state of man, the way of salvation, the doom of sinners, and the happiness of believers. Its doctrines are holy, its precepts are binding,

263

its histories are true, and its decisions are immutable.

Read it to be wise, believe it to be safe, and practice it to be holy. It contains light to direct you, food to support you, and comfort to cheer you. It is the traveler's map, the pilgrim's staff, the pilot's compass, the soldier's sword, heaven opened, and the gates of hell disclosed.

CHRIST is its grand object, our good its design, and the glory of GOD its end. It should fill the memory, rule the heart, and guide the feet. Read it slowly, frequently, and prayerfully. It is a mine of wealth, a paradise of glory, and a river of pleasure. It is given you in life, will be opened in judgment, and remembered forever. It involves the highest responsibilities, will reward the greatest labor, and will condemn all who trifle with its sacred contents.

How do you know the Bible is the Word of God? The Bible is being attacked today more than any other book. It once was a best-seller in a world population of 5.5 billion people, with an adherence of about 6,700 languages. The points which follow may convince you.

1. The preservation of Scripture over the centuries is unaccountable in human thought and cannot be annulled *(Daniel 10:21; Galatians 3:22; II Timothy 3:12-17)*.

2. Archeological findings have proven evidence, e. g., the Dead Sea Scrolls, that the Bible is the Word of God.

3. Conclusive proof of fulfilled prophecy has been discovered in the history of the Bible *(II Peter 1:20-21; Isaiah 53; Mark 15:28-32)*.

> *Galatians 3:22   But the scripture hath concluded all under sin, that the promise by faith of Jesus Christ might be given to them that believe.*

4. The lives of true believers today are radically changed *(Romans 12:1-3; II Corinthians 3:1-18)*.

5. The Holy Spirit makes the Scripture real to the believer. You ask God, who is only good, to fill you with knowledge of His

will, wisdom, and spiritual insights *(Colossians 1:9-10)*.

Study *Psalm 119:9-16*. The Bible is God's inspired instruction book of life. Philippians 2:16 tells us to hold forth the Word of Life. The Bible, termed the Word of God, was written by forty-five authors under God's inspiration who wrote during dispensational periods spanning 1,400 years. The Word of God is the protector of freedom and reminds every generation that the Almighty God is there to reach all men. Christians grow in grace by inviting the lost and saved to eternal faith *(Hebrews 3:12 - 4:16)*. The Scriptures can help anyone with their daily problems, but the plan of salvation must take place as you allow the Holy Spirit to save you.

> *Romans 12: 1 I beseech you therefore, brethren, by the mercies of God, that ye present your bodies a living sacrifice, holy, acceptable unto God, which is your reasonable service.*

> *Colossians 1:9 For this cause we also, since the day we heard it, do not cease to pray for you, and to desire that ye might be filled with the knowledge of his will in all wisdom and spiritual understanding...*

Literature, science, mathematics, social and political science are the uninspired works of humanity that are unable to save you.

Jesus answered the unbelieving Thomas, "I am the way and the truth and the life. No one comes to the Father except through me *(John 14:6)*."

The works of men and the Koran can certainly teach good principles of living, but *it is impossible to deliver a sinner to a sovereign God by good works. The resurrected Christ performed a finished work of grace beyond human effort and offers us His righteousness.*

Supplements and Stratagems

Today every pastor needs to be fully informed about the so-called inspiring new ideas for the growing church. Here is a minimum list offered to churches with all the commercialism the world can offer:

1) Books, magazines, libraries, videos and cassettes of music. Bible subjects and entire readings and studies for all ages.

2) Design services, church plans, organize Sunday School buttons and award ribbons, labels, posters, and other motivators.

3) Election equipment, furniture, software, computers, memberships-ledger systems and attendance stratagems.

4) Fund raising ideas, plans for a new church, tours throughout the world.

5) Youth resources, counseling, outreach claims for all ages.

6) Plans for bridging the communication gaps between the generations and the sexes.

But Stay Close to the Word

Pastors who claim to be sound in doctrine must rethink, along with their church leaders, whether their preaching is vain or meager in reference to Scripture. They must analyze the substance of each message and stay close to the Word. Feeding the congregation is their fundamental calling and impact; not pleasing or entertaining the flock with stories about themselves and others.

Pastors, are you afraid of being rejected? The reality of your calling can be summed up in *I Corinthians 15:1-4*. Music, announcements of social events, and prayer for the sick and dying do take time, but feeding your flock is the essential part of the worship service. It takes at least twenty hours a week to prepare a forty-five minute message with Biblical substance. There never has been a shortcut in the ministry for Christ.

Hebrews, chapter 6, prepares the believers for a permanent trip to heaven. God expects the best from them after salvation. He is mindful of all our labors of love to others as we glorify the Godhead. We have a living faith and cannot become careless in the ministry *(James 2:17-20)*.

Surely we will receive blessings from the Heavenly Father. We do possess faith, hope and love *(I Corinthians 13)*, for the saints and from our kind, loving Father. Lessons are continually forthcoming from the Bible.

Gideon's logic in contrast to God's wisdom of the Mideonite defeat is an example *(Judges 7:1-25)*. What a decisive victory for Israel. They were obedient to God. God gave the blessings. Neither Hebrews nor Gentiles today have learned a lesson from the Mideonite conflict.

God does not approve of frivolous secular attractions for church services. The desire for numbers, human preeminence, participation in secular affairs has seeped into the congregation and cannot be used by God! Men's devices cannot accomplish God's purposes unless God directs.

God will raise up the church flock that is fervently praying and studying the Word carefully—on how to establish values and practice daily living in Christ. Many churches do exert a strong influence and support for the gospel. If entrapments are present, however, they may be hardened in their hearts toward the gospel.

May we suggest that Christians bus people from the outer areas to church or have some branch out from the community. God will raise up a new work among Christians if they spread to other locations. A building should not restrict the Gospel freedom that a good God will advance. Study *Matthew 28:16-20; Mark 16:15-20; Luke 24:48*.

Churches are diminishing because Bible doctrine and

> *Luke 24:48 And ye are witnesses of these things.*

spiritual goals are lacking. Observe the number of older people in churches today. God loves them, but where are the young and the families? What a defeat we are experiencing! God wants you to establish a church in the home, barn, store, even a school bus. Our priorities need to be clear according to God's plan.

The Disappearance of Christian Legacies

The Holy Spirit is missing. The love that is God's legacy is not among us. It is like missing the third verse of a hymn. Here are some examples which are prevalent:

1) Lacking hospitality toward each other *(I John 4:7-10; I Peter 1:9)*.

2) Leaders sitting always at the head table *(I Timothy 5:21)*.

3) Manipulating of saints—using a person for their own purposes *(Matthew 14:1-12; Luke 23:20-24; II Corinthians 6:3-13)*.

4)) Discriminating and rejecting those they dislike *(Esther 3:1-15; Mark 6:1-13)*.

5) Neglecting a person's gifts or not caring about one another *(I Timothy 4:13-15; Romans 1:1-12)*.

6) Having to invite you to dinner to impress others, hugging you when they do not really mean it *(James 1:24-25; Luke 14:7-14; I Samuel 16:1-13)*.

7) Ignoring certain people who have a different view, ignoring phone calls of need *(I Corinthians 4:3-4; Matthew 7:24-29; Mark 7:9)*.

8) Belittling people with snide remarks (that includes ministers) *(John 7:24;; Matthew 15:21-28)*, saying:

    a. They drive an old car.

b. They are on welfare.

c. They are divorced.

d. They lack openness with or ignore the stranger.

e. They are insensitive to their afflictions.

Here is a homely illustration: At a church seminar, the minister feels he has to tell a yarn that may ridicule a person in the group or in society, per se. Such low-level humor, to entertain or loosen up a group or for whatever purpose, is a sin.

Did Jesus tell jokes that ridiculed a person with a handicap or personal idiosyncrasy? Take notice of your tendency to make snide remarks. People may also take offense and speak up. When we hear yarns that ridicule others, we should pray and counsel others who are amused with such behavior. The Holy Spirit is missing also when:

9) You ignore or neglect to know how to discuss values and attitudes according to Biblical teaching *(Matthew 18:15-20; Colossians 2:23)*.

10) You lack trust in the stranger and you are even skeptical about believing in people you have known for years *(Jeremiah 17:5; Psalms 118:9)*.

11) You carry false beliefs, i. e., not believing in the triune God. What you sow you will reap *(II Corinthians 9:6-15; Psalm 112:9; Matthew 13:1-43; Galatians 6:7)*.

12) You forge an image for yourself and deride others who fall short of your selfish purposes and goals. (A power struggle in the church) *(Revelation 9:20; Daniel 5:23)*.

13) You rush from the church fellowship to eat the roast and watch the ball game *(Ephesians 5:11-16)*.

14) You are not utilizing members and nonmembers in the ministry of Jesus Christ. The growing cults do a bet-

ter job of getting people to participate *(I Timothy 4:8-15)*. Because:

a. You need eight months to study a person.

b. You protect the clique from outside influence.

c. You use the person for your own purpose and not for the person's calling. You show no interest in his calling and ministry.

15) You neglect visiting others. There is no time for the stranger, to make him feel comfortable, to invite him home to dinner, to a camping retreat, or perhaps to a potluck. There is no time for witnessing. Therefore, Christian witnessing is seldom done *(Isaiah 10:3; Job 10:12; I Peter 2:12)*.

16) You have neglected his calling and gifts. Instead welcome his help. Here are some suggested assignments *(Proverbs 1:24-27; Amos 7:8)*.

a. Offer him a Sunday School class.

b. Offer him an ushering assignment.

c. Offer him a greeter assignment.

d. Have him prepare the coffee pot, water the plants.

e. Welcome him into the choir.

f. Let him drive the church bus.

Life is a test. When the Holy Spirit does not live inside you, you hinder the other person who has faith in doing good works to glorify God. Encourage him. Help him. Pray for the fruits of the Spirit of God *(Galatians 5:22-26)* as you walk with him in the Spirit. We are careful that our food and water are pure and clean, but often we are neglectful of our spiritual food. Physical nourishment is essential for life, but what goes into our hearts and minds is spiritual and eternal.[6]

Literacy and Issues of the Flesh

Food for Souls

A systematic survey of Bible literacy levels of understanding has been reported with Bible statements. The results identified that some people excel but many are weak in the knowledge of the Scriptures.

It is widely recognized that catering, i. e., teaching better Bible study habits and processes in any Christian body will build and establish solid beliefs, attitudes, and feelings toward a Spirit-controlled life in Christ. Only the Christian who will allow the Spirit of God to reach him through Scripture—licking the wounds of his injured, poor, and undernourished soul with spiritual food—can receive blessings and mercy from Almighty God *(Revelation 1:3)*. What a precious legacy we have.

In this country, abortionists and homosexuals are receiving preferred legal status. Marriage is not sacred and persons of authority are challenged on all fronts. The children of wrath are perishing, and souls and spirits are eroding away.

> *Revelation 1:3 Blessed is he that readeth, and they that hear the words of this prophecy, and keep those things which are written therein: for the time is at hand.*

Christian bodies have limited ability to cope with the social and spiritual dimensions of these life-styles. At the least, they turn their backs on the issues. If they do demonstrate love and attention to the poor, sick, injured and twisted-in-thought, there is much to learn. Seminary, language training, knowledge, and wisdom are of limited value if they do not also nourish the soul.

Societal Issues

A similar damage occurs in this nation's influence upon

the social institutions of other countries. The sexual revolution has been going on throughout the world. The AIDS epidemic is further weakening nations. This terminal disease is cutting across levels of cultural and economical societies. Obviously, the sexual revolution has been accompanied by increased marital infidelity, prostitution and sexually transmitted diseases. Syphilis has risen 45 percent in the last decade of the century. Liberals wonder what to do about this rampage caused by the sexual revolution, since health care programs take care of the rich usually.

Yet we continue to accommodate the presence of these symbols of decay. Some clergy will even marry homosexuals. We countenance guest lectures and workshops on "How to Become a Welcoming Congregation to Homosexual and Bisexual Gentiles and their Partners", and provide participants with the unique opportunity to experience firsthand their counterparts in home hospitality, hiking, mountain climbing, and swimming. The participants entering the welcoming congregation develop special interest in dialogue, social action, and philosophy. There is no food for souls; there is simply no accommodation for lost souls.

In the broader social action, condom distribution and use of the tax dollar are more important than allowing Bible study in any congregation or school. The law of the land is liberal and weak, because man has allowed God to be removed from the sphere of influence. In His place, human reasoning has drafted a sick societal system.

The highest courts of our nation have not tried to achieve consistent sanctions on abortion, homosexuality, fetal-tissue adoption, or euthanasia. Instead these things are held to be legal according to the changed laws of the land. The court officially says any of the above issues can be administered as easily as establishing a charitable trust. The violation is allowing persons to do all sorts of things with their bodies. This ignores constitutional law and especially God's law.

What a mockery this becomes when a government official is sworn in by placing his hand on the Bible. Does he believe the Word of God? Nevertheless, he is taking an oath that he will uphold the laws of God and man. His authority is then final in the view of the world, but not with God.

There are seven things that God hates, for they are an abomination to Him. They are a proud look, lying, murder, a heart that plots wicked schemes, feet that are swift to do evil, a witness who tells lies, and a person who causes trouble among his brothers *(Proverbs 6:12-19)*.

Yet, the number-two killer in this nation is abortion. Coronary heart disease is first. Abortion deaths have reached 1.6 million each year in this ungodly nation of people. Read the ungodly life-style of Jerusalem *(Ezekiel 16:32-48.)*. They believed in false prophets while the truthful prophets warned them of their sin and the fall of Jerusalem. Is this not a lesson we can learn in our own lives as our nation has gone astray?

Since this country was built upon one nation under God, we must subject all the sad and sinful happenings in our present day to the counsel He gave us in His holy Word. When there is no counsel we will be flawed *(Proverbs 11:14)*. II *Chronicles 7:14* teaches us that if people are called in His name and submit themselves, pray, seek God's will and repent of their sin; then our gracious God will forgive sin, heal and correct the problems of the land.

Men may dress the wounds of humanity, but God heals them. Few believe in seeking the mind of God. Why? Because natural man is strong-willed and filled with desires and ambitions to follow his own notions. He has strong

> *Proverbs 11:14 Where no counsel is, the people fall: but in the multitude of counsellors there is safety.*

psychological drives and vigorously desires to achieve his goals with the energy of the flesh. In so doing he will not hesitate to put others down.

Money and power are gods of mankind. They build with hay, stubble and wood that can be destroyed quickly. Observe how poorly they plan homes, floodplain sites, etc. They build a memorial to themselves and money. The energy of the flesh is on parade.

How quickly men suffer when they encounter a loss of temporal goods. Many reach out and help those with a great loss in floods, earthquakes and fires accompanied by sorrow, grief and death.

A greater loss in human life, however, is reported regularly in the abuse suffered in schools, in gay clubs, in prostitution, and in the use of controlled substances that are devouring people. Commentators may want to discuss a hot issue, or they may bury their heads in the sand, but the issues do not go away.

Television personalities report and entertain us with problems involving morality without mentioning names. Those authors who do address the truth of today's conditions and report immorality according to the scriptures are subject to litigation. Private immorality is protected.

Evil flourishes and the citizens of our nation, for the most part, do nothing. We are out of control with our language, thought patterns, living values, addictions, and with our possession of the weapons of evil.

Some concerted efforts, however, to combat publicly-sanctioned immorality are being made. Pro-life, antiabortion groups march and lobby against the killing of babies. They ask those who condone such practices, "Why are you so blind to God's truths? Your parents did not abort you! They loved you. Jesus loves and forgives. Jesus does not want you to sin and abort others."[7] Others are rescuing lives, like premature babies, the separation of Siamese babies, etc.

Others are losing the battle to combat euthanasia. Dr. Jack Kavorkian is playing God by helping people to take their own lives. Physician assistance has turned into a reality in the State of Oregon.

What are Christians doing? Not enough, apparently, for the cause of Christ. On God's report card you are failing, collectively, in your witnessing to souls about salvation and about the burning issues of life. Is it not enough that we have war, famine and disease? We must now allow new evils! The reason a majority have now condoned euthanasia is that people do not believe that life is sacred. They may say they believe in God, but they would allow another to go to their death abandoned by Him.

How can we survive as a nation with the collapse of our Judeo-Christian belief system, and its attendant lack of respect for law. Liberal judges are removing prayer, the Ten Commandments, and the Bible from schools, public forums and governmental bodies. As we fall in moral ruin and decay, we are unable to sustain responsibility for our people. Our whole society will crumble. Yes, and then the United States of America may fall under a foreign military power.

When we turn away from God we will surely fall into ruin. Biblical and secular history have chronicled the destruction of great civilizations of the past. Why should America be an exception?

Wait till God shakes the heavens and earth. It will take place faster than a flood or earthquake registering eight to twelve points on the Richter scale. Even the Richter scale is outdated.

God is in control and He will strengthen you as you continue to speak out against abortion, homosexuality, anti-Christian TV, and international Internetting of wickedness and violence. The media and film industry offer glimpses of the most sinister activities they can imagine. They build temples of evil, because it is profitable to destroy the minds and souls of people.

But there is hope when we witness to those who are wayward. Love them. Help them to turn from their ungodly ways and unbelief.

The Believer Questions

Know, however, that the true believer is himself the temple of a Holy God and the Holy Spirit abides in him. Study *I Corinthians 3:10-23* and *II Corinthians 6:16-18* carefully and then ask yourself these priority questions:

1. How am I building my affairs? *(II Timothy 2:4; Philippians 1:27)*

2. Are my affairs going to be tested by fire *(James 1:12)?*

3. What could I lose? *(Matthew 10:39; 16:24-26)*

4. Which temple am I? *(Acts 17:22-25; I Corinthians 3:16-18)*

5. Am I easily deceived? *(Deuteronomy 11:13-16; Luke 21:8-12)*

In whom have you placed your trust? In yourself, others, God, secular organizations, etc.? With what misconception and alienation have you allowed the world to cloud your mind and understanding?

You keep taking courses to improve yourself, to earn a college degree, to build up old and new skills so you can be employed, to be successful and have a future with others—ever-learning, but are you never coming to the knowledge of God's truth?

What will you do with your life? Will you stay married? Why not? You think you are all right. Life and time will catch you in a snare because you are so right, so beautiful, so smart that you can tell God to condemn anything or anyone. But you may have this emptiness in your life.

Continue indulging like the Romans—in food, in drinks, in drugs, your coffin nails. Your ego, your morals, and your loose talk at the work place are sickening. The Romans thought their morals and life-style were complete. Complete in what? *Only God who made you can complete you (II Corinthians 13:5-9; Hebrews 6:1)*, not your complacency, not a cult leader or a religious order.

What about vanities? What sacrifices are you making in the vain pursuit of the right look and the most impressive feat in order to exalt yourself? Vanity, an offshoot of pride, is a sin problem that is constantly flaring. What work of the Lord are you neglecting in your preoccupation with:

1. Face and body lifts?

2. $100 bungee jumps?

3. Tracking "big foot"?

4. Abrupt suicide, which you are advocating—a clean demise in order to make a fastidious departure?

5. Gradual suicides, such as overeating, tobacco, drugs, alcohol and even stress?

You name the vanities and you have defined some of your problems with sin. Sin is disobeying the God who will righteously judge and punish you after physical death. Believe it, or you will discover God's judgment, with no appeals.

Reflect on the condition of your life. Turn your life and time over to God. Then your life will become meaningful because you have turned your body, mind and heart over to God who loves you. In turn you will be preparing yourself to be answerable to Him at your appointed judgment time. In the meantime, God will make you a blessing to others during your probation here on earth *(I Corinthians 10:13-17)*.

ENDNOTES

1. *The Unchurched America.* The National Council of Churches of Christ in the USA. Princeton, NJ: The Princeton Religion Research Center and the Gallup Organization, Inc., 1978, pp. 1-19.
2. *Ibid.,* pp. 1-19.
3. *The Unchurched American, 10 Years Later.* Princeton, NJ: The Princeton Religion Research Center, 1988, pp. 25-47.
4. Baker, Don. *Restoring Broken Relationships.* Eugene, OR: Harvest House, 1989.
5. Adler, Mortimer and Charles Van Doren. *How to Read a Book.* New York, NY: Simon & Schuster, Revised 1972, pp. 223, 293.
6. Leuthold, Reuben. *What Happened When You Believed?* Grand Rapids, MI: Bible Doctrine Publications, Inc. Third Printing, 1996, p. 72.
7. Baker, *op. cit.*

CHAPTER THIRTEEN: False Teaching

The apocalyptic passion of the Branch Davidians ended in tragedy *(Ephesians 4:13-27)*. David Koresh and his followers went on to destruction, having devoured themselves through their own reasoning.

That episode pointed out two dangers inherent in their religious vision. First, people can become so entrapped by the control mechanisms of charismatic leadership that they forget the difference between humanity and God Almighty. His followers had no qualms in obeying Koresh's orders—the self-declared Jesus Christ.

What a waste that the blessings and legacies of a Sovereign God are lost! The cult baits, brainwashes and intimidates the followers *(Job 5:6-8; II Kings 17:7-18)*. Their error can be discovered for they did not follow the fruits of the Spirit.

A second danger is present when a group believes a Gospel other than that of Christ. David Koresh and his followers thought that they were the only pure souls

> *II Kings 17:12 For they served idols, whereof the Lord had said unto them, Ye shall not do this thing.*

battling the evils of this world. Any day now, according to their fearless leader, the world would soon end. They were fighting the last great war of the Lord, and would not mind dying in the Lord's service. Koresh distorted, twisted and made merchandise of the Word of God *(Galatians 1:6; Ephesians 4:14-15; II Timothy 3:1-14; Titus 3: 1-6, 9-11).*

> *Galatians 1:6 I marvel that ye are so soon removed from him that called you into the grace of Christ unto another gospel...*

What a gruesome, ungodly bloodbath that inferno turned into. It cost $1.31 million in restitution to the families of the slain law enforcement officers of state and federal governments. What a waste of human life, time, and effort it required to put down such a disorder.

Reject in love any man that is a heretic, after the first and second cautionary warning *(Titus 3:8-14)*! Some of the surviving Davidians received a maximum sentence of forty years from a Texas jury and judge. Others received less, while others were acquitted of all charges. Some were convicted of voluntary manslaughter and weapons charges.

God will judge the sins of all. Sin will surely be judged more severely than any earthly court judgment. There will be no appeals and truth will defeat all distortions and falsehoods that men can devise. Jesus cares! Oh, how he will punish the unredeemed sinners!

David Koresh and others build idols to themselves in their persuasive teaching. A biblical example was Aaron and the golden calf *(Exodus 32:1-9)*. In a moment of backsliding, the Israelites worshipped the calf. It became the only thing they cared about in life.

Judaism had to strive with this problem. Who did they glorify? The excuse they gave was that they were human, not perfect. They did not acknowledge their sinful condition.

Aaron managed to work through his failings by repenting of his sins. He had to have a faith relationship with God and turn away from striving for the causes of his flesh and human reasoning.

When a leader establishes a model, shouldn't we be skeptical of another human's claim to divinity?

An interest in man and his capabilities should never be confused with the will of God and Bible doctrine. Though we have had false leaders through the centuries who have set themselves up as deities, we would never let ourselves follow them.

The unschooled or the easily-coerced individual may be hoodwinked into another Jonestown mass suicide, a humiliating Rajneesh departure, or a flaming end such as was experienced in Waco, Texas. When we discovered they were duped, we are outraged, but we must brush ourselves off and get back to the real business of true Christianity, living by the grace of God. Nevertheless it is well that we never forget the possibility of such a debacle happening again, and that we are on guard to help anyone thus enslaved.

Many of us are unsure every day. Some people try to innovate, activating all of the nineteen senses,[1] while others try to retain traditions. Every day is a day of reckoning, a day of accountability. Applewhite, Koresh, Jones, Bhagwan Shree Rajneesh, Father Divine, etc. are all personalities who have influenced people through religion, teaching, music, sexual deviation, and a personification of divine power that engulfs lives and thinking.[2] People submit themselves to such a leader, endure the mind manipulation, and finally even desire a certain indoctrination into abuse.

It may begin by a denial of self for the cause of the leader. Next comes a surrendering of material goods and services to the leader organization, until the individual has no one to turn to for support and approval outside. There may be an attraction to illicit sex and a breakdown of inhibitions in the person. Finally, he tolerates violating the traditions and laws of the land, and even taking his own life to justify the reasoning of the leader. Such actions and behaviors are in great conflict with Biblical teachings.

Although we may imagine that such forces are in the past, are identifiable and manageable, we may be alarmed to realize that such manipulations are ever with us, especially for vulnerable individuals, and they may be in the throes of large and powerful organizations that even our government is powerless to curb.

A large powerful cult group recently blackmailed the IRS into returning their tax-exempt status and first sued, and then bought out the Cult Awareness Network which had been a safeguard against such activity!

Many are buying their way into approval, step by step, with such organizations, letting them determine what are the sins and contaminations of their souls and bodies for which they are punished and degraded. Someday we may wonder why we did not pursue our fears of this rich and powerful group further.

Caveats Against False Teaching

Pride is conceit, arrogance, and an inflated self-opinion. It makes us all vain. In *Isaiah 14:12-15*, pride can be seen to blind the hearts of men. It started when Lucifer boasted that he would be the most high in heaven. After humanity was created, he would have preferred that God control man, that man would ever be proud and self-sufficient. But God allowed man to fall, to eat of the tree of good and evil, and to know sin, so that he could also learn repentance and humility *(Genesis 3:1-10)*.

Sin is deadly. In it we miss the mark of God's righteous and holy standard. "For all have sinned and come short of the glory of God *(Romans 3:21-26)*." And "he that committeth fornication sinneth against his own body *(I Corinthians 6:18-20),*" so how, except by God's wisdom, can we escape? Godly counsel helps us to flee from sin. Greed leads to other sin. Sin is outside and inside the body. Practiced sin leads to other sin. Sin leads to addiction and devastation. Yes, we are on target for Satan!

Beware of being locked into arrogance and violence as revealed in the media, such as white supremacist groups throughout the country. Presently they have an intolerance for cultural diversity. They reject the premise that God created all people from one blood and the life is in the blood *(Leviticus 17:11-14).* We are all God's offspring.

In today's world, the Prince of Power, called Satan, taints every avenue of human endeavor and every element that was meant for the good of man. Man then tests God, and every element and endeavor, with his own experience and folly. His old nature is an alienation against God. He is at war against God with his education and his psychological philosophies.

The Greeks and Romans possessed the same blind ignorance of God. *Ecclesiastes 1:15* reads "that which is crooked cannot be made straight" and that which is lacking, missing and even defective cannot be supplied and registered. Study *James 1:13-18.*

The true church is not an political-economic institution. Men lose sight of the primary nature of the church as a "called out" body of people for God's use in this world. Christians are God's ambassadors, with a superior covenant with God in heaven and Jesus Christ as the head *(Ephesians 1:22).*

Many people have come to know Christ truly, even after having been ensnared in a cult or religious membership for years. Though faithful supporters of an earthly church organization, they have never really experienced the truth of *II Corinthians 5:21*, where Paul exclaims, "For He hath made Him to be sin for us, who knew no sin; that we might be made the righteousness of God in Him." So there is a new creation when any man is in Christ. The old life has passed into submission and a new regenerated life lives within us.

All this is from God, who through Christ reconciled you to Himself, and gave you the ministry of reconciliation *(II Corinthians 5:17-19)*. He has entrusted the message of a changed relationship between God and man through the redemptive work of Jesus Christ.

Therefore we are representative ambassadors. God is using real Christians to witness and appeal to the world, just as if Christ were here pleading and begging unbelievers to be reconciled to God through our Lord Jesus Christ. Christ is the sinless God-man, and God poured on Christ our sins. Then, in exchange, Christ poured His goodness into each true or real Christian. We are clothed in the righteousness of Jesus Christ.

God's superior love, called *agape* love, which He gave to His Son and the human race *(John 3:16; John 17:26; Romans 12:1-3)*, rests in each of us. The love of Christ overmasters us, and we live no longer for ourselves, but for Him.

> *John 17:26 and I have declared unto them thy name, and will declare it: that the love wherewith thou hast loved me may be in them, and I in them.*

Spiritual Expectations

Spiritual expectations may include believers bearing one another's burdens in the Spirit. God wants real Christians to meet together *(Hebrews 10:24-25)*. When they choose to join a church, they assume there is an open truthful attitude *(Ephesians 4:15-27)* in God's kind of love *(Luke 6:27-38)*. They may ask:

1. Are their expectations of the church and those of the prospective member the same?
2. Are sincerity and honesty enough to clarify the church's expectations?

3. Is there a time and place for each person to respect another in the Lord and clarify their expectations *(Galatians 6:1-10)*?

4. Is truth in love more powerful than the leader's control?

So what happens if we ignore the issues? What happens when our expectations clash? Consider a case in point, is in the following example:

A group was going to study the Bible lesson that was assigned the previous week. Did the class of thirty adults come to hear the personal experiences of the teacher or to hear and discuss the Bible lesson? The teacher felt he must talk about his experiences during two Sunday class sessions.

A husband remarked that he came to class to study and discuss the assigned lesson. The teacher ignored the husband's remark. Therefore the husband, with his wife, asked permission to leave, since the lesson was not being taught. Permission was granted, while the remaining class members remained silent.

The teacher for the next few weeks was upset and did not teach. The pastor informed the couple they were wrong in leaving the class.

What went wrong? Who was right? The couple? The teacher? The Pastor? Why didn't the pastor arrange a conference with the couple and the teacher? These questions would grieve the heart of any sincere Christian.

If two or three had gathered in sincere prayer, the spirit of forgiveness and restoration might have occurred. Instead, there was ignorance, strong wills, and frustration on the part of each party. Sin severed fellowship in this episode. No wonder people do not attend or participate in church activities to glorify God.

At the end of his first missionary journey Paul gathered with the church and they rejoiced together for the many blessings God had given them. It was not a closed group, nor was the Bible class the couple decided to leave. The saints had allowed an open door for the stranger (a gentile) and extended fellowship and hospitality for a long time with the disciples *(Acts 14:26-28)*.

Relationships must be open, and charity and forbearance must be practiced with each servant of God. We are not meant to evaluate each other's performance constantly, but to encourage one another in whatever calling he may attempt. This must be observed among true Christians who are Spirit-lead and God-controlled in their relationships. Only the love of God through His Spirit can maintain each believer in peace and love with his fellowman.

Gifts Versus Lost Legacy

Teaching is a gift, whether one is exposing students to secular or spiritual truths. In the beginning, wisdom is given to the person with the ability and a call to teach, though he must study continuously *(Proverbs 1:5, 7)*. God has given that person the ability to communicate and the patience to apply the knowledge and understandings he has gained from study to his lesson and everyday living.

A person may have the ability to play the violin by ear, but arduous study is necessary to refine that God-given gift *(Ephesians 4:11-15; I Corinthians 12:28; Acts 11:26; 15:35; 18:11, 25-28; 28:31; Ecclesiastes 2:26)*. Give God the total credit. Then you will be blessed.

Search the Scriptures for your gift(s). A good study Bible and a concordance will help you search for the gift God has given you. A suggested partial list could be:

1. Management *(Acts 6:2; I Timothy 3:8-13; Genesis 31:38-40)*
2. Leadership *(Hebrews 13:17)*
3. Evangelism *(Acts 8:26-40)*
4. Encouragement of others *(I Corinthians 14:1-5, 24-25)*

5. Giving of temporal goods *(Philippians 4:15-16; Acts 4:36; II Corinthians 4:12-15)*

6. Hospitality *(Acts 16:14-15)*

Herbert Lockyer[3] stressed two vital principles concerning gifts which were applicable in the early church and also in our present day body of believers. They are:

1. Gifts bestowed upon people may be used at the service of the community *(Romans 12:5)*. The church is made up of many members, who are to render a service to others within the body of Christ and use their gifts to honor and glorify God *(I Corinthians 12:21)*.

2. Also, gifts are to be esteemed and coveted in the body of Christ in proportion to the usefulness which they have. Lockyer derived from Paul a number of lessons in regard to spiritual gifts that are to be encouraged and used:

   a. Everyone has a gift and should be able to use it.

   b. We must be humble to use our gift.

   c. Remember that the gifts are to be harmonious and to be used within the body of Christ (the Church).

   d. Be satisfied with your gift. For God has given you that gift to glorify Him and His church.

   e. All gifts are mutually helpful and needful, therefore they should be used faithfully for His glorification.

   f. All gifts promote the health and vitality of the church; none of them can be removed.

   g. Our use of God's gifts depends on His power, and we need to stay close to Him.

Some scriptures that reinforce the use of God's gift to each person are expressed plainly:

1. *I Corinthians 12:4-11*: "Now there are diversities of gifts but the same Spirit, the same Lord, the same God which *works in all*." The passage explains that the Spirit works in one person with a specific gift; and in another with a different gift. None of the gifts operate at cross purposes.

2. *I Corinthians 13:2*: "I may have the gift of *prophecy* and comprehend all the mysteries, and all knowledge; I even have trusted faith, but I do not have love for others." Do I really have anything? In the sight of God, I have nothing. God's love and wisdom are absent.

3. *Ephesians 4:7*: God has given to each one of us grace according to the measure of Christ's gift. When Jesus ascended on high, He held captivity captive, and gave gifts to all men. Can man now be given the grace, and the opportunity to express his gift to glorify God?

Some confessing Christians do not know or refuse to use others' gifts in the church. They refuse to recognize the gift a specific person has.

It may be that the leader is so enthralled with himself and his program that the gifts of others in God's ministry are neglected and their spiritual needs are neglected. Many ministers do not want to acknowledge gifts that would compete with their authority.

Does the minister ask various members what their gift is? Does he and the fellowship of believers accept or invite the stranger to use his gift in the church? Or do they wait and observe the stranger for months? Do they then ignore that person? Here are a few examples of discrimination:

1. The stranger is not given hospitality or friendship. He is not one of their ethnic background.

2. The stranger is not in the same socioeconomic status as the group. Members know his name, where he lives, what he does, and the type of vehicle he drives. If his dress is different or if he is mentally different, the church may ignore, reject and even belittle that person.

Members may discriminate against a person who has a strong body odor, drives a late model car, is obese, or who may discuss controversial subjects in the narthex of the church or Bible class. Such controversial subjects make church members mock, judge, ignore and even distance themselves from the stranger who may long for salvation. In order to gain acceptance, church members should try to discover:

a. his knowledge and wisdom from the Word of God.

b. his outgoing personality despite their conservative less-social tendencies, or vice versa.

c. the reason for his outward appearance, if different from theirs.

d. his ability to discuss and agree with their views on the issues they should care about:

1) abortion rights
2) contraceptive devices
3) birth control drugs
4) *homosexuality
5) the aged, euthanasia
6) health costs and long-term care
7) planned parenthood
8) family values vs spiritual values
9) politics
10) economics
11) public schools vs. home schools
12) retirement
13) mental & physical cruelty
14) rape
15) harassment
16) death

The Issues Which Divide

*There are scriptural examples which remain relevant today only when we visualize God's wrath on the unbelieving and disobedient person. The Bible does judge homosexuality to be a sin and the doer as a sinner. We cannot condemn or judge, but God certainly does in His word. When a person corrects his sin behavior, a loving God forgives. The real

Christian in turn accepts and restores fellowship with the person regardless of the sin. However, the issue is a dividing issue in the way we view our fellowmen.

Human nature is observed in gender studies. The revelation and redress of the oppression of women awakens revolution in some persons. Similar oppression of African-Americans is based on perceived inequalities and differences. Centuries of studies in secular and Biblical history expose Jewish persecution. Some are brought about by God, and some are caused by people and abhorred by God. In each study of all the time periods, people have been exploited, persecuted and executed by the hatred of their oppressors.

Attempts to correct such problems have never brought satisfaction or peace. Throughout many historic periods, people have reviewed the above problems and issues and have failed in their endeavors to solve them. Nothing but discontent and/or war has been fermented. It is so much easier to make war than peace.

War is expressed in many ways. War is always destructive, and it is doubtful that God endorses any war, even when elements are thought to be just or constructive. Some wars are not wars at all. For example, there is a war against disease. There has been a war against poverty.

Heart disease kills thousands yearly. The Food and Drug Administration claims to regulate tobacco as an addictive drug, yet disease from smoking, chewing, and snorting this substance continues to claim the lives of over 400,000 Americans annually. Tobacco-financed studies, however, provide every attempt to reduce our perception of such destruction. Surgery and hormonal and chemical therapies may prolong lives that are damaged by heart and lung disease or cancer.

At the other end of the spectrum, humans have the strong will to take a sacred life that God has placed on earth and even clone a life. People with the technology intercede and forcefully want to control life. Birth control, practiced since the dynasty of Egypt, has become commonplace today. Abortive measures have taken over to block out life. Those with terminal diseases can abruptly end their lives, with a deliberate overdose of a lethal chemical.

Man violates God's law to end a sacred life. Humans with knowledge, technology, and ingenuity desire to control every facet of life. In the now-generation of New Age believers, God is lost in the experience of living in the moment. Yet what they do and say may be radically irrational, unreasonable, and immoral.

We come upon the absurdity of human reasoning and logic in regard to moral values and integrity. Without the wisdom of God, men will make choices based only upon sinful desires and and self-interest. However, when men and women study and pray, they enter into a constant trust to seek the Lord God with all their heart and soul *(II Chronicles 15:12)*. When we study the Psalms, Proverbs and Ecclesiastes, from our youth onward, we are constantly reminded by our Creator to retain His commandments. The wisdom of God will reveal to you that there is no pleasure in evil *(Ecclesiastes 12:1-14)*.

People want immediate answers rather than to allow natural ways to manage life and death. God will give us answers if we patiently await them. For example, leaves dropping off a deciduous tree in the fall is analogous with certain insects losing their wings or a man experiencing a natural release of his sperm by nocturnal emissions. Prior to the death rattle, pain medication and/or loss of appetite allows the body gradually to shut itself off. Such a natural practice does not violate God's will and commandments. The experience of death is not so terrible that we have to hasten it!

From the beginning of life to the end of life, some people are determined to end life. They have made mistakes, and they believe they can correct them in this way or they doubt they have the patience and courage to let life run its course.

Therefore, they manage what they consider their rights, which supercede God's will!

If such human-centered phobic thoughts on rights, fear, sex, war, prejudice, poverty, disease, death, etc., could be resolved by men, then Almighty God would not have to enter our lives. People indulge in ruinous mistakes and demand their willful rights. Yet they deny that sin is the center of their problems.

Religion, philosophy, and psychology are only partial aids to life's problems. We talk about symptoms, causes, behaviors and therapies. The New Age movement or some other new trend by the year 2000 will try to teach you that you are a god and can improve daily. Even definitions change with cults of a contemporary mindset.

For example, the definition of abortion has been altered for the new generation. Forty years ago abortion (not natural miscarriage) was termed criminal abortion when a fetus was unlawfully removed prior to birth. As we approach the end of the 20th century, words like criminal, unlawful, and murder no longer apply to induced abortion. An induced abortion by any means, including the RU-486 hormonal technique, has arrived and is legal.

Can we hold insensitive anti-God persons to high leadership positions and gain God's divine plan for this world? Trying times are here. Leaders in high places continue to uphold unethical practices and values. An agenda—that is both pro-homosexual and anti-life—is deviously looting our households to pay for ungodly programs.

It is easy to be indifferent and ignore burning issues when we are not directly affected. However, if we are truly concerned for our families, we need positive changes for our children and grandchildren. We must be highly concerned to quell the rising tide of amoral sentiment that threatens us all. We are aware of high sentiments of people wanting to go another way, but the others want to go any way but God's way.

We need more courage and patience to endure it all! Consider David with all his blunders and Paul who was chastised—both needed to be sifted for service so God could use them in His plans. Daniel and Jeremiah prayed and did obey Almighty God. They were used victoriously in God's way. All people need to understand lessons God is teaching us, that we might follow and obey Him. He is preparing us for a better life of peace, joy and rest. Are we unable to put this in our thoughts and ways?

Is it an obsessive stance to be a fool for Christ? Every real Christian yields to God, who is all truth and cannot lie or deceive. He consistently chastens His believers so they may love and obey Him without any excuses. It is man's logic that is imperfect *(Hebrews 12:5-10; Revelation 3:19-22)*.

Centuries of history have proven that fact. Religion, philosophy, government, war, poverty, disease, etc. emerge from sin. Man ignores sin because of depravity and unbelief. He thinks he is all right. Embittered man wars against man.

Man also is at war with God. Secular and biblical history support this view. Man with all his abilities and energies has strived for utopian ambitions for centuries. But the sin problem is not acknowledged and cannot be managed by man.

Proof of that is revealed in history. The world has had very little peace except when Christ lived among us. The world, with all its understandings, finds explanations for everything but sin. Terms such as evil, carnality, error, and false pride define the fallen condition of all men, but they are not even identified. Do you ever hear people in the world talk about these when they discuss problems? Sin is a separation from God and disobedience to the will of God *(Romans 3:23)*.

Man will cleave unto his sinful nature until Christ returns to establish His kingdom. Study carefully Daniel and Revelation. Christ will reign and no one who has salvation will miss the mark of the glory of God.

ENDNOTES

[1]. Kovalik, Susan and Associates. *Integrated Thematic Instruction: The Model.* 3rd edition. Kovalik Publishers, 1994, pp. 79-83

[2]. Enroth, Ronald M. *Churches That Abuse.* Grand Rapids, MI: Zondervan Publishing House, 1992, pp. 93-108.

[3]. Lockyer, Herbert. *All The Doctrines of the Bible.* Grand Rapids, MI: Zondervan Publishing House, 1964, p. 246.

CHAPTER FOURTEEN: As Christ Works In You

Some people who really want to hear the Word of God preached and taught in accordance with His will find it difficult to find a church home. Sometimes people in churches are not very accepting of strangers. They may exhibit antisocial tendencies, such as a subtle rejected silence toward the newcomer.

They may ask in a kindly manner:
1.   What is your name?
2.   Where do you live?
3.   How long have you lived there?
4.   What do you do?

Then they go back to their familiar cronies and talk about nothing, or what someone said on a talk show. Do people have the heart's desire to evangelize, to be zealous to build up the church of Jesus Christ, and to embrace others whom Christ loves?

Lets face it: Most people dislike to hear the truth or change. It disturbs their mindset. Whether it is government, economy, education or morality, Rush Limbaugh can stir practically anyone within hearing distance. But you may not want to hear him. And you may agree with him or disagree.

Human nature is puzzling to understand. People believe what they want to believe *(Ephesians 4:11-16)*. They believe their political party or denomination is fine. Their system can do no wrong. Their system is their comfort zone. People are subject to systems, distinctives, traditions, and even prejudices.

Conservative? Or Advancing the Cause of Christ?

Many evangelical Christians, in name only, have referred to themselves as conservatives. Was Jesus Christ a conservative in his teaching and ministry as God-man?

Christ did not come to offer peace upon the earth, but a sword (the word of God) to divide mankind. There is a conflict of truth, and the Word will finally settle all spiritual warfare *(Matthew 10:32-42; Micah 7:1-9)*. The early believers, called Christians, were radical fundamentalists like Christ. They turned the world upside down.

How could they be conservative and advance the cause of Christ? Today, we too, with a divine nature, should be radical in the Spirit as we live and witness. Christ living in us extends beyond church membership, or attending a church with a big organ, or one with fine furniture and a commercial kitchen that can cater any affair in the community. Longtime members may be so committed to the organization of the denomination that they completely lose focus on Bible truths and team witnessing.

Many churches have different pastors for people of all ages, outreach programs and family services. In reviewing the seven churches in chapters two and three of Revelation, six of the churches fell into apostasy. The seventh church remained faithful and obedient to the ministry of Christ.

Apostasy Through Worldly Outreach

Listen to the Spirit as He addresses the churches. Today similar apostasy is discovered in many churches, and the doctrine of the Spirit is ignored.

David Jeremiah remarks,[1] "Today there are many Christians who are bent on changing society through government programs, lobbying activities, civil disobedience, and pressure groups. I do not find any place in the Bible that says this is the mission of the Church of Jesus Christ. The mission of the Church is witnessing to lost souls about the redemption provided by the Lord Jesus Christ. This mission is being replaced by those who believe the kingdom of God can be established here and now by our human activities."

David Jeremiah expresses it well. Are Christians being exploited by the world? If so, the Christian is allowing it to happen. Are they a target for Satan? If they are addicted to the activities of this world, and run with the trends of this world, they have no recourse but to weaken and eventually lose the faith.

While you are occupied with worldly concerns you may be too busy to be a Christian. How much concern do you have for serving your church? Ask yourself:

1. Do you ever entertain church members or strangers in your home?
2. Have you been an officer in the church?
3. Has the husband or wife taught a Bible study in their church?
4. Have you been invited to a church member's home for a meal or dessert?
5. Have you substitute-preached in your church?
6. Have you held church meetings in your home? Examples would be:

a. Mission or Bible groups

b. Hosting overnight church guests in your home *(Ro mans 12:13; Titus 1:8; Hebrews 13:2)*

7. Have you ever asked an evangelist out for a meal?

So many of us can be tempted by the devil. You are the free moral vessel to settle the one greatest decision in life. You have made many important decisions in life but the single decision to accept Christ as your Savior, King, Priest and Judge is an eternal decision you can make *(Revelation 14:6-7; 16:4-7; 20:11-15; II Corinthians 5:6-10)*. After physical death no one will be able to make an eternal decision for Jesus Christ. It will be too late to change your mind!

A seminarian was hardened when he was invited to read this manuscript about the apostate church. He claimed he was brought up on Bible doctrine in seminary. He believes the Christian today is confronted with a whole new challenge, namely that our rights as Christians are being taken away. However, he had no fears of apostasy.

Fifty years ago Bible-believing churches were separate from the apostate church, but the apostate church was identifiable. There are ministers who do not or will not recognize apostasy within their denomination.

Where have they been? Not involved, certainly, in the struggle to gain souls for Christ. Apostate organizations are growing rapidly. There are over 6000 apostate groups in the world. The church is not soft seats, indirect lighting, pipe organs, church bells and chimes, a big debt, a large budget, and an impressive membership with a historical past. It is not the burning of the mortgage or music programs with paid performers to entertain and hold the interest of the congregation. If it is not changing lives, its attractions are hollow.

Here are the possible criteria that will not be popular with most people attending church. Unless you turn partiality into participation and truly love your brethren *(I John 3:16; Hebrews 13:1-2)* your faith may wither.

Do you:

1. Participate in prayer?

2. Participate in Bible study in the home and church?

3. Participate as a faithful spiritual leader humbly understanding all sorts of people?

4. Participate in building up the membership in Bible understandings for a disciplined life-style in Christ?

5. Participate in a sustaining Christian service for all people in worshipping God and carrying out good works and truths for the glory of God?

> *I John 3:16 Hereby perceive we the love of God, because he laid down his life for us: and we ought to lay down our lives for the brethren.*

Grace believers must glorify God now! One must listen to the heart of God. Time is wasting. People do not look forward to age forty. All you have is old age waiting for you! The child will remark that thirty-five is old. The forty-year-old will think the seventy-year-old as "old" while the ninety-year-old may perceive him as a young kid. But the time is now to love God and participate in his ministry.

Age is relative. The only way to keep from growing old is remaining involved in the affairs of the Lord. Robert Browning, an English poet, reminds us with this thought: "Grow old along with me, the best is yet to be."

One can do much to help his fellowmen. God wants you to take one step further and focus on the affairs of the Lord. With this in mind, one can be a blessing to God and mankind. When we glorify God, we can focus on the sensitivity and complexity of mankind. God's love takes the stress out of man's ordeals. God's love allows us to pour out our love and attention to others who are needful of our ministry.

Do you ever tell someone you love them? What is the response you receive? When people know you love them, God loves them, whatever they have done. Do you love yourself? If you love yourself, then you can love your neighbor as yourself.

It is the quality of love we give to each other and the quantity we experience. Do not expect anything back in return. Now study *Luke 15:11-24* about a father who was ever-loving to his sons. Our Heavenly Father has an everlasting, unconditional love for us. Some people cannot return love, but, with unconditional love, you do not expect the person to reciprocate.

God wants balance in your life as the Spirit leads and establishes for you a Christ-centered life-style. Some Christians overextend themselves with activities outside the church in addition to their ministries. No wonder people feel burnout in their lives. Don't they recognize they are sinning to satisfy their own drives and interest? Unless he has health problems, it is also a sin when a person does nothing for the Lord but sit in a pew and tithe, regardless of age.

Neglect of Older Adults

So often older people spend their personal time in solitude. They have maturity, experience, and hardship behind them. Some Christians consider older people as "death warmed over," but the elderly can be mentors like Paul was to Timothy and others *(Ecclesiastes 4:9-12)*.

> *Ecclesiastes 4:9-10*
> *Two are better than one; because they have a good reward for their labour. For if they fall, the one will lift up his fellow: but woe to him that is alone when he falleth; for he hath not another to help him up.*

Older people usually are good mentors to young people who have problems in life. Among Christians, there should be no generation gap. Youth may not have had the experiences of relating well with their parents and grandparents; therefore mentoring can be a blessing.

The providence of God's purposes works in us and through

us. Since we are God's servants, let's not be giving ourselves excuses to shun older people with excuses such as:

1. They are retired
2. They may take over the activities
3. They are not attractive
4. They may be boring to young people
5. They have old-fashioned ideas and traditions contrary to the activities of younger people
6. They can be used, but only if they can be fitted conveniently into our church activities
7. They are set in their ways
8. They are so talkative
9. They don't have the time

No wonder there is a generation gap among believers! The allegations are not necessarily true and are tinged with sin in thought and deed. The older adult is often made to feel invisible at the dismissal of the worship service. After the service, no one really comes to them and visits as to a friend.

Can you love each other as much as Christ loves you? I *Samuel 4:9* and *I Corinthians 16:13-14* teaches us to keep the faith, be alert and courageous as we grow in the grace and strength of the Lord Jesus Christ. Despite the clear teaching of the Scriptures, thousands cling to the law of preference instead of being bathed in the free grace of God *(Galatians 3:3-14)*.

Of course, if a person has money, sings or plays an instrument, they might fit in. How can the church remain anti-social (silent) with some and social with others? Surely this is a troublesome dilemma in most churches. Skeptical of strangers, the older adults, the poorly dressed, the obese, and those of a different race, the church needs to address the double-minded prejudices of discrimination.

Love each other to the end that he will be a living testimony to others, sound in faith and in love, ever patient with others, and teachers of good things that are a blessing to the

Lord and others *(Titus 2:2-3)*. *Psalm 92:14-15* reminds us that when they are old they will still produce fruit *(Proverbs 22:6)*. For the Lord is their Rock of Salvation and there is no error in Him.

The church ought to use the full potential and experience of older people. Robb[2] offers a number of suggestions that can be modified and utilized among older adults in the local church. The Bible deals with real issues of the heart. Seek the truth in love. If you claim to believe in God your motives in faith will gleam as a true child of God.

Philippians 2:3-4; 4:2-9 strongly urges that we work together in harmony for the Lord. Accept each other in the Spirit and cooperate, without having anxiety and forming barriers with anyone. Pray and petition with thankful hearts in Christ for each other.

For many of us, one of the last things on our minds, as we scramble about this life that God has bestowed upon us, is sympathy. All the aged want from us, however, is a sympathetic acceptance, fellowship with saints of all ages, social and spiritual involvement, and participation in the ministry— not necessarily to be elected an officer in the church.

Human goals and superego will certainly discourage our attendance to the will of our Lord Jesus Christ. Those associating with the aged must realize that their motives are the same as ours. Is love really present when we ignore this segment of the congregation?

Search our hearts, Lord. Reveal what is below the surface of our hearts. Desires can be our downfall. Let us submit ourselves to God and then our Spirit-controlled lives will overcome fleshly desires. "Resist Satan and he will flee from you *(James 4:7)*." When we give in to our own desires and fleshly goals, we are vulnerable to Satan.

Accepting All Peoples

Getting the most from church means involving everyone in the responsibilities and activities of the church. The church that will *accept everyone* is leading them—singles, families, and the aged into a loving fellowship. When we know God's Word and experience the presence of the Holy Spirit, all of His children are one.

Every church has faithful people who attend every service. They reap great dividends. Others attend Sunday service, but seldom come to midweek Bible and prayer services. Why? When they are not actively participating, they do not gain a maximum blessing from church. The more secular our society becomes, the more believers need to expose themselves to the Word of God and prayer.

There are 168 hours in a week. What you can do? Surely you want to help. It is time to stop complaining and start trying to do something about it. Obviously one or two hours spent in the Lord's house, studying the Bible, is meager compared to the time devoted to life's *other* activities. Most do not give it nearly as much time as they devote to reading the newspaper or viewing television.

We do not hesitate to attend school, art or music courses, fishing and hunting activities. We visit the dentist and doctors for self-preservation. Parents and children, however, desperately need the spiritual/social opportunities the church can offer in terms of worship and praise according to God's will.

The Greek word *parakletos*, meaning one who gives support, comes to mind. Jesus was the first *paraclete*, who promised a replacement to carry on His teaching and testimony *(John 16:7-15)*. That replacement, or *paraclete*, that Christ promised is the indwelling Holy Spirit in every true believer.

Ministers and other church officials need to improve their strategies in a *get-involved policy* toward everyone, and not just talk about it.

It is often the hypocrisy in a church that makes a mockery of the true body of Christ. We know the church is not perfect, but we can improve it for the Glory of God. It is often expressed, "The church needs you." Then why don't church officials enlist more church participation? Also church members do not make a commitment to serve for any length of time. Substitues or group teams may be enlisted to remedy the church that wants to grow spiritually.

Never criticize the church or its leaders. Let's pray for each other and then do something about it. And there appears to be a silent, restraining influence toward certain people who want to be part of the action. Others could not care less; therefore they remain part of a captured congregation. For those who want to be involved, let them!

Accepting a Calling

The church may be conscious, unconscious or even evasive when it fails to tap the reservoir of experiences available in any church. Does the minister and/or church board make an attempt to search out the conscientious? Do they ask the believer, "Do you feel the Lord has called you to do a faith work for God? What might be your calling?" A suggested list might be:

1. Preach
2. Teach
3. Witness to the lost without an argument
4. Usher
5. Assist in collecting the offering
6. Assist in the communion service
7. Catalog books in the church library
8. Clean the church and grounds with others
9. Call on others in the community
10. Read and tell Bible stories in church school

11. Take part in Vacation Bible school
12. Help younger people with their prayer life
13. Advise and counsel others about finances
14. Perform to glorify God with your talents
15. Help and pray with the grieving
16. Record a variety of church activities
17. Drive a bus
18. Be a greeter
19. Take care of the visitors' book
20. Write a welcome card to a visitor and encourage them to return to worship and fellowship with the church.
21. Visit shut-ins
22. Help others with family values
23. Sing in the choir
24. Write to the sick, shut-ins, missionaries
25. Collect food, Bibles for local and overseas needs
26. Educate people biblically about the intents of abortion, homosexuality, euthanasia, divorce, drugs, alcohol, illicit sex
27. Baby-sit children, read to an adult and vice versa
28. Supervise parking for cars
29. Grow and/or furnish flowers for the church
30. Minister to youth of all ages in regard to their needs

No matter how hard it will be to have a called-out ministry, the Lord wants you to do it for His glory. There is much talent the Lord has given each of us. Let us all be allowed to use it.

There seems to be a hesitancy to call on those who have a formal education. The church does not usually use highly trained professionals (doctors, dentists, lawyers). Even retired ministers and professors sit as sterile spectators in a captured congregation because the minister and board may not want to be influenced by their training and experiences. If a learned man demonstrates humility his wisdom should be welcomed.

Let us recognize that world influences can contaminate a church, but never the *true* Church. Some churches will deny that contamination occurs. Therefore, we must recognize that the church is not perfect, but it can improve as an earthly organization, or better yet, into a biblical or spiritual one.

Examples of Biblical Ministry

In studying the Bible and observing the church at work throughout history, we see many ministries that furnish examples for us. This list is important, and none of these stand alone.

It may be the need to add hospitality, or socialization to the stranger, the family, or the aged in your life of ministry. Remember we want them to return, worship, and have fellowship with us. How can we best become ministers to each other?

As you study examples of godly men in the Bible, consider how the Lord might use and bless you as you emulate them. These are the biblical examples:

1. *Abraham*: God called Abraham to leave his family to follow God to Canaan and there to establish his family as the beginning of the Jewish people. At one point Abraham asked the Lord why He would sweep away the righteous with the wicked in the destruction of Sodom. In this ministry one would intercede with prayer for God to deliver the elect.

2. *Asaph*. He was appointed by King David as a director of choral music in the house of the Lord, and was retained in the same capacity by Solomon in the temple. At first Asaph and his clan composed the temple choir and then were set apart specifically for that purpose. This ministry plans the musical parts of worship services.

3. *Andrew*. Andrew was the first of Jesus' twelve disciples. After his call by Jesus, Andrew promptly enlisted his

brother, Simon Peter, as a follower. Andrew, as one bringing others to Jesus, was in a sense the first missionary.

4. *Barnabas*. Barnabas was instrumental in bringing the newly-converted Saul from Tarsus to Antioch and was influential in having him received by the apostles in Jerusalem. Later, the two were commissioned by the church at Antioch to conduct missionary tours. In this ministry is the call to hospitality, encouragement, and welcoming new brethren.

5. *Bezalel and Aholiab*. An artist designer, Bezalel took Moses' inspired ideas about the tabernacle and produced the finished product. In this ministry we see commitments to glorify God through building design, craftsmanship, decoration, and beauty.

6. *Ezra*. Ezra was a strong-minded leader-priest-scribe in the period after the fall of Babylon who led a group of expatriots back to Jerusalem. After the resettlement, Ezra was selected to teach the people God's Word. He did so with such skill that they stood and listened attentively for days. In this ministry was a commitment to teaching the Bible and providing applications of it to all ages.

7. *Jethro*. Moses' father-in-law, Jethro was the priest and chief of a clan who wandered the desert areas of the Sinai. Jethro advised Moses to return to Egypt and join the wandering Israelites. He counseled Moses to delegate responsibilities to others and acted as a desert guide for a time. His ministry included management, administration and director of Christian education for all ages.

8. *Nehemiah*. This Nehemiah was the great patriot and leader who tirelessly pushed a group of dispirited Jews returned from exile in Babylon to rebuild the walls of the devastated Jerusalem. Included in this area of ministry was a commitment to build and organize, and it can be applied to the maintenance of churches and Bible study.

9. *Philip*. He was originally one of the first "deacons," the group of seven set apart to look after the welfare of eld-

erly widows. He was also instrumental in helping the earliest Christians proclaim the gospel to the Gentiles as well as to the Jews. Not only does this ministry serve the needy, but it concerns itself with witnessing and carrying out the Great Commission.

10. *Stephen*. One of the seven initial deacons chosen to look after the widows and the needy, Stephen was told not to neglect the ministry of the Word of God. In this he was very active. So the Word of God spread and a large number of people became obedient to the faith. He was the first Christian to die for his belief. Stephen's ministry was in converting, and also in caring for the temporal needs of the afflicted.

11. *Timothy*. An early convert, Paul trained Timothy to be a pastor and gave him instruction that would move the church from merely adding members to multiplying them. He was well-qualified for meeting with new believers, for individual teaching, discipleship, and training to take someone else through instruction later. This is indeed a worthy ministry to acquire.

The Spirit of Individualism

In 1991, a news medium reported the largest opinion poll ever conducted on religious affiliation in the United States. Does Oregon have the highest proportion of atheists? Oregon does lead the way when it comes to people without any religious affiliation.

Why is Oregon the most unchurched state in the nation?[3] Next in line are Washington and California. Is it true that people in the western states are almost twice as likely to have no religion as people in the rest of the country? Is this a fact?

We all know that there is a spirit of individualism and independence in the nation. The pluralistic society exhibits a mentality that disregards God, as the media portrays. Daily review of the media exhibits this image. After all, to believe in God means admitting that we are not in control and that is not easy for self-made people to admit. We do not want to account to anyone but ourselves.

All this is to admit that we live in a spiritually depraved world.[4] For "Oregon launched a long-range program for restructuring and improving its educational system, called the Oregon Educational Act for the Twenty-First Century. Under the plan, high school students would receive a 'certificate of mastery' in the tenth grade and then be steered towards a college preparation or vocational training. The reforms would also lengthen the school year from 175 days to 220 days by the year 2010." The program prepares one for the world system. There is no provision for character education or moral value judgments.

Are character, education, spiritual values, and morals learned? Radio and television talk-show spokespersons provoke people daily to respond and discuss local and national issues of a pluralistic society. This country needs God and that puts those of us who profess Christ on the line. More than ever, we need to be the "salt" and "light" in a spiritually impoverished society.

Specifically, it is people who need God desperately. The Bible expresses in numerous ways that we need God and He has a special purpose for us. Surely He wants to conquer the spiritual resistance in every community in the nation; as a matter of fact, in the whole world. Revival is long overdue. God's unconditional love is extended to every part of the world. As you pray and study your Bible, God wants you to be part of it!

In our present world of social, economic, and psychological problems, we have not addressed our spiritual problems. The oldest news medium in the world, the Bible, repeats that man is at war with God on all fronts.

We are promised that the Messiah shall return to judge and settle all disputes among the nations! Nations shall beat their war toys into implements of peace. Finally, all war will end, but only his chosen ones will experience it. The wonder of this last dispensation will be addressed in the next chapter.

The Whole Armor of God

First, however, there is a direct appeal to you in God's plan and time. People will walk in the light and obey God and learn of war no longer *(Isaiah 2:3-5)*. Therefore, put on the whole armor of God, that you as an individual may be capable with God's help to resist the devil and all its manifestations *(Ephesians 6:11)*.

> *Ephesians 6:11   Put on the whole armour of God, that ye may be able to stand against the wiles of the devil.*

We see how God spared Job's life, but allowed Satan to dominate his life. But his integrity *(Job 1:6-12;20-22; Matthew 2:3-5;23:37-39)* and blamelessness were not preserved beyond the influence of Satan and his own friends. The finale of the narrative conveys that Job had not been really listening to God. Yes, Job complained of his suffering. But he had to turn himself wholly over to a sovereign Heavenly Father. When Job did this his sufferings were removed, and he once again regained the blessings of God! Even Job was justified by faith, not works.

This is a good lesson for each of us. We must have total faith in God and then He can use us for His glory. Pride, however unconscious, controlled this patriarch. But repentance bent him into shape, to decrease self and increase God. Read *Job, chapters 28-42*. Pride was his problem; the suffering was secondary.

Elijah, David, and Paul and others had to learn hard lessons in life also. We too, must decrease our individualism and allow God to use our divine nature for His glory. Very few of us learn the lessons Job learned from God. We need to smother our pride or whatever sins are of grievance to the Lord, in order to achieve the full-blown purposes of God.

The perplexity of mankind to believe and obey God is impossible. The Holy Spirit through the teaching of the Word convicts the unsaved to acknowledge he is a sinner. He is willing to surrender his will for the will of God. Then the Spirit can save the sinner by grace through faith.

Remember God can chose who he may *(Ephesians 1:4-14; John 15:16-19; 13:18-21)*. Although man possesses a limited free will, he is not to be ashamed. Scripture offers examples of human responsibility *(Genesis 13:9; 14:23; 18:5; 21:24; 22:2-8; 27:9-12; Leviticus 19:5; 22:29; Luke 9:23-26; I Corinthians 7:36-37; Mark 8:38)*.

In the epistle of John, Christians are reminded to confess a sin immediately. Don't wait! Confess anger, false pride, falsehood, etc. and turn from that sin as the Holy Spirit comforts and directs your heart and life. The Spirit places you under conviction.

> *Luke 9:23 And he said to them all, If any man will come after me, let him deny himself, and take up his cross daily, and follow me.*

You deal personally with that sin, for God loves you and chastens you *(Hebrews 12:6-8; Revelation 3:19)*.

God is faithful and just. He will forgive your sin and literally cleanse you from all wrong doing through the Advocate's blood. God's light will shine in your life, for a loving Christ will continue to cleanse and lead you *(I John 1:5, 2:2; Matthew 7:13-14; Luke 13:22-27)*.

Habakkuk 1:5-6 warns of the Babylonian invasion of Judah. Today the warning is re–sounded. We are warned[5] that our nation, too, will be punished for sin and indifference. People are out there pounding the streets and repeating the scenario that Judah experienced. See how many wrangle for civil rights, women's rights, gay special rights to perversion, abortion rights, animal rights and the G.I. Bill of Rights.

People contend and strive over all sorts of human rights. The first ten amendments of the constitution written by America's founding fathers permits every person certain inalienable rights. The freedom and protection given each individual insures the strength and sovereignty of the nation.

Today we are witnessing our nation on a collision course. Is it not possible that our nation's decline is connected to a loss of individual freedom? People have been given all sorts of freedom but are demanding a wider latitude of freedoms.

This is an age, like all ages, that man falls into the trap of his own righteousness. His freedoms have declared him to be righteousness as long as he is not breaking the law. Moses warns Israel to listen to God in *chapter six* of *Deuteronomy. Verses 2, 4, 6, 16, 18* and *20* command us to follow the right laws of God for they are perfect.

Contrast that with *Proverbs 14:8-12*, where men never learn the lesson that their exercised freedom of righteousness is the way of torment *(Romans 6:21-22)*. The positive end of man's sin, however, is that he is covered by the Lamb of God.

The free gift from Christ is everlasting life of joy. *Ephesians 1:11* stresses absolute freedom of the will belongs to God. We resist His will and seek to extend our rights and freedoms, ever learning man's remedies and cures, but never relying on the knowledge and wisdom of an unmovable, stable, loving and merciful God *(Malachi 3:6; Hebrews 13:8; James 1:17)*.

Ephesians 1:11 In whom also we have obtained an inheritance, being predestinated according to the purpose of him who worketh all things after the counsel of his own will:

Therefore, people strive over all sorts of rights, freedoms, and make frontal attacks when the death rattle is staring them in the face. Can we afford to travel a collision course of entrapments? Jesus tells the truth *(John 8:30-47)*. The truth is that absolute permanent freedom that really is a gift of God.

This country is failing daily. Russia and other countries have opened up churches, at least for a short period of time, but then have persecuted them. Right now, much of the newly-free world is teetering. The Russian people struggle with democracy for the first time in their long history.

> Malachi 3:6 For I am the Lord, I change not; therefore ye sons of Jacob are not consumed.

They are questioning the value of western capitalism. Also, the church has been denied the freedom of biblical teaching in its churches. The new regime has not brought happiness and prosperity as hoped.

Russian politicians are not enforcing freedom from oppression. The crime rate is up. Understandably, many people are thinking the old communist system was not so bad. Yes, they did not have freedom and the secret service was everywhere! They had shoddy goods and services and long lines to buy what was available. But tomorrow would bring as much.

The new freedom is scary. Old folks have lost their pensions. The young have no security. Nothing seems to be working, even the military goes unpaid. So much money is being poured into space travel while the people are neglected economically, spiritually and socially.

Foreign influences and spiritual ministries are making an impact to revitalize Russia, Poland, India, Zimbabwe and many other countries. Such foreign projects and interests are teaching the people how to start businesses—creating jobs and better living conditions and encouraging a return to God without persecution.

Bibles are being distributed but also destroyed. People hunger for the Word of God. They have been starved physically and spiritually for the unvarnished truth. It was removed from their culture.

As a nation we have had the Bible and have used it since the New World discovery over 500 years ago. Even the Conquistadors came in the name of Christianity. For a long time it was the foundation of settlement in the New World and the governing principle in the new nations.

The Liberal Media

Public libraries have many good books and resource materials, but moderates and liberals have allowed lewd literature and pornography to be introduced in the name of freedom of expression. The rights of the spiritual for protection against such influences have been trampled by the many who seek sensual pleasures and sexual titillation from such novels, magazines and other media. For profit these have been devised, bringing society the downfall of minds and bodies of all strata of people, encouraging them to have depraved sexual fantasies and out-of-wedlock experiences The greatest pleasure for the greatest number is the theme of the permissive majority, but this concept is untenable and ungodly because God refuses to enter human debauchery.

The liberal press aggressively uses and advocates free speech, supported by amendment rights. But just let a person witness for Christ in a public setting and he is warned to move or be prosecuted. Moral instruction has a somewhat better chance. Mental hygiene, philosophy and psychology are acceptable forms of expression in schools, libraries and peaceful marches, but not Christ.

We are reminded, as the apostle Paul closes his letter to the Ephesians church, that we are not yet in heaven. We have not reached the point of rest that remains for the saints of God. He reminds us, "Finally, my brethren, be strong in the Lord, and in the power of His might *(Ephesians 6:10-12)."*

Be steadfast, faithful, and endure the sufferings as Moses did against humanistic understanding *(Hebrews 11:25-35).*

We are constantly receiving strength from the Lord's Spirit—redeeming the time, for the days are evil. A portion of Israel is stubborn and the Gospel is hard. Through God's mercy, conditions will change. This has happened to help Gentiles receive and accept the gospel. We must be dependent upon His mercy today, for the power is not in we ourselves, but in close communion with Christ *(Matthew 23:23; James 3:17; Micah 6:6-8)*.

Billy Graham[6] concurs with prophecy scholar John F. Walvoord that the world is entering a period of crisis that is traumatic and ominous. The purpose of this book is to prayerfully jolt, poke, and encourage the best in man to study the Bible carefully so as to change your life.

Prayer assists us to get close to God. The church needs to go forward, whether you are kneeling, walking, or driving your car. God will always hear your prayers. God answers prayer in His way, not the way you think He should answer. You need to wait upon the Lord always.

We really are on a course of turmoil in the passage of time. We must speak up and explain the gospel to those who are indifferent, ignorant and out of touch with God. And do also plead the cause of the desolate, defenseless, poor and needy *(Proverbs 31:8,9; Job 29:15-16; I Samuel 19:4; Jeremiah 22:16)*.

Face the truth, for God forgives anyone who will believe the Gospel of Christ. The time is short and we need to tell the Good News in God's way. God will show you in His Word that you can do it[7] regardless of conditions—wars, riots, floods, earthquakes, the growth of dangerous religious groups and cults, government, business, bank leadership failures, and the exploitation of human and natural resources.

> *Proverbs 31:9 Open thy mouth, judge righteously, and plead the cause of the poor and needy.*

Stay Close to Biblical Truth

Is the church ignoring biblical principles? Evaluate your church and spiritually screen yourself as a grace believer in the true body of Christ. The born-again child of God possesses the Holy Spirit in his witness and daily living. He accepts the free gift of God. It is Jesus who died for your sins and mine. Because there was the shedding of His blood, there is remission of your sins. *You who believe are given eternal life!*

The Christian has gained a divine, regenerated nature. He grows spiritually as the Holy Spirit comforts, directs, and nurtures his life each day. Scripture teaches that true Christians love one another *(I Corinthians 13:1-13; I Peter 1:22; I John 4:7, 11; Colossians 2:2 and 3:14).*

> *Colossians 2:2   That their hearts might be comforted, being knit together in love, and unto all riches of the full assurance of understanding, to the acknowledgment of the mystery of God, and of the Father, and of Christ*

How?

We are to *admonish* each other *(Romans 15:14)*

Comfort one another *(I Thessalonians 4:18)*

Serve one another *(Galatians 5:13)*

Bear one another's *problems (Galatians 6:2)* At least you can pray, *encourage* and *help* to reduce the burden.

Try to be *kind* and understand each other *(Ephesians 4:32)*

Submit to one another *(Ephesians 5:21)* According to the will of God.

We rarely confess our sins to each other. Why not? *James 5:16* instructs us to do this. Do we possess false pride, feel embarrassed, on the spot? Remove the mask of pride that blinds you daily.

Our human nature conflicts with our new nature *(Galatians 5:16-18; Ephesians 6:12)*

We do well in praying for each other *(James 5:16; John 15:7-10)* silently and in public.

How do we encourage one another *(Hebrews 3:13)*?

Is it hard for us to forgive one another *(Colossians 3:13)*?

The Lord is our example to follow. Jesus teaches us many principles in life. Study *Matthew, chapters 4 to 6.* Now grow in the wisdom of God.

Teach and admonish one another with God's wisdom *(Colossians 3:16).*

Learn to be content and thankful in any and every situation for He strengthens you *(Philippians 4:12-13).*

James 5:16   Confess your faults one to another, and pray one for another, that ye may be healed. The effectual fervent prayer of a righteous man availeth much.

Lessons That Lead

How do I learn the lessons that lead to contentment? Do we respond anxiously or do we respond with spiritual stability? When everything is falling apart, do I have contentment? Listen, said Paul, my needs are not being met, but I am content *(Philippians 4:11-13; Psalm 16:6; Luke 3:14; I Timothy 6:8; Hebrews 13:5; II Corinthians 10:12-18).*

Therefore I am truly content when all my needs are not met. God's sovereign power is in my weakness. Christ, who is sufficient, directs my life. His power is available for us and for our

Colossians 3:16 Let the word of Christ dwell in you richly in all wisdom; teaching and admonishing one another in psalms and hymns and spiritual songs, singing with grace in your hearts to the Lord

problems in order to take care of all circumstances.

We are *called* into fellowship with our Savior. God is faithful and always with us *(I Corinthians 1:9)*.

It is more blessed to give, in service, monetarily, and with deep concern *(Acts 20:32-35)*.

John 15:3-10 teaches that the Word cleanses us as the indwelling Spirit works in us. When we abide in Christ, all mysteries presented in Scripture are explained. In this text, positive Christian behavior expresses love, good judgment, great spiritual wisdom, and unmatched intelligence in bearing fruit for the glory of the Lord*(I John 3 & 4; John 15: 4-5, 8)*.

John 14:16, 17 teaches us that we have fellowship with the Holy Spirit *(Romans 8:16; John 14, 16, 17)*.

Holy living means speaking the truth one member to another. Abstain from all forms of evil for you do not want to grieve the Holy Spirit of God. You have been sealed by the Holy Spirit until the day of redemption *(Ephesians 4:25-30)*.

The Christian loves to confess Christ before men *(Matthew 10:32; I John 4:15; Romans 10:9-10)*.

Be merciful, even kind to all as your Father is merciful *to you (Luke 6:35-36)*.

Precious is my meditation of Him. How precious are your thoughts unto God the Father *(Psalm 104:34; 139: 17-18)*.

Beloved brethren, always be steadfast, unmovable, always succeeding in the work of the Lord. Your labor is not wasted in the Lord *(I Corinthians 15:58; I Corinthians 16:13)*.

Remember to allow the Word of Christ to live in you richly with *all* wisdom *(Colossians 3:16-17)*. Then you can teach and encourage others in praise as it is in your heart. You are glorifying God.

You are requested to bless God daily and praise His name for eternity *(Psalms 34:1-4, 145:2)*. Also acknowledge the greatness of God. Praise Him for His mighty acts *(Psalm 150)*.

Ask Him through prayer to show us His mercy and loving kindness. "Give us Thy salvation, Lord *(Psalm 85:7)."* Recognize that you are a sinner. Ask for mercy for your depraved condition, for he that humbleth himself shall be exalted *(Luke 18:13-14).*

Men think like men. Therefore must they "stand fast in the faith, quit you like men, be strong *(I Corinthians 16:13-20)."* Men may sink lower in their acts than the animals. Animals don't punish or beat their mates or use alcohol and drugs. Still man boasts about being more intelligent than the lower species. *Who is more sinful than man?*

"O that my ways were directed to keep thy statutes *(Psalm 119:5)!"* You have loved me and I am unable to love you. Order my steps in life from your Word. May iniquity *have* not dominion (control) over me *(Psalm 133).*

Hope is revealed when one is not *ashamed* of the Gospel of Christ. One recognizes his condition and then simply believes by faith that he will receive salvation from God through His Son. Yes, we have all hope and faith in the promises of the Scriptures *(Romans 15:4-5; Romans 1:16-17; Habakkuk 2:4; I Peter 3:13-16).*

Love not the world, neither the things that are in the world: the drunken driver, the child and woman abuser, the drug addict, the person seeded with pride, etc. If a man or woman loves the world, the love of the Father is not in him.

> *Habakkuk 2:4 Behold, his soul which is lifted up is not upright in him: but the just shall live by his faith.*

How can it be? For all that are in the world, the lust of the flesh and the pride of life, is not from the Father, but the world system. These are the pleasures of the world. The world and its lusts are passing away, but he who ever does the will of God lives forever, and so we must witness daily *(Matthew 7:13-14; Luke 13:23-27).*

Believers and skeptics, many Antichrists will come and

go. People will consistently break the laws of the land.

What privileges and duties have you in this life? If you are in Christ, you have a Holy Spirit life-style. You cannot burn out. Christ is your focus. What manner of love the Father has given us in allowing us to be called children of God! Whoever continually abides in Christ does not habitually sin; inasmuch as whoever lives in sin has not seen Christ nor come to know him.

Let no one deceive you, children of God. He who is committing sin is of the devil. He drives like a demon on the highway, ruthlessly cutting off people, and speeding to the traffic light. Disobeying the rules of driving is one manifestation of sin, but he who is righteous has the righteousness of Christ. This applies to rich and poor alike.

You are a child of God. God loves you. The police are God's agents and that is why an officer confronts you. God does not want you to make a deadly decision on the roadway. When we make a living decision for Christ, we have migrated out of death into everlasting life.

Christian Influence Among Nations

The merits of true Christianity go far beyond the virtues of moralists, atheists, agnostics, Muslims, Jews, Confucians, Buddhists, Hindus or any religious cults. Martin DeHaan of Radio Bible Class Ministries reports Muslim Turkey as having less than 0.1 percent claim of any kind of Christian affiliation.[8] Turkey was once a land of the Bible. Within its borders:

1. Noah landed on Mt. Ararat.

2. Abraham received God's call from Haran.

3. Paul was born in Tarsus and returned to that city after his conversion. He planted many churches in that country.

Chapter 14:As Christ Works In You

4. Peter addressed his first letter to Christians dispersed in Pontus, Galatia, Cappadocia, Asia, and Bethynia. Here we discover Colosse, Hierapolia, along with the seven churches of Revelation.

5. In AD 312 Roman Emperor Constantine legalized the Christian faith.

6. For 1000 years Christian dominance reigned. You will note the seven churches in Revelation maintained their presence and spiritual effectiveness in the world. Revelation reports the spiritual deterioration of most of those churches.

How can we forget the failure of the church and the rise of modern Turkey in Muslim thought and belief? The author has observed the establishment of numerous neighborhood mosques in America. Every Christian is to serve our Lord and witness to the unsaved in a loving manner until the Lord returns to every region on the globe.

Over 850 million Indians are followers of Hinduism. Only a few basics are held in common by almost all Hindus, one of these beliefs being that if a person is born a woman or is poor or suffers in this life it is because he or she has sinned in former lives (karma).

All Hindus believe that there is a God, but that belief ranges from God as an impersonal reality to God being within one's heart. Buddhism, Sikhism and Jainism are considered by many to be reforms of Hindu belief. Since most Hindus believe that the divine power has been incarnated many times, Jesus Christ is seen as one more holy man like Buddha or Muhammad; Christianity is considered just one more acceptable way of life.

Adding another god to their pantheon of 33 thousand gods is simple. One may proselytize and convert a person to Christianity in those religious groups only to find that they then consider themselves a better Muslim or Hindu.

Rejecting all other religions to claim Jesus Christ as the only Way is repugnant to Hindus. *Christianity does not make the world a better place. It is Christ living within a person's life that makes a difference.* No one else has been recognized as a God-man who died for our sins, arose from the dead and is now in heaven with God.

The above-mentioned bodies certainly may be helpful in improving the world as a better place. All the bodies, including Christianity, do consider the favorable merits of teaching kindness, consideration, compassion, hospitality, love, etc. Also, they considered the negative aspects and implication of sin, such that they must not lie, cheat, curse, murder, hate, etc.

Steps to Eternity

How does true Christianity go far beyond ordinary virtues *(I Timothy 2:5)*? The recognized Berean example in *Acts 17:11-12* was that they tested every fact against the prophets. The Bereans did not act on impulse and arrive at simple solutions. The Bereans, as well as the true Christians today, lived in a discordant world, but became inheritors of eternity.

I Timothy 2:5 For there is one God, and one mediator between God and men, the man Christ Jesus...

Here are the beliefs and steps, then as now, that one must accept and initiate for eternal life.

1. Jesus Christ as God-man entered this world conceived by the Holy Spirit in the virgin Mary.

2. Jesus Christ, God in the form of man, died for the sins of this world (past, present, future).

3. Jesus Christ shed His blood once on the cross for the remission of sin so anyone, anywhere could have eternal

life.

4. Jesus Christ arose from the dead; God in the form of humanity came to minister and to give His life a ransom for many.

5. Because of the sovereignty of God, Jesus Christ can elect anyone to receive the free gift of salvation. Anyone can acknowledge he is a sinner. When the sinner confesses his sins, God, through the Savior the Lord Jesus Christ, will give anyone the free gift of eternal life by simply believing by faith in a merciful loving God who offers grace (unmerited favor) to all that are chosen by Him.

6. In both cases cited, there is a remission of sin only through the blood of Jesus Christ.

7. The free gift of salvation is not achieved by being good or by working yourself into heaven for everlasting life. You cannot do anything but accept the free gift or reject it!

8. By confessing your sins, and believing Christ is loving and merciful to forgive you of all your sins and cleanse you from all unrighteousness.

9. Christ gives you a new nature as the Holy Spirit enters and lives within you. The person walks, talks, works, lives as the Holy Spirit comforts, directs, leads, your life daily as a child of God.

10. Still the old nature of the mortal believer possesses the perishing sinfulness of the flesh *(II Corinthians 4:16-18)*. By God's grace the Spirit counters our choice to sin. The soul and spirit (inner man) is immortal and is saved from torment. Soul and spirit are fully conscious between physical death and resurrection of the body. The newly resurrected body lives into all eternity *(John 6:51; Galatians 5:13-26; I Peter 1:3-23)*.

In the meantime stand firm in your faith for the strength and power of the Lord is within you. Resist Satan and he will flee from you *(Ephesians 6:11-18)*. God calls us for one purpose, to serve Him and to equip each of us for the building up of the church, the body of Christ *(Ephesians 4:12-16)*.

Sins are covered by the constant washing of your sins through the shed blood of Christ. Without the shedding of Christ's blood, there is no remission of sins. The true Christian is sealed by the Spirit until the day of redemption, when the believer joins his soul and spirit and receives a glorified body *(Ephesians 4:30; Philippians 3:20-21; I John 1:9)*.

For now, whoever has the world's goods and beholds his brother in need and shuts his heart against him, how can the love of God abide in him? Let us not love in word nor in talk, but in deed and in truth. By this we shall come to know that we are really of the truth and shall be persuaded in our hearts of His presence whenever our hearts condemn us *(James 1:26-27)*.

How? Because God is greater than our hearts and knows *all* things. Beloved, if our hearts (conscience) condemn us, we have living confidence toward God that whatever we ask we are receiving from our Savior Jesus Christ, because we are keeping his commandments and doing those things that are pleasing in his sight and not in our own understanding of life.

We should believe in the name of the Son of God, Jesus Christ, and love one another as He instructed us to do. Do not believe every spirit, beloved, but test the spirits to see whether they are of God *(I John 4:1)*.

> *I John 4:1 Beloved, believe not every spirit, but try the spirits whether they are of God: because many false prophets are gone out into the world.*

There are many false teachers. By this you know that the Holy Spirit of God and every other spirit that confesses that Christ came in the flesh is from God. Therefore every spirit which confesses him not, is not from God.

Yungen expresses it in current vernacular; "One of the most common New Age attitudes is that there are many paths to God and that it is wrong to judge or condemn another person's path because not all people are suited for the same one. They argue that each one should find the path best for them."[9]

Read *Matthew 7:22-23*. To those who cried Lord! Lord! Christ professed He never knew them and tells them to depart from Him. Your work is a work of iniquity! Study *John 14:6-27*, for Christ is the only way. Remember children of God, you have conquered the children of wrath because He that is within you is greater than he that is in this world *(I John 3:20-23; Matthew 6:33)*.

They are of the world; they think and act like the world; and for this reason they speak as of the world with their vile remarks, finger gestures, body exposures, and willful disregard for your freedoms. Yes, and the world listens to them.

Pagans and some Neo-Christians are so busy they would not give you the time of day. The point is to listen and understand God.

Test Every Precept

The Christian follower of Jesus Christ tests every principle on which his faith is grounded in the Scriptures. True Christians hold to the Word of God in order to keep their minds in Christ *(Philippians 2:5)* and avoid heresy *(Colossians 2:4,18; Isaiah 29:2)*. Study each passage prayerfully *(I Corinthians 2:14-16; Isaiah 55:6-13)*.

No other teaching group has a living Savior today. They do not receive from a Savior the free gift of salvation, for they do not have a God who came through a divine virgin birth from heaven. No other leader has been physically resurrected after His blood was shed for everyone's sins.

It is impossible to work yourself into heaven, but it is by simple faith that you agree you are sinful and you turn your life over to the loving Savior. He has done everything for you. Remember, good works come out of your faith *(John 3:18; Nehemiah 13:14; John 8:41; Acts 7:22; 19:18-20; Colossians 3:17; James 1:25; Proverbs 16:3; Matthew 5:16; Deuteronomy 4:28-29).*

> *Nehemiah 13:14*
> *Remember me, O my God, concerning this, and wipe not out my good deeds that I have done for the house of my God, and for the offices thereof.*

Remember, to test the reasoning that the Spirit of truth is contrary to the spirit of error *(Matthew 6:33; 7:7; John 5:20; John 8:50).* In a 100 years from now it will not matter—what kind of house you live in—what kind of car you drive—how much money you saved in a bank account or bond collection—nor what your clothes looked like.

How shall we escape if we do not pay attention to the God-given free gift of salvation for all men. Striving to be a little bit better because you were an important person in this life is an expression of righteous complacency *(Hebrews 2:1-13).* Learn in the Spirit to imitate God and be His beloved child *(Ephesians 5:1-14).* Believers, with a divine nature, will not eliminate besetting sin in their lives completely, but will seek the wisdom of Almighty God by which moral and spiritual living can be experienced daily *(Romans 1:16-17).*

Who shall separate us from the love of Christ? Shall anguish, or calamity, or persecution, or famine? Shall nakedness, or peril, or sword? As it is written in *Psalm 44:22*: "For your sake we are killed all the day long; we were accounted as sheep for the slaughter."

But in all these things we have full victory through the grace of a good God who demonstrated his love for us. "For I am truly persuaded that neither death, nor life, neither angels, nor principalities, nor powers, neither this present world nor the world to come, neither height nor depth, nor anything else in all creation, shall be able to separate us from the love of God, which is in our Lord Jesus Christ *(Romans 8:38-39)*."

May you open your mouth boldly, and make known the mystery of the Gospel. You are an ambassador in chains. Pray that you may proclaim it boldly as you ought to speak *(Ephesians 6:19-20; John 16:24-30)*. May the beauty of Jesus Christ be seen in you as you walk with Him daily in this life into eternity.

Love your enemies *(Matthew 5:44)*, as difficult as it may be. Some of us have already suffered, we proclaim places of fierce persecution. It will become worse in the future. Observe world and local situations. We must ardently love even his worst enemy, in spite of the evil they do us *(II Corinthians 4:7-10)*.

Stop reading this page and write down on the margin the names of those who have hurt you the most. Then write next to the name(s) "Beloved" and "Forgiven." God looks upon forgiven scarlet sins as if they were white as snow. Exercise yourself by doing the same, especially since you know that all things, absolutely all things, including those that tear your heart, work together for the good if you love the Lord. Love is the badge of a Spirit-controlled Christian. Christian rights have no place in the love of the Lord.

Christ taught us to make a distinction between sin and sinners. Hate lies, but love liars, is an example. Not all Christians agree with us. Christians want to reach people in the field, love them, and feed them while God harvests people Himself through His workers. *In Matthew 28*, Jesus commanded the disciples to "Go teach all nations!"

Words cannot express how excited we are with the opportunity to live out His command of the Good News for the few years He has given us. Many appeals have been made to accept the plan of salvation of God. After death, no appeals are possible. Remember, God loves you!

A potpourri of ideas loosely connected to the sin question that affects every individual, social, business and government institution might be mentioned: Samuel Bannister Harding's text entitled *New Medieval and Modern History* ; a 1438-page volume entitled *Chronicle of the 20th Century* edited by Clifton Daniel, 1987; and Newt Gingrich's book entitled *To Renew America* . There are many other examples of sin-in-review one could mention.

Carry The News!

Away to the east of us;
Away to the west of us;
Away to the south, and the north,
Are folks who are seeking
Relief while we're speaking,
And the Master had bid us "Go Forth!"

To all lands He sends us,
For all peoples lends us
The gift of His son to present;
'Tis the love He has for them,
His gift will restore them
From anguish to Peaceful content.

Then go, if the call come,
Or, send of your income,
To nations in heathendom's thrall;
Fill mite boxes cheerfully;
Give them out prayerfully
That Jesus may come to them all.

For all heathen nations
Are our obligations;
Cease not, then, an earnest appeal;
And, as sister and brother,
We'll help one another,
Then Jesus in us we'll reveal.

by Lillie Flanders Overholt

ENDNOTES

[1]. Jeremiah, David and C. C. Carlson. *Escape the Coming Night.* Dallas, TX: Word Publishing, 1990, p. 58.

[2]. Robb, Thomas B. *Growing Up: Pastoral Nurture For The Later Years.* New York, NY: Haworth Press, 1991.

[3]. *The Unchurched American.* Princeton, NJ: Princeton Religion Research Center, 1971.

[4]. Colson, Chuck and Jack Eckerd. *Why America Doesn't Work.* Dallas, TX: Word Publishing, 1991, p. 107.

[5]. Jeremiah, David and C. C. Carlson. *The Handwriting On The Wall.* Dallas, TX: Word Publishing, 1992; p. 25.

[6]. Graham, Billy. "Our One Bright Hope." in *Decision.* Minneapolis, MN: Billy Graham Evangelistic Association, Vol. 34, No. 9; Sept., 1993; pp. 1-3.

[7]. Gutzke, Manfred George. *Help Thou My Unbelief.* Nashville, TN: Published by Thomas Nelson, Inc.,1974, pp. 75-85.

[8]. DeHaan, Martin II. *Times of Discovery.* Vol 3: Number 3. Grand Rapids, MI: August/September/October, 1996, pp. 1-2.

[9]. Yungen, Ray. *For Many Shall Come In My Name.* Woodburn, OR, 1991: Solid Rock Books Inc., Revised Edition, 1991, p. 106.

CHAPTER FIFTEEN: End of the World System

The Last Dispensation

With kind permission, the writer uses a sequence of Scriptures selected by Paul Liberty[1] to describe and narrate God's plan for the end of the world system. The writer takes the liberty of following the King James version of Scripture and of paraphrasing certain phrases and verses (in italics) in order to preserve the narrative quality.

Herein we see a wonderful correspondence—between the stories that were told by each of the disciples, and those foretold by the Old Testament and coming to pass in the New Testament.

The Destruction of the Temple

The "King of Kings," our Lord Jesus Christ, gave a detailed account to the disciples of his persecution which would commence in their own generation and continue through end-of-time events—just preceding His return and the Last Judgment.

This "Lord of Lords," our Savior, withdrew from the lavish temple, rebuilt by Herod to pacify the Jews, which the

331

disciples admired. "And Jesus went out, and departed from the temple: and his disciples came to him for to shew him the buildings of the temple (taken from *Matthew 24:1)." Mark 13:1;* and *Luke 21:5*; parallel this Scripture).

"And as some spake of the temple, how it was adorned with goodly stones and gifts... *(Luke 21:5)."*

"...One of his disciples saith unto him, Master, see what manner of stones and what buildings are here *(Mark 13:1)!"*

"But will God indeed dwell on the earth? Behold, the heaven and heavens of heavens cannot contain thee; how much less this house that I have builded *(1 Kings 8:27)?"*

Jesus, the "Greatest Prophet," makes a startling prediction about the temple's destruction. "And Jesus said unto them, See ye not all these things? verily I say unto you, There shall not be left here one stone upon another, that shall not be thrown down *(Matthew 24:2)."* See also *Mark 13:2; Luke 21:6.*

"Except the Lord build the house, they labor in vain that build it; except the Lord keep the city, the watchman waketh but in vain *(Psalm 127:1)."*

Aroused by the prophecy from the "Master of Time and Eternity," His "Earliest and Most Seasoned Disciples" are prompted to ask a multiple-part question about the near, and distant future *(Matthew 24:3; Mark 13:3,4; Luke 21:7).*

And later as He sat upon the Mount of Olives, over against the temple, Peter and James, and John and Andrew asked Him privately "And he spake many things unto them in parables, saying, Behold, a sower went forth to sow... *(Matthew 13:3)"* Saying, "Master... *(Luke 21:7),"*

1) "Tell us, when shall these things be *(Mark 13:4)?"*

2) "and what sign will there be when these things shall come to pass Luke 21:7?"

3) "...and what shall be the sign of your coming

4) and of the end of the world *(Matthew 24:3)?"*

"And he said, Behold, I will make thee know what shall be in the last end of the indignation: for at the time appointed the end shall be *(Daniel 8:19)."*

The "All Knowing" Christ temporarily set aside their question about specific timing and cautioned His "Dutiful Servants" about self-proclaimed saviors *(Matthew 24:5; Mark 13:5,6; Luke 21:8).*

"And Jesus answering them began to say, Take heed lest any man deceive you *(Mark 13:5):"*

"For many shall come in my name, saying, I am Christ; and shall deceive many *(Matthew 24:5)."*

"...and the time draweth near: go ye not therefore after them *(Luke 21:8)."*

I am come in my Father's Name, and ye receive me not: if another shall come in his own name, him ye will receive *(John 5:43)."* " Little children, let no man deceive you: he that doeth righteousness is righteous, even as he is righteous *(1 John 3:7)."*

Therefore, the disciples, as "Soldiers of the Cross," are not to fear wars and rebellions, but regard them as false signs about the end of all things *(Matthew 24:6; Mark 13:7; Luke 21:9).*

"And when ye shall hear of wars and rumours of wars *(Mark 13:7),"*

"...and commotions, be not terrified: for these things must first come to pass... *(Luke 21:9);"*

"...but the end is not yet *(Matthew 24:6)."*

"The Lord is my light and my salvation; whom shall I fear? the Lord is the strength of my life; of whom shall I be afraid?... Though an host should encamp against me, my heart shall not fear: though a war should rise against me, in this will I be confident *(Psalm 27:1,3)."*

"God is our refuge and strength, a very present help in trouble... The Lord of hosts is with us; the God of Jacob is our refuge... Be still, and know that I am God... *(Psalm 46:1, 7, 10)."*

But major wars, accompanied by earth-shaking disasters (which are not man-made), will signal the very *beginning of the end (Matthew 24:7,8; Mark 13:8; Luke 21:10,11).*

Then said He unto them, "Nation shall rise against nation, and kingdom against kingdom *(Luke 21:10a);*"

"And great earthquakes shall be in divers places, and famines, and pestilences; and fearful sights and great signs shall there be from heaven *(Luke 21:11).*"

"...and troubles... *(Mark 13:8).*"

"ALL THESE (this combination) ARE (just) THE BEGINNING OF SORROWS (of the tribulation) *(Matthew 24:8).*"

The Beginning of Sorrows

"And nation was destroyed of nation, and city of city: for God did vex them with all adversity *(II Chronicles 15:6).*" "And I will show wonders in the heavens and in the earth, blood, and of fire, and pillars of smoke *(Joel 2:30).*" "This know also, that in the last days perilous times shall come *(II Timothy 3:1).*"

"And there went out another horse that was red: and power was given to him that sat thereon to take peace from the earth, and that they should kill one another: and there was given unto him a great sword... And I beheld, and lo a black horse; and he that sat on him had a pair of balances in his hand... and I looked, and behold a pale horse: and his name that sat on him was Death, and Hell followed with him *(Revelation 6:4, 5b, 8a).*"

God's "Suffering Servant" alerts His "Faithful Followers" to expect religious and secular trials and mistreatment before the global disturbances begin *(Mark 13:9; Luke 21:12).*

"But take heed to yourselves... for... *(Mark 13:9),*"

"...before all these, they shall lay their hands on you, and persecute you, delivering you up to the synagogues and into prisons... *(Luke 21:12).*"

"… they shall deliver you up to councils; and in the synagogues you shall be beaten… *(Mark 13:9).*"

"And when they had preached the Gospel to that city, and had taught many... confirming the souls of the disciples, and exhorting them to continue in the faith, and that we must through much tribulation enter into the Kingdom of God *(Acts 14:21a, 22).*" "Yes, and all that will live godly in Christ Jesus shall suffer persecution *(II Timothy 3:12).*"

Severe testing will give "True Believers" an opportunity to declare where they stand regarding the "Lord and Savior" until the gospel is offered to every person *(Mark 13:9b, 10; Luke 21:12).*

"And you shall be brought before rulers and kings for my sake… *(Mark 13:9).*"

"And it shall turn to you for a testimony *(Luke 21:13)*"

"… against them *(Mark 13:9).*"

"And the gospel must first be published among all nations *(Mark 13:10).*"

"...and when they had called the apostles, and beaten them, they commanded that they should not speak in the name of Jesus, and let them go. And they departed from the presence of the council, rejoicing that they were counted worthy to suffer shame for his name. And daily in the temple, and in every house, they ceased not to teach and preach Jesus Christ *(Acts 5:40b, c, 41, 42).*" "And they overcame him *(Satan)* by the blood of the Lamb *(Jesus)* and by the word of their testimony; and they lived not their lives unto death *(Revelation 12:11).*"

"People of the Light" are to maintain their composure by trusting and relying on the "Spirit of Truth" to guide them through, and to convince and to convict *(Mark 13:11; Luke 21:14, 15).*

"But when they shall lead you, and deliver you up *(take you to trial)*, take no thought *(don't worry)* beforehand what he shall speak, neither do ye premeditate: but whatsoever shall be given *(occur to)* you in that hour, that speak ye *(say simply)*: for it is not ye that speak but the Holy Ghost *(spirit of God) (Mark 13:11)*."

"Settle it therefore in your hearts not to meditate before what you shall answer *(in your defense) (Luke 21:14)*."

"For I will give you a mouth *(an eloquence)* and *(divine)* wisdom which all your adversaries shall not be able to gainsay *(contradict)* nor resist *(Luke 21:15)*."

"And the Lord, He does go before you; He will be with you; He will not fail you, neither forsake you; fear not, neither be dismayed *(Deuteronomy 31:8)*." "And they were not able to resist the wisdom and the Spirit by which he *(Stephen)* spake *(Acts 6:10)*." "...the word that God puts in my mouth, that I shall speak *(Numbers 22:38b)*."

"And Moses said unto the Lord, O my Lord, I am not eloquent, neither heretofore, nor since thou hast spoken unto thy servant: but I am slow of speech, and of a slow tongue. And the Lord said unto him, Who has made man's mouth? or who makes the dumb, or deaf, or the seeing, or the blind? have not I the Lord? Now therefore go, and I will be with thy mouth, and teach thee what thou shalt say *(Exodus 4:10-12)*."

The Great Divider

Unlike international conflicts and civil wars, the final struggle becomes much more individual and personal, as loyalty to the "Great Divider" causes a wide gap among relatives and friends *(Matthew 24:9; Mark 13:12; Luke 21:16)*.

"Now the brother shall betray the brother to death, and the father the son: and children shall rise up against their parents, and shall cause them to be put to death *(Mark 13:12)*."

"And ye shall be betrayed both by parents, and brethren, and kinsfolk, and friends *(Luke 21:16)*."

"Then shall they deliver you up to be afflicted *(Matthew 24:9)*."

"…and some of you shall they cause to be put to death *(Luke 21:16)*."

"Precious in the sight of the Lord is the death of His Saints *(Psalm 116:15)*." "…no man should be moved by these afflictions; for yourselves know that we are appointed thereunto. For verily, when we were with you, we told you before that we should suffer tribulation… *(I Thessalonians 3:3, 4a)*."

As the persecution intensifies, many apostates attempt to mislead the flock, to bring about a more rapid separation of the "good from the evil" *(Matthew 24:10-12)*.

"And then shall many be offended *(turned away)* and shall betray one another, and shall hate one another *(Matthew 24:10)*."

"And many false prophets shall rise and shall deceive many *(Matthew 24:11)*.

"And because iniquity shall abound, the love of many shall wax (grow) cold *(Matthew 24:12)*."

"Now the Spirit speaketh expressly, that in the latter times some shall depart from the faith, giving heed to seducing spirits, and doctrines of devils *(I Timothy 4:1)*." "For it had been better for them not to have known the way of righteousness, than, after they have known it, to turn away from the holy commandment delivered unto them *(II Peter 2:21)*."

"Imitators of Christ" are told that in spite of bitter hatred, each must individually remain steadfast to the very end *(Matthew 24:9b,13; Mark 13:13; Luke 21:17-19)*.

"… and you shall be hated of all men for my name's sake *(Luke 21:17)*."

"But he that shall endure unto the end, the same shall be saved *(Matthew 24:13)*."

"But there shall not a hair of your head perish *(Luke 21:18)*."

"In your patience possess ye your souls *(Luke 21:19)*."

"…but we glory in tribulations also; knowing that tribulation worketh patience *(Romans 5:3)*;" "Wherefore, let them that suffer according to the will of God commit the keeping of their souls to him in well doing, as unto a faithful Creator *(I Peter 4:19)*."

"For what shall it profit a man if he shall gain the whole world, and lose his own soul *(Mark 8:36)*?" "Take, my brethren, the prophets, who have spoken in the name of the Lord, for an example of suffering affliction, and of patience *(James 5:10)*." "Fear none of those things which thou shalt suffer: behold, the devil shall cast some of you into prison, that ye may be tried; and ye shall have tribulation ten days; be thou faithful unto death, and I will give thee a crown of life *(Revelation 2:10)*."

Go Unto All the World

The "Living Word," which is Christ, informs His "Holy Ambassadors," who are His beloved disciples, that worldwide saturation of the gospel must first take place for all to choose, before the final days of human history *(Matthew 24:14)*.

"And this gospel of the kingdom shall be preached in all the world for a witness unto all nations; and (only) then shall the end (of the world) come *(Matthew 24:14)*."

"… Peace be unto you: as my Father hath sent me, even so send I you *(John 20:21)*." "...freely you have received, freely give (Matthew 10:18b)." "... occupy till I come *(Luke 19:13b)*." "...He that winneth souls is wise *(Proverbs 11:30b)*."

"Go you into all the world, and preach the Gospel to every creature *(Matthew 16:15)*." "Go out into the highways and hedges and compel them to come in, that my house may be filled *(Luke 14:23b)*." "Herein is my Father glorified, that ye bear much fruit; so shall you be my disciples *(John 15:8)*."

"I must work the works of Him that sent me, while it is day; the night comes, when no man can work *(John 9:4)*."

"But the Lord said unto him, Go thy way: for he (Paul) is a chosen vessel unto me, to bear my name before the Gentiles, and kings, and the children of Israel: For I will shew him how great things he must suffer for my name's sake *(Acts 9:15,16)*."

"Jesus said unto him, Let the dead bury their dead: but go and preach the Kingdom of God... And Jesus said unto him, No man, having put his hand to the plough, and looking back, is fit for the kingdom of God *(Luke 9:60, 62)*."

The pending destruction of Jerusalem, and the Antichrist being revealed, are clear indications for "Those Sensitive to the Spirit" to escape to, and take refuge in, the high country *(Matthew 24:15, 15; Mark 13:14; Luke 21:20a, 21)*.

"And when ye shall see Jerusalem compassed with armies, then know that the desolation thereof is nigh *(Luke 21:20)*."

"But when ye shall see the abomination of desolation spoken of by Daniel the prophet, standing where it ought not… *(Mark 13:14)*,"

"… in the holy place (whoso readeth, let him understand) *(Matthew 24:15)*,"

"… then let them that be in Judea flee to the mountains *(Matthew 24:15)*."

"And the king shall do according to his will; and he shall exalt himself and magnify himself above every god, and shall speak blasphemies against the God of gods, and shall prosper till the indignation be accomplished: for what has been determined shall be done *(Daniel 11:36)*."

"And I heard another voice from heaven, saying, Come out of her, my people, that ye be not partakers of her sins, and that ye receive not of her plagues *(Revelation 18:4)*."

Abandon All Possessions

Therefore, "Workers of the Day" are urged to abandon all material possessions as they are led out to avoid God's punishment upon the wicked *(Matthew 24:17, 18; Mark 13:15, 16; Luke 21:21b, 22).*

"And let him that is on the housetop not go down into the house, neither enter therein, to take anything out of his house *(Mark 13:15)*."

"Neither let him which is in the field return back to take his clothes *(Matthew 24:18)*,"

"... and let them which are in the midst of it *(the city)* depart out and let not them that are in the countries enter there into *(Luke 21:21)*,"

"... for these be the days of vengeance, that all things which are written may be fulfilled *(Luke 21:22)*."

"Remember Lot's wife (Luke 17:32)." "But my God shall supply all your need according to his riches by Christ Jesus *(Philippians 4:19)*." "...and you shall flee to the valley of the mountains *(Zechariah 14:a)*."

Those who decline God's righteousness and grace are left behind to suffer immense personal anguish *(Matthew 24:19; Mark 13:17; Luke 21:23,24).*

"But woe unto them that are with child and to nursing infants in those days! For there shall be great distress in the land, and wrath *(God's anger)* upon this people *(Luke 21:23)*."

"And they shall fall by the edge of the sword, and shall be led away captive into all nations. And Jerusalem shall be trodden down of the Gentiles until the times of the Gentiles be fulfilled *(Luke 21:24)*."

"Behold, the day of the Lord comes, and your spoil shall be divided in the midst of you. For I will gather all nations against Jerusalem to battle; and the city shall be taken, and the houses rifled, and the women ravished; and half of the city shall go forth into captivity *(Zechariah 14:1a)*."

So the "Word of God," which is Christ Jesus, tells His "Wandering Pilgrims," to pray specifically for their timely evacuation and safety until God's mercy brings the terrible times to a close *(Matthew 24:20-22; Mark 13:18-20).*

"But pray that *your* flight *(to the mountains)* be not in the winter, neither on the sabbath day *(Matthew 24:20)."*

The Great Tribulation

"For then shall there be *great* tribulation such as was not since the beginning of the world... *(Matthew 24:21),"*

"... which God created unto this time *(Mark 13:19),"*

"... and except that the Lord had shortened those days, no flesh should be saved but for the elect's sake, who he has chosen, he hath shortened the days *(Mark 13:20)."*

"And shall not God avenge his own elect, which cry day and night unto him, though he bare long with them? I tell you that he will avenge them speedily. Nevertheless, when the Son of man cometh, shall he find faith on the earth *(Luke 18:7, 8)?"*

"For the Lord said, The whole land shall be desolate; yet will I completely destroy it *(Jeremiah 4:27)."* "Watch you therefore, and pray always, that you may be accounted worthy to escape all these things that shall come to pass, and to stand before the Son of Man *(Luke 21:36)."*

Even so, the "Executors of His Will" are to be suspicious of anyone attempting to direct them to fake messiahs and impressive miracle workers attempting to mislead and corrupt *(Matthew 24:23,24; Mark 13:21,22).*

"And then if any man shall say to you, Lo, here is Christ; or lo, he is there; believe him not *(Mark 13:21)."*

"For there shall arise false Christs and false prophets, and shall shew great signs and wonders; insomuch that, if it were possible, they shall... *(Matthew 24:24)"* "lead the very chosen astray *(Mark 13:22)."*

We read in *II Kings 17:7-8* that same, early lesson in regard to other gods.

"Little children, it is the last time: and as you have heard that antichrist shall come, even now are there many antichrists:

whereby we know that it is the last time *(1 John 2:18)*." "I am the good shepherd, and know my sheep, and am known of mine *(John 10:14)*." Also *Hebrews 13:20-21; I Peter 5:4.* "And I saw three unclean spirits like frogs come out of the mouth of the false prophet. For they are spirits of devils, working miracles *(Revelation 16:13, 14a)*."

The Second Coming

The "People of the Light" should disregard rumors about the "Glorious Son of God" having returned, because His Second Coming will be quick and obvious for the entire world to witness simultaneously *(Matthew 24:25-27; Mark 13:23)*.

"Wherefore if they shall say unto you, Behold, he is in the desert; go not forth: behold, he is in the secret chambers; believe it not *(Matthew 24:26)*."

"For as the lightning comes out of the east and shines even unto the west, so (suddenly and most visible) shall also the coming of the son of man be *(Matthew 24:27)*."

"But pay attention: Behold, I have foretold you all things *(Mark 13:23)*."

"For yourselves know perfectly that the day of the Lord so comes as a thief in the night... But ye, brethren, are not in darkness, that this day should overtake you as a thief *(I Thessalonians 5:2, 4)*." "Behold he comes with clouds; and every eye shall see him, and they also which pierced him: and all kindreds of the earth shall wail because of him. Even so, Amen *(Revelation 1:7)*."

Many will become terrified with consuming anxiety as the "Lion of Judah" uses His creation to bring judgement upon a sinful world *(Matthew 24:28; Luke 21:25,26)*.

"And there shall be signs in the sun and in the moon, and in the stars and upon the earth distress of nations with perplexity: the sea and the waves roaring *(Luke 21:25)*."

"Men's hearts failing them for fear, and for looking after (fearfully anticipating) those things which are coming on the earth... *(Luke 21;26)*."

"For wheresoever the corpse is, there will the vultures be gathered together *(Matthew 24:28)*."

"And the slain of the Lord shall be at that day from one end of the earth even unto the other end of the earth: they shall not be lamented, neither gathered, nor buried; they shall be dung upon the ground *(Jeremiah 25:33)*."

Soon after that time of difficulty the world will be thrown into darkness, then they will see the symbol of the "Light of the World," and *Christ is recognized (Matthew 24:29, 30; Mark 13:24,25; Luke 21:26b)*!

"Immediately after the tribulation of those days shall the sun be darkness and the moon shall not give her light... *(Matthew 24:29)*."

"And the stars of heaven shall fall (be driven from their courses), and the powers that are in heaven shall be shaken *(Mark 13:25)*."

"And then shall appear the sign of the Son of man in heaven: and then shall all the tribes of the earth mourn... *(Matthew 24:30)*."

"Then spake Jesus again unto them, saying, I am the light of the world: he that follows me shall not walk in darkness, but shall have the light of life *(John 8:12)*." "The earth shall quake before them; the heavens shall tremble: the sun and moon shall be dark, and the stars shall withdraw their shining... Therefore also now, saith the Lord, turn you even to me with all your heart, and with fasting, and with weeping, and with mourning *(Joel 2:10, 12)*."

"And in that day they shall roar against them like the roaring of the sea: and if one look unto the lad, behold darkness and sorrow; and the light is darkened in the heavens thereof *(Isaiah 5:30)*." "And when these things begin to come to pass, then look up, and lift up your heads; for your redemption draws near *(Luke 21:28)*."

The "Prince of Peace" will return in awesome splendor as the "King of Glory" for the resurrection and ascension of all "Heirs of the Kingdom" *(Matthew 24:30,31; Mark 13:26,27; Luke 21:27)*.

"And then shall appear the sign of the Son of man in heaven... coming in the clouds of heaven with power and great glory *(Matthew 24:30)*.":

"When the Son of man shall come in His glory, and all the holy angels with him, then shall he sit upon the throne of his glory *(Matthew 25:31)*." "And behold, I come quickly: and my reward is with me, to give every man according as his work shall be... I am the root and the offspring of David, and the bright and morning star *(Revelation 22:12, 16b)*."

"Lift up your heads, O ye gates; even lift them up, ye everlasting doors; and the King of glory shall come in. Who is this King of glory? the Lord of hosts, He is the King of glory... *(Psalm 24:9, 10)*."

"And he shall send his angels with a great sound of a trumpet, and they shall gather together his elect from the four winds *(North, South, East, West)... (Matthew 24:31)*."

"For the Lord himself shall descend from heaven with a shout, with the voice of the archangel, and with the trumpet of God: and the dead in Christ shall rise first: Then we which are alive and remain shall be caught up together with them in the clouds, to meet the Lord in the air: and so shall we ever be with the Lord. Wherefore, comfort one another with these words *(1 Thessalonians 4:16, 18)*."

"Behold, I show you a secret truth: we shall not all sleep, but shall all be changed. In a moment, in the twinkling of an eye, at the *last trumpet sounds*; for the trumpet shall sound, and the dead shall be raised incorruptible, and we shall be changed. O death, where is your sting? O grave, where is your victory? Therefore my beloved brethren, be steadfast, unmovable, always abounding the work of the Lord, for as you know that your labor is not in vain, in the Lord *(I*

Corinthians 15:51, 52, 55, 58)."

"I tell you in that night there shall be two men in one bed; the one shall be taken, and the other shall be left. Two women shall be grinding together; the one shall be taken, and the other left. Two men shall be in the field; the one shall be taken and the other left *(Luke 17:34-36)*."

"Marvel not at this: for the hour is coming, in which all that are in the graves shall hear his voice, and shall come forth; they that have done good, unto the resurrection of life; and they that have done evil, unto the resurrection of condemnation *(John 5:28,29).*

"...From the uttermost part *(most remote regions)* of the earth, to the uttermost part *(furthest reaches)* of heaven *(Mark 13:27)*."

"Then shall the righteous shine forth as the sun in the kingdom of their Father. Who has ears to hear, let him hear *(Matthew 13:43)*." "The heavens declare the glory of God; and the firmament shows his handiwork *(Psalm 19:1)*."

"He tells the number of the stars; he calls them all by their names *(Psalm 147:4)*." "For since the beginning of the world men have not heard, nor perceived by the ear, neither hath the eye seen, O God, besides you, what he has prepared for him that waits for him *(Isaiah 64:4)*." "And he that overcomes, and keeps my works unto the end, to him will I give power over the nations... And I will give him the morning star *(Revelation 2:26, 28)*."

"I Jesus have sent my angel to testify unto these things for the churches. I am the root and the offspring of David, and the *Bright and Morning Star (Revelation 22:16).*

Here endeth our reading of the Scriptures, a holy and consistent promise God has made throughout recorded time.

A Prayer of Gratitude

Our kind loving God, "Holy" be Your name; we thank you for counting us among the many you served by dying on the cross for our sins. Today we want our gratitude to exceed word by offering ourselves as living sacrifices in your great mission of seeking and saving the lost.

Give us more faith, wisdom, enthusiasm, and above all grant us servant sensitive hearts and spiritual vision so that we will respond to the lost as you did, Jesus.

Send us out in the power of the Holy Spirit to live and serve in a way that pleases you, produces fruit in the lives of others and for your glory, in the matchless name of our Lord and Savior Jesus Christ. Amen.

ENDNOTE

[1]. Liberty, Paul L. *Peter and Paul Ministries.* Toledo, OH: Unpublished Manuscript. Used by permission, and adapted, by Ralph Cater, 1997.

BIBLIOGRAPHY

Adler, Mortimer and Charles Van Doren. *How to Read a Book*. New York: Simon and Schuster, Revised 1972.

Aldrich, Joseph C. *Life-Style Evangelism*. Portland, OR: Multnomah Press, 4th printing 1983.

Arvine, Kazlitt. *Cyclopedia of Moral & Religious Anecdotes*. New York: Funk & Wagnalls, 1890.

Baker, Don. *Restoring Broken Relationships*. Eugene, OR: Harvest House, 1989.

Bancroft, Emery H. *Elemental Theology - Doctrinal and Conservative* Grand Rapids, MI: Zondervan Publishers, 1970.

Barrett, David B. "Annual Statistical Table on Global Mission." *International Bulletin of Missionary Research*, January 1997.

Best, W. E. *The Church - Her Authority and Mission*. Houston, TX: Best Book Missionary Trust.

Boyd, Gregory A. *Oneness of Pentecostal and the Trinity*;. Grand Rapids, MI: Baker Book House, 1992.

Bush, Luis. "Focusing on the 10/40 Window," *Dallas Insider*, Dallas, TX. Winter Issue 1991; Vol. 14; No. 1; Spring Issue 1991; Vol 14, No. 2, Part 2.

Cater, Ralph F. "A Systematic Approach in Student Reading," *Improving College and University Teaching*. International Quarterly Journal. Corvallis, OR: Oregon State University, Autumn, 1962.

Cater, Ralph. "Sexual Harassment is a Centuries Old Problem," Salem, OR: *Statesmen Journal*, letter to the editor, Section A. Oct. 22, 1991.

Chafer, Lewis S. *Major Bible Themes*. Findlay, OH: Dunham Pub. Co., 1953.

Colson, Charles. *Loving God*. New York: Harper Paperbacks, 1987.

Colson, Chuck and Jack Eckerd. *Why America Doesn't Work*. Dallas, TX: Word Publishing, 1991.

DeHaan, Martin R II. *Times of Discovery*. Vol 3; Num 3. Aug/ Sept/Oct 1996. Grand Rapids, MI.

Dunn, Bruce; *Divorce And Remarriage*. Peoria, IL: #45: The Grace Worship Hour.

Egner, David. *What Will Make My Marriage Work?*; Grand Rapids, MI: Radio Bible Class, 1986.

Enns, Paul. *The Moody Handbook of Theology*. Chicago, IL: Moody Press, 1989.

Enroth, Ronald M. *Churches That Abuse*. Grand Rapids, MI: Zondervan Publishing House, 1992.

Evans, William. *The Great Doctrines of the Bible*. Chicago, IL: Moody Press, Rev. 1939.

Fausset, Andrew Robert. *Bible Encyclopedia and Dictionary - Critical and Expository*. Grand Rapids, MI: Zondervan Publishing House, 1902.

Feit, Edward, Contributing editor. "Government and Leader," *An Approach to Comparative Politics*. Boston, MA: Houghton Mifflin Co., 1978.

Graham, Billy. "Our One Bright Hope," *Decision*. Minneapolis, MN: Billy Graham Evangelistic Association, Vol. 34, No. 9; Sept. 1993.

Green, Jay P. Sr. *The Interlinear Hebrew - Aramaic Old Testament*. Peabody, MA: Henderson Publishers, 1985.

Griffin, John Howard. *Black Like Me*. Boston, MA: A Signet Book, Published by Haughton Mufflen, 1960.

Grubb, Norman. *C.T. Studd Cricketer and Pioneer*. Washington, PA: Christian Literature Crusade, 1985.

Gutzke, Manfred George. *Help Thou My Unbelief*. Nashville, TN: Thomas Nelson, 1974.

Hammond, T.C. *In Understanding, Be Men*. Downers Grove, IL: IFCA Press, 1978.

Ironside, H.A. *Wrongly - Dividing the Word of Truth - Ultra Dispensationalism Examined in the Light of Holy Scripture*. New York, NY: Loizeaux Brothers, Inc., Bible Truth Depot, 1938.

Jamieson, Robert. Commentary. *Practical and Explanatory in the Whole Bible*. Grand Rapids, MI: Zondervan Publishing House, 1962.

Jeremiah, David and C.C. Carlson. *Escape the Coming Night*. Dallas, TX: Word Publishing, 1990.

Jeremiah, David and C.C. Carlson. *The Handwriting on the Wall*. Dallas, TX: Word Publishing, 1992.

Jordan, Richard. *Macedonian Trip Report: The Grace Journal*, Vol. 7, No. 3, Bloomingdale, IL: December, 1994.

Kovalik, Susan, and Associates. *Integrated Thematic Instruction: The Model*. 3rd edition. Kovalik Publishers, 1994.

Kuiper, Rienk Bouke. *The Glorious Body of Christ*. Grand Rapids, MI: Wm. Eerdmans, 1958.

Kusumoto, Kay. "Remarks reveal hostility beneath Civil Society." Salem, OR: *Statesman Journal*, Dec. 9, 1993.

Larkin, Clarence. *Dispensational Truth*. Philadelphia, PA: Rev. Clarence Larkin, 1924.

Leuthold, Reuben. *What Happened When You Believed?* Grand Rapids, MI: Bible Doctrine Publications, Inc., Third Printing, 1996.

Liberty, Paul L. *Peter and Paul Ministries*. Toledo, OH: Unpublished Manuscript. Used by permission, and adapted, by Ralph Cater, 1997.

Life Application Bible, The. The Living Bible. Wheaton, IL: Tyndale House Publishers, Inc. and Youth For Christ/USA, 1988.

Lockyer, Herber. *All the Doctrines of the Bible*. Grand Rapids, MI: Zondervan Publishing House, 1964.

Lundin, Robert W. *Personality - An Experimental Approach.* New York: The MacMillan Company, 1961.

Marshall, A. *The Interlinear Greek - English New Testament.* London: Samuel Bagster & Son Ltd., 1960.

McGee, J. Vernon. *Joel.* Pasadena, CA: Thru the Bible Radio, 1978.

Mead, Frank S., Revised by Samuel S. Hill. *Handbook of Denominations in the United States.* 9th ed. Nashville, TN: Abingdon Press, 1990.

Menninger, Karl. *Whatever Became of Sin?* New York: Hawthorne Books, Inc., 1973.

"Morality And Homosexuality." *The Wall Street Journal*; Thursday; Feb. 24, 1994; Section A.

Nash, Ronald M. *The New Evangelicalism.* Grand Rapids, MI: Zondervan Publishing House, 1963.

Philadelphia Confession of Faith With Catechism,The. Grand Rapids, MI: Associated Publishers and Authors, Inc., 1869.

"Readers share views about death penalty." Salem, OR: *Statesmen Journal*, August 31, 1996.

Reid, Daniel G., Consulting Editor and Others. *Dictionary of Christianity in America.* Dowers Grove, IL: Inter-Varsity Press, 1990.

Robb, Thomas B. *Growing Up: Pastoral Nurture For the Later Years.* New York: Haworth Press, 1991.

Roche, George. *How government Funding is Destroying Americans Higher Education.* Hillsdale, MI: Imprimis—Hillsdale College, Oct. 1994, Vol. 23, No. 10.

Saucy, Robert L. *The Church in God's Program.* Chicago, IL: Moody Press, 1972.

Scofield, C.I. *The New Life in Jesus Christ.* Chicago, IL: The Bible Institute Colportage Assn., 1915.

Scofield, C.I. *Rightly Dividing the Word of Truth.* Neptune, NH: Loizeaux Brothers Publications, 1986.

Scott, Thomas. *Scott's Commentary on the New Testament.* Philadelphia, PA: J.B. Lippincott & Co., 1857.

Sekulow, Jay. *Casenote*. Atlanta, GA: The American Center For The Law And Justice. June, 1994.

Singer, Charles W. *A Testimony of God's Grace and Faithfulness*. Los Angeles, CA: International Refugee Mission, Inc.

Solomon, Muriel. *Working with Difficult People*. New York, NY: Prentice Hall, 1992.

Stam, C.R. "Bible Study in 1880 and Now," Vol. 51, No. 1. Germantown, WI: *The Berean Searchlight*, February 1991.

Strong, Augustus Hopkins. *Systematic Theology*. A Compendium and Commonplace Book - Three Volumes in One. Philadelphia, PA: The Judson Press, 1907.

Tenney, Merrill C. ed. *The Zondervan Pictorial Bible Dictionary*. Grand Rapids, MI: Zondervan Publishing House, 1964.

Thiessen, Henry Clarence. *Introductory Lectures in Systematic Theology*. Grand Rapids, MI: Eerdmans Publishing Co., 1949.

This We Believe. Westchester, IL: Independent Fundamental Churches of America. Vol. I, 1970.

This We Believe. Grandville, MI: Independent Fundamental Churches of America, Vol. II, 1980.

Thompson, Frank Charles. *The New Chain-Reference Bible*. Third Improved Edition. 41st Reprint; King James Version Indianapolis, IN: B.B. Kirkbride Bible Co., 1951.

Tidwell, Josiah Blake. *The Bible Period by Period*. Nashville, TN: Broadman Press, 1923.

Timby, Ruth J. *The Living Word*. Raleigh, NC: Your Bookstore, 1955.

Torry, R.A. *What the Bible Teaches*. Ada, MI: Fleming H. Revel Co., 1898-1933.

Tucker, Bruce. " Are Oneness Groups Cultic?" *The Standard*. Arlington Heights, IL: The News Magazine of the Baptist General Conference, Vol. 82, No.3, April 1992.

Unger, Merrill F. *Unger's Guide to the Bible*. Wheaton, IL: Tyndale House Publishers, Inc., 1974.

Unchurched American, The. The National Council of Churches of Christ in the USA. Princeton, NJ: The Princeton Religion Research Center and the Gallup Organization, Inc., 1971.

Unchurched America, The. Princeton, NJ: The Princeton Religion Reseach Center and the Gallup Organization, Inc., 1978.

Unchurched America 10 Years Later, The. Princeton, NJ: The Princeton Religion Research Center, Inc., 1988.

Van Gorder, Paul R. *The Church Stands Corrected: A Solution For Today's Church Problems.* Wheaton, IL: Victor Books, 1967.

Vine, W.E.; Unger, M &.F.; White, W. *Expository Dictionary of Biblical Words*, New York, NY: Nelson Publishing, 1985.

Walvoord, John F. and Roy B. Zuck editors. *Bible Knowledge Commentary*, Vol 1 and Vol ll. Wheaton, IL: Victor Books, 1983-1985.

Walvoord, John F. "Prophesy and the Seventies." Edited by C.L. Feinberg, in *Where is the Modern Church Going?* Chicago, IL: Moody Press, 1971.

White, Tom. *The Voice of the Martyrs.* Bartlesville, OK, April 1997.

Whitney, Donald S. *Spiritual Disciplines for the Christian Life.* Colorado Springs, CO: NavPress, 1991.

Wilson, Neil, editor. *The Handbook of Bible Application.* Wheaton, IL: Tyndale House Publishers, Inc., 1992.

Winston, Patrick Henry. *Artificial Intelligence.* Second edition. Reading, MA: Addison Wesley Publishing Co., 1984.

Worrell, A.S. *The New Testament Revised and Translated.* Philadelphia, PA: American Baptist Publication Society, 1904.

Yungen, Ray. *For Many Shall Come In My Name.* Woodburn, OR: Solid Rock Books, Inc., Revised and edited, 1991.

Zuck, Roy B. *Basic Bible Interpretation.* Wheaton, IL: Victor Books, Div of Scripture Press Publishing Inc.,1991.